Social Psychology of Helping Relations

Contemporary Social Issues

Contemporary Social Issues, a book series authored by leading experts in the field, focuses on psychological inquiry and research relevant to social issues facing individuals, groups, communities, and society at large. Each volume is written for scholars, students, practitioners, and policy-makers.

Series Editor: Daniel Perlman

Multiculturalism and Diversity: A Social Psychological Perspective
Bernice Lott

The Psychological Wealth of Nations: Do Happy People Make a Happy Society?
Shigehiro Oishi

Women and Poverty: Psychology, Public Policy, and Social Justice
Heather Bullock

Stalking and the Cultural Construction of Romance
H. Colleen Sinclair

Social Psychology of Helping Relations: Solidarity and Hierarchy
Arie Nadler

Ableism: The Causes and Consequences of Disability Prejudice
Michelle R. Nario-Redmond

Forthcoming

In the Midst of Plenty: Homelessness and What To Do About It
Marybeth Shinn and Jill Khadduri

Taking Moral Action
Chuck Huff

Social Psychology of Helping Relations

Solidarity and Hierarchy

Arie Nadler

WILEY Blackwell

This edition first published 2020

Registered Office
John Wiley & Sons, Inc., 111 River Street, Hoboken, NJ 07030, USA

Editorial Office
111 River Street, Hoboken, NJ 07030, USA

For details of our global editorial offices, customer services, and more information about Wiley products visit us at www.wiley.com.

Wiley also publishes its books in a variety of electronic formats and by print-on-demand. Some content that appears in standard print versions of this book may not be available in other formats.

Library of Congress Cataloging-in-Publication Data

Names: Nadler, Arie, author.
Title: Social psychology of helping relations : solidarity and hierarchy / Arie Nadler.
Description: Hoboken, NJ : Wiley-Blackwell, [2020] | Series: Contemporary social issues | Includes bibliographical references and index.
Identifiers: LCCN 2019030289 (print) | LCCN 2019030290 (ebook) | ISBN 9781118521519 (hardback) | ISBN 9781119124610 (paperback) | ISBN 9781118521403 (adobe pdf) | ISBN 9781118521526 (epub)
Subjects: LCSH: Helping behavior. | Social psychology.
Classification: LCC BF637.H4 N33 2020 (print) | LCC BF637.H4 (ebook) | DDC 302.3–dc23
LC record available at https://lccn.loc.gov/2019030289
LC ebook record available at https://lccn.loc.gov/2019030290

Cover Design: Wiley
Cover Image: © vernonwiley/Getty Images

Set in 10.5/12.5pt Galliard by SPi Global, Pondicherry, India
Printed and bound in Singapore by Markono Print Media Pte Ltd

10 9 8 7 6 5 4 3 2 1

TO ETTA KEREN AND GILI

Contents

Acknowledgment

Preparation of this book was supported by a grant from the Israeli Science Foundation.

1

General Introduction

The questions why and when people help or do not help others in need have preoccupied humans since they began carving their thoughts in stone. Religious teachings admonish their adherents to help their fellow human beings, and discussions about human helpfulness and selfishness are pivotal in the writings of Plato, Aristotle (Annas 1977), and Seneca (cf. Griffin 2013), to name a few. The same concern with the reasons and circumstances of helping or failing to help has dominated the writings of more recent philosophers and stimulated the growth of a vibrant field of research in modern social psychology (Dovidio et al. 2006; Keltner et al. 2014). Throughout, these moral teachings, scholarly treatises, and research efforts have centered on the question of generosity, i.e. helping others in need. The present book goes beyond this emphasis on help-giving to consider the recipient's perspective and the broad spectrum of giving, seeking, and receiving help in interpersonal and intergroup situations.

1.1 Helping Relations: Social Belongingness and Social Hierarchy

The departure point for the present understanding of helping relations is that they reflect the workings of two fundamental human needs: to belong and to be independent. The need for belongingness is reflected in the desire to form and maintain significant social relations

Social Psychology of Helping Relations: Solidarity and Hierarchy, First Edition. Arie Nadler.

(Baumeister and Leary 1995). Helping others in need and relying on their help when we are in need are behavioral expressions of belongingness: they express solidarity, which is the glue that binds people together in relationships and groups. In *Civilization and Its Discontents*, Freud (1930) attributed people's general need to feel connected to others to the sex drive and processes within the family. Subsequent psychoanalytic approaches placed an even greater emphasis on people's need for belongingness as a central psychological force in life (e.g. Klein 1984). Humanistic psychological theories also emphasized the need to belong. Abraham Maslow (1982), for example, theorized that only existence-related needs were more primary than people's need for love and belongingness.

Yet alongside the need to belong, people also want to be independent. Independence from significant others such as one's parents is a marker of successful development (Rogoff 2003). People are proud of their achievements when these are individual achievments (McLelland 1967), and self-reliance is a central value in work and organizational settings (Miller et al. 2002). In fact, because helping is associated with having more skills or resources, giving to others in the group promotes the helper's prestige and status, whereas dependency is considered a marker of one's lower prestige or status. Thus, helping relationships represent a combination of belongingness and hierarchical relations in social interactions.

The duality of these needs is reflected throughout the life cycle. We begin life by being dependent on the caregivers with whom we share belongingness; later, during adolescence, we express a strong need to be independent from them; and in adulthood, the need to belong dominates again as we establish intimate relationships and start new families. In old age, the pendulum swings again and in the face of deteriorating mind and body that make us dependent on others' help, our need to maintain self-reliance dominates.

The central role of these two needs is echoed in several current social psychological theories. Self-determination theory posits that people are motivated by three basic psychological needs: competence, autonomy, and relatedness (Ryan and Deci 2000). Although not synonymous with the need for self-reliance, the needs for autonomy and competence are closely related to it, and the motivation for relatedness parallels the need for belongingness. Research on human values cites benevolence and achievement, paralleling belongingness and independence, respectively, as two basic and universal values (Schwartz 1992). Moreover, the Big Two conceptualization of human motivation regards the needs for communion and agency, corresponding to belongingness and independence, as dominating social life (Abele et al. 2008). Finally, recent research on reconciliation has noted that conflict poses threats to these needs, and that removing these threats increases the prospects of interpersonal and intergroup reconciliation (Nadler and Shnabel 2015; Shnabel and Nadler 2008).

Helping relations are the stage on which the two fundamental needs play out. On the one hand, helping and being helped are the behavioral expressions of belongingness that binds individuals and groups together. On the other hand, being independent in times of need implies that one is strong and competent. Consistent with this, helping others increases the helper's prestige, while depending on others' help is frowned upon (Nadler and Halabi 2015). Thus, while the need for belongingness and communion motivates people to give and receive from others, the need for agency and competence motivates them to remain self-reliant even in times of adversity, thereby maintaining their place in the social hierarchy as able and competent relative to others.

This dual message has been captured in the poem "Ye Wearie Wayfarer," by the Australian poet Adam Lindsay Gordon (1893, p. 28):

> Question not, but live and labour
> Till yon goal be won,
> Helping every feeble neighbour,
> Seeking help from none;
> Life is mostly froth and bubble,
> Two things stand like stone,
> Kindness in another's trouble,
> Courage in your own.

To overcome people's selfish tendencies, society tells them that they should "help every feeble neighbor," but to encourage active coping people are told that they should "seek help from none" when they are "feeble." Therefore, to preserve others' view of them as competent, people often prefer to pay the price of continued hardships rather than receive the help they need to overcome them (Nadler 1986). A new employee may reject an offer of assistance from a colleague in solving a problem he or she cannot solve alone (e.g. Geller and Bamberger 2012); and a student struggling with difficult course material may avoid requesting help from peers or teachers (Karabenick and Gonida 2018), even if this increases the likelihood of failure. Thus, our *social* nature propels us to help and be helped, while our *individual* nature leads us to prefer self-reliance in our time of need.

This theme of helping relationships as reflecting the interplay between people's need to belong and their need to be independent is a powerful undercurrent in social psychological studies of helping. Much of past theory and research has been devoted to the question of generosity, and the first part of the book is accordingly devoted to variables and processes that explain giving help to others in need. Subsequent sections will consider the consequences of giving and receiving help, and the final section will be devoted to research on intergroup helping.

1.2 "Helping" in Social Psychology: Definitions and Concepts

Helping comes in all shapes and sizes. Risking oneself to save a stranger who has fallen on the tracks of an approaching train, spending time to instruct a new employee about organizational politics, and volunteering in soup kitchens for the poor are all examples of helping. These three examples vary, among other things, in the degree of *risk* involved, the *duration of* helping, and the *decision processes* leading to it. Saving another individual from an approaching train is risky, while spending time with a new employee or volunteering to feed the hungry involve little risk, if any. Regarding duration, pulling the fallen person off the tracks may take a few seconds, talking to the new employee might last minutes or hours, and volunteering may represent a commitment of months or even years. Finally, the decision processes involved in each of these three examples are different. Saving a person from the advancing train represents a split-second decision. If one were to ask the rescuer to describe how he or she had decided to put their life on the line and help, one would likely be told something like "I don't know – I just acted." The other two examples represent lengthier and more elaborate decision processes. The decision to tell the new employee who should be avoided in the workplace is likely to have come about after some thought, and the decision to volunteer for an extended period is the outcome of an even more complex decision process.

The wide variety of human social behavior that falls under the concept of helping calls for a definition. The need to define "helping" goes beyond what is required by academic conventions. The definition is important because it informs us what is within and what is outside the boundaries of the phenomenon under study. One way of dealing with the complexity of a concept such as helping is to define it broadly. Defining helping as "doing good to others" is an example. This definitional strategy runs the risk of conceptual ambiguity regarding what is *not* helping (i.e. the danger of "conceptual stretching"; Meierhenrich

2008). In fact, "doing good to others" would include a successful business transaction with another person – after all, by facilitating such a transaction, we "did good" to another. Yet although benevolent intentions may be an important ingredient of successful business deals it is clear that we do not aim to analyze successful business transactions when we consider helping.

The opposite definitional strategy would be to limit the definition to a relatively small set of behaviors. Defining helping as "volunteering in the community" represents such a strategy. Here we run the opposite risk: in the effort to clearly demarcate the phenomenon, we restrict it. Although it is an important topic, the social psychology of helping contains more than research on volunteering. In sum, a definition of helping needs to navigate between the Scylla of conceptual stretching and the Charybdis of conceptual restrictiveness if it is to steer research about helping successfully.

In the present book, we define helping as *volitional behavior directed at another person that benefits a person in need without expectation for a contingent or tangible return*. This definition is not ideal, but it helps minimize the twin dangers of conceptual stretching and restrictiveness. On the one hand, it excludes giving that is contingent on the expectation of tangible return, e.g. an economic transaction; on the other hand, it allows consideration of a wide variety of behaviors that benefit others in need (e.g. rescue, donation, or support). While the emphasis on the tangibility of a contingent reward excludes economic transactions, it includes helping interactions where people expect and receive *intangible* rewards. As discussed more fully in a subsequent section that centers on the motivations for help-giving, one reason people help is their wish to gain prestige as generous group members, or to feel good about themselves. The definition's emphasis on helping as a volitional behavior excludes benevolence that is not based on volition. Thus, it excludes in-role helping, but includes helping that is beyond role demands (e.g. a social worker comforting her client during office hours vs. doing so outside office hours).

Before concluding this section, note that scholars working in the helping area have also used the concepts of prosocial behavior and altruism to guide their theorizing and research. The first concept represents a broader perspective than that of helping. Thus, Dovidio et al. (2006) titled their review of the field as *The Social Psychology of Prosocial Behavior* and viewed any behavior that benefits another as prosocial (e.g. cooperation between individuals and groups). Similarly, in their volume titled *Prosocial Motives, Emotions, and Behavior*, Mikulincer and Shaver (2010) included chapters on reconciliation processes between individuals and groups. Finally, Sturmer and Snyder (2009) included chapters on the political aspects of social solidarity in *The Psychology of Prosocial Behavior.*

Altruism is a third concept often used by researchers in this field. It serves to identify two relatively independent phenomena. The first is related to evolutionary analyses of self-sacrificial behaviors, mostly but not only in the animal world. Altruism is used by evolutionary theorists who seek to explain the seemingly irrational behavior where an individual organism sacrifices itself to save others in the pack or nest (e.g. dolphins who put themselves in danger by carrying a wounded individual to safe waters). This "evolutionary altruism" is distinguished from "psychological altruism" (Sober and Wilson 1998) that does not describe a particular behavior (i.e. self-sacrifice) but the *intention* that propels it. Helping driven by the helper's motivation to increase the other's well-being as opposed to the desire to gain psychological or social rewards is defined as altruistic (Batson 2011). Because the present volume does not confine itself to the topics implied by the concept of altruism nor addresses the broader array of topics implied by the concept of prosocial behavior, the concept of helping is more appropriate.

1.3 Perspective on Helping Relations and Outline

1.3.1 Present Perspective on Helping Relations

The title of the present book includes the phrase "helping relations" and not the more commonly used phrases "helping behavior," "prosocial behavior," or "altruism." This change in language reflects the present book's move of going beyond the past focus on the question of generosity to consider the fuller spectrum of relationships between helper and recipient. This perspective reminds us that a helping interaction involves a transaction involving material or non-material resources between a person in need and a resourceful, helpful other. This broader perspective on research on helping is evidenced here in the *scope*, *temporal dimension*, and multiple *levels of analysis* on which helping relations are considered.

The extended scope is reflected in that the book goes beyond (i) the study of help-giving to consider the seeking and receiving of help, and (ii) beyond the dichotomous distinction between "help" and "no-help" to the consideration of different kinds of help (e.g. autonomy-/dependency-oriented help). The first section centers on help-giving.

It begins with answers provided in the past to the question of generosity as evidenced in philosophical discourses and early psychological theories. In the main, these philosophical and early psychological theories centered on the nature of human beings: are people helpful because they are innately good, innately selfish and "forced" to be good, or do they learn to be selfish or caring?

This broad outlook is followed by an overview of the evolutionary origins of generosity, after which the book turns to consider social psychological research on giving help. This research highlighted the multi-causal and complex nature of who, when and why people help. Subsequently, the book considers the other side of helping, i.e. seeking and receiving help. This section addresses processes and variables that explain and predict people's decision to seek outside help to cope with difficulties, and the positive and negative consequences of being dependent on others' help.

The second aspect of the greater breadth of the present coverage is help itself. Most of past research in this field has centered on the dichotomy between help and no-help. Thus, research on help-giving assessed whether or not help had been given. Here, however, we go beyond this dichotomy to consider different kinds of help. A key distinction is between dependency-oriented and autonomy-oriented help, i.e. solving the problem for the needy or giving them the tools to solve it. This and other distinctions (e.g. assumptive vs. requested help) play out in the present coverage of helping relations.

Regarding the *temporal dimension*, unlike most other reviews of the field this book does not stop at the point in which help had or had not been given or received. Rather, we consider the short- and long-term consequences of giving (e.g., helper's affect and physical well-being) and receiving help (e.g. gratitude and higher or lower social status).

Finally, the book also extends the *level of analysis* of helping relations. For the most part, past research on help-giving has assessed generosity in interpersonal relations. The common research paradigm has focused on an individual who had or had not helped another person. Building on empirical and conceptual developments in the social psychology of intergroup relations, the present book goes beyond the interpersonal to the intergroup level of analysis by describing research on willingness to give and receive help across group boundaries. Generally, while the level of analysis changes and the specific variables on both levels are different (e.g. ingroup commitment and interpersonal proximity in intergroup and intra-group contexts, respectively), the basic processes are the same on both levels, with helping relations viewed as affected by people's needs for belongingness and independence.

1.3.2 Outline of Book Contents

After an introductory chapter that centers on the definition of helping, early philosophical analyses, and the evolution of human generosity, the book will move to address social-psychological research on help-giving. This research has addressed *situations* in which people are more likely to respond to others' predicament by helping them, *personal characteristics* of those who are more helpful than others, and the different *motivations* for generosity (i.e. When, Who and Why people give help, respectively: Dovidio et al. 2006). We will conclude this review of the literature on help-giving by attending to research on the effects of help-giving on the helper's psychological and physical well-being.

The emphasis of past research on help-giving has led to viewing the recipient of help as a passive receptacle of the helper's benevolence. The next part of the book will shift the focus onto the recipient and consider readiness to seek and receive help. Here again, we begin with the belongingness aspects of receiving help by reviewing research on the antecedents and consequences of recipients' gratitude and move on to the other side of the helping equation: the self-threatening aspects inherent in dependency that lead people to not be willing to seek or receive help from others.

The third part of the book moves from the interpersonal to the intergroup level of analysis. Whereas previous parts centered on seeking, giving, and receiving help between two individuals, this part considers helping relations across group boundaries. It reviews research showing that while giving across group boundaries can reflect shared belongingness with an out-group, it can also be a mechanism through which groups create, maintain, and challenge hierarchical relations. Thus, for example, the habitual dependence of one group on an out-group may constitute the behavioral expression of structural inequality. The implications of intergroup helping relations for social change in structurally unequal contexts will also be addressed. A final section addresses the conceptual implications of research on interpersonal and intergroup helping relations, points at future research directions, and considers the practical implications of this body of knowledge.

To help the reader navigate through the different aspects of helping relations covered in this book, a map of its contents is provided in Figure 1.1. The map also reflects a chronological development of research and theory on helping. Much of the material covered in the first part of the book (i.e. broad philosophical and early psychological answers) predates social psychological research. The next part that

- ***Introduction:*** The move from help-giving to helping relations
    - o Social belongingness and social hierarchy in helping relations
    - o What is "helping"? Definitions and concepts
- "In the beginning": ***Philosophy, early psychological theory*** and ***evolutionary analyses*** of help-giving
- Social Psychological Research on Help-Giving
    - o ***When***: Bystander intervention, norms and cultural differences
    - o ***Who*** helps: Development, demographics and personality
    - o ***Why*** help: Empathy, prestige and attributions
- From Giving Help to Helping Relations: ***Effects of giving and receiving*** help
    - o Short- and long-term consequences of *giving* help for the *helper*
    - o Positive and negative consequences of *receiving for the recipient*: Gratitude and threat to self-esteem
    - o Kind of help, recipient characteristics and culture affect reactions to receiving
- From Interpersonal to ***Intergroup Helping Relations***
    - o Giving in the group
    - o Discriminatory helping
    - o Helping relations between advantaged and disadvantaged groups.
- Summary and Conclusions

Figure 1.1 Map of the contents of the book.

considers social psychological research on help-giving covers the period that began with research on bystander intervention in the second half of the twentieth century. The third part that addresses the consequences of helping for the helper and the recipient focuses on research pursued at the turn of the twenty-first century. Finally, most of the research described in the last part, on intergroup helping relations, has been conducted in the last two decades.

The boundaries of this proposed chronology are flexible (e.g. research on recipient reactions has already been conducted in the 1970s). Yet it serves to demonstrate how research developments have been affected by sociocultural changes outside the realm of social psychology. Thus, for example, the cultural changes in the Western world in the 1960s are responsible, partly at least, for the attempts to understand and overcome human apathy in the face of others' sufferings (i.e. bystander intervention research). Within the field of social psychology, developments in research and theory on intergroup relations (i.e. the social identity perspective on intergroup relations: Turner and Reynolds 2001) constitute an important reason for the growing interest in intergroup helping relations in the early twenty-first century.

2

Broad Perspectives

Philosophical and Psychological Theory, Evolution, and Overview of Social Psychological Research

The next sections review theory and research on help-giving. We begin with aspects of belongingness and independence in helping relations as they appear in philosophical treatises, early psychological theories, and anthropological observations. Many of these efforts have predated the development of social psychological research and theory on helping, hence the first part of this section's title. The section begins with a focus on giving as an expression of mutual belongingness, and moves on to helping relations as hierarchical relationships where the helper gains and the dependent recipient loses status and prestige. The next section reviews the main themes in evolutionary analyses of helping. The third and final section will bring us closer to the central theme of the book by providing a bird's eye view of the short history of social psychological research on helping from the middle of the twentieth century to the present.

2.1 Early Philosophical and Psychological Theory

2.1.1 Helping: Belongingness and Solidarity

On the individual level, giving to others or risking oneself on their behalf beg explanation. They are inconsistent with the idea that the basic human motivation is to ensure self-preservation and maximize one's own resources. Yet, as already noted, on the relational level,

Social Psychology of Helping Relations: Solidarity and Hierarchy, First Edition. Arie Nadler.

giving assistance to others in need, and seeking and receiving help from them when one is in need, are the sine qua non of solidarity. The breadth of solidarity or the feeling of shared belongingness varies. For some people, in some sociocultural contexts and under certain circumstances, it applies to a relatively narrow circle of relationships (e.g. family or tribe). For others, solidarity is broad and includes members of an entire society or even the whole of humanity.

Three broad answers have been offered to the question of why people act against what seems to be their best interests and give help or take personal risks to increase others' well-being. Each of the answers offers a different view on human nature. The first represents an optimistic view: the motivation that underlies giving to others is attributed to the innate benevolent nature of humankind. Jean Jacques Rousseau (1712–1778) voiced this position most poignantly (Damrosch 2007). If this is so, one might ask, how is it that we are not always good, generous, and helpful? In fact, some people often, and most people under certain circumstances, are indifferent to the plight of their fellow humans. Rousseau answered this question by suggesting that this reflects the corrupting nature of society. The pressures and oppressive character of families, groups, and cultures are the reasons why we sometimes act selfishly against our innately noble and helpful character.

This optimistic approach to human nature is shared by humanistic psychology. Both Carl Rogers (1961) and Abraham Maslow (1954) emphasized social connectedness and sensitivity to others' needs as vital for psychological well-being. Maslow lamented the relative lack of interest of the psychological science of his day in studying these positive aspects of social relationships. He criticized his contemporaries for their preoccupation with the negative aspects of interpersonal relations and wrote that "kindness, generosity, benevolence, and charity have too little place in the social psychology textbooks" (Maslow 1954, p. 371).

More recently, similar emphasis on social solidarity and interpersonal connectedness has been made by research subsumed under the title of positive psychology. This development, spurred by Seligman and his associates, seeks to shift psychology's focus on the pathological and maladjusted to people's happiness and well-being, and view a person's social ties with others as a central aspect of human welfare (Seligman and Csikszentmihalyi 2000; Seligman et al. 2005).

English philosopher Thomas Hobbes (1588–1679) gave a more pessimistic answer to the question "why help?" Whereas Rousseau held that civilization interfered with our innate benevolence, Hobbes argued that civilization made it possible. To him, the "state of nature" consisted of "war of all against all" (Malcolm 2014). Even if two people seemed on good terms with each other, there was no guarantee that one would not attack the other because he or she coveted what the other had. According to Hobbes, solidarity and helpfulness, and respect for others' property and rights are forced upon people rather than emanating from within them. This grim world of *homo homini lupus est* (man is wolf to man) is transformed into a livable society because an external, powerful entity forces us to curb our murderous instincts and act responsibly toward each other. This entity can be the king or a religious leader who lays down laws that force people to cooperate. To emphasize the enormity of this "enforcer of goodness," Hobbes metaphorically called that sovereign the *Leviathan* – the title of his best-known work (Malcolm 2014).

Some three centuries later, Sigmund Freud (1930) suggested that human beings were selfish by nature and if left to develop outside the constraints and values imposed by society they would seek immediate gratification at the expense of others' well-being. Freudian theory goes beyond the Hobbesian ideas by suggesting the intra-psychological dynamics through which these societal constraints and values are internalized. Like Hobbes, however, the Freudian view regards helpfulness as alien to human nature and dependent on external rules, norms, and values internalized in childhood.

The third answer to the question "why help?" falls between the two extremes represented by Rousseau and Hobbes. It is articulated most famously in the writings of English philosopher John Locke (1632–1704) (Wood 1992). Locke tells us that we are neither innately concerned with other people nor innately selfish and unconcerned with them. Our nature is neutral. We are born into the world as a proverbial *tabula rasa*, onto which parents and teachers "write" a story of solidarity and shared belongingness, or one of selfishness and lack of concern for others. We *learn* to be good and caring toward others: "nine parts of ten of what [people] are good or evil, useful or not [are determined] by their education" (John Locke (1796) in Grant and Tarcov 1996, p. 10). Again, if we skip to the twentieth century we can find a psychological parallel – in this case, behaviorism. Applying behavioristic principles to explain generosity toward others, B.F. Skinner (1981), the father of behaviorism, notes that "We value [helping] behavior, and indeed reinforce it, by saying 'Good!'" (p. 503).

2.1.2 *Helping Relations as Hierarchical Relations*

The dual nature of helping relations as reflecting solidarity *and* inequality was noted as early as the fourth century BCE by Aristotle, who coined the concept of *megalopsychia*, or magnanimity, defined as "that crowning ornament of virtues, meaning conferring benefits but being ashamed to receive them as well as to try to outdo one's benefactor in return in order to retain a position of superiority" (in Griffin 2013 pp. 18–19).This description captures both the belongingness- and independence-related hierarchical elements in giving and receiving help. While giving to others can be a "crowning virtue" it can also be an assertion of superiority, and dependency on others is shameful.

Four centuries later, Seneca wrote an essay titled "De Beneficiis" (On Giving), which would be well received by the Church Fathers and translated into English and French in the nineteenth and twentieth centuries (Griffin 2013). Seneca highlights the Janus-faced nature of helping by distinguishing between *beneficius* and *munus*. *Beneficius* represents genuine giving that is driven by a concern for the recipient's well-being, where the giver expects no benefits to him- or herself. This giving is captured in the Latin phrase *ego illud dedi, ut darem* (I gave in order to give). *Munus*, on the other hand, represents giving that is driven by the desire to gain fame, honor and prestige in return for kindness. The goal of such giving is not to help others but to express the giver's pride; it does not alleviate the pain of others but subdues them (Goux 2002).

Fast-forwarding to the early modern era, German philosopher Immanuel Kant (1724–1804) notes that people are humiliated by having to depend on others' assistance. Receiving help results in feelings of inferiority and indebtedness and therefore people with a "noble spirit" refuse assistance from others. Moreover, indebtedness and inferiority can turn into hostility toward the helper and lead the recipient to "bite the hand that feeds" (Kant 1930). Echoing a similar sentiment, Friedrich Nietzsche (1844–1900) describes "gift giving as the lust to rule."

In the French-speaking world, two twentieth-century scholars focused on the inequality associated with dependence on others' help. Pierre Bourdieu (1930–2002) coined the concept of *symbolic violence*, which refers to assertion of control and dominance through non-violent means, hierarchical help giving being one common example (1989). In a subsequent section on intergroup helping relations as status relations, we will return to this topic, equipped with the conceptual and empirical tools of experimental social psychology. In his writings on gift giving, Jacques Derrida (1930–2004) notes that since every act of giving help includes an act of receiving, the recipient is inferior and indebted to the giver, who derives the benefit of being the more dominant creditor. Thus, gift-giving is inherently paradoxical, because for there to be a gift it is necessary that the gift "not [be] perceived or received as gift" (Derrida 1992, p. 16).

Helping as an expression of hierarchical relations was also noted by the French scholar Alexis de Tocqueville (1805–1859) who summarized his observations of the young USA in a book titled *Democracy in America* (1834/1956). In this book, he wrote that members of the American ruling class exercised dominance over the underprivileged classes by providing them with assistance, and that the acceptance of such assistance constituted "servitude of the regular, quiet and gentle kind" (p. 303).

In the early twentieth century, Marcel Mauss (1872–1950), one of the founding fathers of anthropology, described the hierarchical aspect of giving and receiving in his seminal contribution *The Gift* (1907/1954). Mauss wrote about the custom of *potlatch* among the indigenous people of the Pacific Northwest, which consists of lavish displays of gift giving by a clan leader to other clan leaders, and wrote that the "motives for such excessive gifts ... are in no way disinterested. ... To give is to show one's superiority" (p. 72). Conversely, by being the willing recipients of these gifts other tribal leaders acknowledge their relative lower social position. He wrote that "to accept without returning ... [is] to become client and subservient" (Mauss 1954).

More recent anthropological studies have made similar observations. On Melanesian islands, the family of the deceased offers an elaborate feast during which guests receive gifts which they are not expected to reciprocate, and the more the family serves the relatively rare turtle meat the higher its esteem and reputation (Smith and Bliege Bird 2000). In a similar vein, Stephen Lyon describes the *dég* ritual practiced in Punjab, Pakistan, whereby excessive giving of food by one group to another is a nonviolent means of asserting the givers' dominance (Lyon 2004).

The preceding sections reviewed some of the deep roots of the Janus-faced nature of helping relations. Helping relations constitute behavioral expressions of social solidarity and hierarchy. Giving and receiving help can be an expression of belongingness in interpersonal and intra-group relations. Yet they can also be a vehicle through which people create and maintain an unequal social hierarchy. Social psychological research has shed light on the variables that determine which of these two facets of the same social interaction dominates. Before we move on to this research, the next section considers the evolutionary aspects of these two sides of the helping coin.

2.2 Evolutionary Perspectives on Helping Relations

2.2.1 The Evolutionary Basis of Generosity

Although Charles Darwin (1809–1882) himself emphasized the evolutionary importance of caring within the group (Darwin 2004/1871), social Darwinism became synonymous with a world dominated by brute force and selfishness. Thomas Henry Huxley (1825–1895), nicknamed Darwin's Bulldog for his early and steadfast support for Darwin's theory of evolution, held that because of evolutionary pressures, organisms in general and humans in particular were innately violent and uncaring creatures, and when they behaved generously, they did so because they obeyed social norms and cultural values (Huxley 1989/1894). This view is consistent with Hobbesian and Freudian views and is captured in the saying, "Scratch an altruist and watch a hypocrite bleed" (Ghiselin 1974, p. 247). If this is so, how can we explain generosity among animals and humans?

As early as the beginning of the twentieth century, Peter Kropotkin (1842–1921) challenged the Darwinian view of competition as the driving force of evolution. A Russian prince who had served as liege to Czar Alexander II and later resettled in London to become one of the leaders of the anarchist movement in Europe, Kropotkin published a book titled *Mutual Aid* (2009/1904), where he wrote that wherever he looked in nature he saw solidarity within species. He opposed the emphasis on the theme of "naked aggression" he saw in Darwin's theory, as well as Rousseau's naïve optimism. While not denying that struggle for survival existed in nature, he added that mutual aid was an equally important evolutionary force. Based on observations in the harsh environment of Siberia, he concluded that organisms developed patterns of cooperation within their groups to combat the perils posed by other species and by nature. For example, although a male deer would compete with other males for the right to procreate with a receptive female, it would put itself at risk by alerting others in the pack against an approaching predator.

More recent challenges to the unidimensional view of evolution as propelled by ruthless competition have led to conceptual refinements of the evolution of helpfulness. Consistent with Kropotkin's observations, scientific reports indicate that many species, from social insects such as bees and ants to predatory mammals such as wolves and lions place their lives on the line to benefit others in the group (de Waal et al. 2009). Bee and ant "soldiers" "commit suicide" by attacking intruders to the nest, and nesting birds are known to attract a predators' attention by limping away from the nest, thereby putting their lives in danger and saving their chicks (Dovidio et al. 2006a). Humans also engage in self-sacrificial behavior to save others who may not be genetically related to them. Examples include soldiers committing suicide by falling on an unpinned grenade to save their comrades (Riemer 1998). All these examples reinforce Kropotkin's (1904) observation: cooperation and self-sacrifice are abundant in nature. How can evolutionary theory that hails the principle of "survival of the fittest" account for the fact that altruism is so widespread in nature?

2.2.1.1 Kin Selection and Inclusive Fitness W.D. Hamilton (1964) proposed a solution to the altruistic puzzle by moving the forces of evolution from the individual to the genetic level of analysis. He suggested that the force that drives evolution forward is not individuals' but genes' "motivation to replicate" themselves. According to this view, genes are the true masters of evolutionary destiny, and the individual is nothing more than a "mobile unit" on which the genes travel into the future. This idea was subsequently refined by Richard Dawkins (2006) and captured in the title of his bestselling book *The Selfish Gene*.

Hamilton (1964) suggested that genes could be transmitted into the future by the survival of the individual or by the survival of his or her genetically related relatives. Further, the probability that the genes would "travel into the future" may be higher if a sufficient number of genetically related kins survive than if the individual survives. To illustrate, when a nesting bird saves its four chicks by sacrificing itself, the 100% of its genes that perish are replaced by 200% of the same genes that survive with the living chicks (50% of the mother's genes in each of the four chicks). Therefore, the mother bird's "altruistic" self-sacrifice has a sound – and selfish – evolutionary logic, because it raises the probability that its genes make it to the next generation. The strategy of transferring the genes to the next generation by ensuring the survival of the individual is labeled *direct fitness*, while doing so by increasing the survivability of genetically related kin is labeled *indirect fitness*. The joint consideration of the two strategies represents *inclusive fitness*.

Are these distal gene-level explanations of self-sacrificial altruism relevant to human helpfulness? An investigation by Burnstein, Crandall and Kitayama (1994) suggests a positive answer. Consistent with the principle of kin selection, in a scenario that depicted a life-or-death situation (e.g. rescue from a burning house), the higher the genetic relatedness of the protagonist (e.g. siblings more than cousins) the higher the tendency to put oneself at risk and intervene. Furthermore, the tendency to rescue a genetically related individual was higher when the person in need had higher reproductive potential (e.g. a genetically related protagonist in childbearing age vs. a similarly related other beyond it). Another support for the role of kin selection in sacrificial altruism is that although people may feel emotionally closer to an intimate friend than to a sibling (Kruger 2003), they are readier to give high cost help (e.g. donating a kidney) to a sibling than to a close friend (Stewart-Williams 2007).

These findings demonstrate the complex nature of distal explanations, such as gene survivability, in explaining helping. On the one hand, they constitute an impressive demonstration of the parsimonious merits of the concept of inclusive fitness. The same principle can be used to explain a bird's self-sacrificial altruism and people's tendency to save a relative. It also serves to remind us that humans and other organisms are made up of the same biological material and that the assignment of "beastly nature" to the latter and heavenly compassion and helpfulness to former represents an idealized and distorted view of social life in nature (de Waal 2006).

Are evolutionary-based principles the only mechanism that explains why we are ready to sacrifice all for the sake of genetically related others? If all we see is genetic relatedness, we may overlook the fact that belongingness, love and intimacy are also reasons why people commit self-sacrificial acts. This becomes obvious when the emotionally close other is genetically unrelated. Indeed, Korchmaros and Kenny (2001, 2006) found that the relationship between kinship and helping is mediated by emotional proximity. Reliance on evolutionary principles alone would have suggested less helpfulness between an adopted child and his or her parent, than between parents and their genetically related children. Yet research indicating that parents of adopted children are no less devoted to them than parents of genetically related children are, suggests that this is not the case (Murray 1996). As humans, we care and take personal risks for the sake of those with whom we spend much time and share a sense of belongingness. Often, these individuals are genetically unrelated to us.

2.2.1.2 Reciprocal Altruism The evolutionary principles used to explain helping focus on help given to genetically related individuals. However, helpfulness is also common between genetically unrelated individuals (de Waal et al. 2009). For example, an individual monkey would alert its pack to incoming danger by making warning calls, thereby putting itself in danger of being attacked. How can the principle of inclusive fitness explain helping genetically unrelated others?

Robert Trivers' concept of *reciprocal altruism* (1971) attempts to do just that. He proposes that individuals help genetically unrelated others with the expectation that they would be helped by them when in need. Such expectations are the basis of cooperative relationships that increase the individual's prospects of overcoming external enemies and the challenges presented by nature. For example, if I help you irrigate your dry field today, you would do the same for me when my field goes dry, and this would increase the probability that both of us and our kin would survive. Phrased in the language of evolutionary theory, the principle of reciprocal altruism suggests that I detract from my evolutionary fitness today, with the expectation that if in the future the need arises you would detract from yours to increase mine. For reciprocal altruism to be a successful and stable evolutionary strategy, all interactants must conform to this rule of conduct and punish free riders who had received help but fail to reciprocate it when their benefactors are in need (Fehr and Rockenbach 2004; Gintis et al. 2001). Human beings whose cognitive capacities allow them to bridge across temporal distances are especially adept in detecting and punishing "free riders" who receive but do not reciprocate (Cosmides and Tooby 1995). In human social life the evolutionary principle of reciprocal altruism finds expression in the norm of reciprocity that governs social relationships (Gouldner 1960). Direct reciprocity means that recipients are obligated to return in kind to those who have helped them, and *indirect* reciprocity that they are obligated to help others in the group who may or may not helped them in the past (Schroeder and Graziano 2015).

2.2.1.3 Group Selection The evolutionary process of natural selection has traditionally been applied to competition between individuals. Recent conceptual developments have suggested that natural selection can also occur on the *group level* (Boehm 1999; Sober and Wilson 1998). The previously described concepts of kin selection and inclusive fitness constitute individual-level mechanisms whereby helping genetically related individuals enables the individual to increase the prospects of evolutionary success. The concept of indirect reciprocity refers to a group-level mechanism that increases the group's evolutionary fitness through increased intra-group cooperation and helpfulness, combined with suppression of aggression and competition within the group. This tends to characterize groups that are smaller, have limited migration to and from outside of their borders, and when they are in conflict with outgroups (Gintis et al. 2003). Under these conditions, the human capacity to build a strong sense of solidarity and feelings of shared belongingness between group members is high. Such ingroup solidarity translates into normative structures that reinforce helpfulness and cooperation within the group. In turn, this group culture creates a moral community that is based on prosocial values of cooperation, trust, and helpfulness that in the context of intergroup competition translate into increased inclusive fitness of its individual members vis a vis other groups (Boehm 2012; Wilson et al. 2008) (i.e. gene-culture coevolution theories; Simpson and Beckes 2010).

2.2.2 Evolutionary Basis of Helping as Hierarchical Relations

In a book titled *The Ant and the Peacock*, Helena Cronin (1991) notes two puzzles that are left unanswered in Darwin's theory of evolution. The "ant puzzle" refers to the intricate patterns of cooperativeness and self-sacrifice to protect against intruders in ant colonies, that the face of it, are inconsistent with the evolutionary-based competition that allows the better adjusted individual to flourish. The evolutionary principles of increasing collective fitness and group-selection discussed previously suggest an explanation for this puzzle.

The "peacock puzzle" refers to the inconsistency between the male peacock's lavish display of its heavy and beautiful tail during courtship rituals and the fact that it makes it harder for the peacock to flee from predators. The *handicapping principle* (Zahavi and Zahavi 1999) suggests an answer to this puzzle. It holds that individual organisms are willing to incur short-term costs in order to advertise their long-term fitness as mates and allies. By spreading its tail, the male peacock tells onlooking peacocks, "I am strong and fit enough to survive and prosper even with this handicap." Applied to the realm of helping relations, giving to others is a self-imposed handicap, indicating to onlookers that the helper has enough resources to take care of their own, *and* others' needs.

Observations of animal behavior support this idea. Birds have often been observed to engage in the evolutionary wasteful behavior of feeding genetically unrelated chicks (Brown et al. 1978). When considered within the logic of the handicapping principle this behavior is a costly signaling of one's resourcefulness to other onlooking birds. It is a costly behavior in the short run that establishes the organism's standing as a superior mating partner in the long run. Thus, this seemingly evolutionarily inconsistent behavior follows the rules of a well-planned advertising campaign. In order to be detected by its conspecifics, the "altruistic" bird waits until a bird audience has gathered before feeding the genetically unrelated nestlings. It also spends more time holding the prey in its beak before feeding it to the genetically unrelated chicks than natural parents do when feeding their offspring (Doutrelant and Covas 2007). This does not imply that the advertising bird preplanned its "altruism in the service of fame" campaign in a local ad agency. Rather, millions of years of evolution have shaped this link between giving and prestige as a successful tactic to gain a mate and guarantee the transfer of one's genes into the future.

The social behavior of the Arabian babbler – a cooperative, group territorial bird living in desert habitats – provides another demonstration of the evolutionary basis of the link between help-giving and status (Carlisle and Zahavi 1986). In most interactions, the more dominant individual bird brought food to the subordinate individual. If the subordinate bird refused to take the food, it was hit or chased by the dominant bird. In cases where this top-down pattern of giving was interrupted, i.e. the subordinate tried to feed the dominant one, the latter refused to take the food and reacted aggressively by chasing or hitting the subordinate. These observations demonstrate how giving is an evolutionary based behavior associated with higher status, while dependence on others' giving is associated with lower status. Carlisle and Zahavi (1986) conclude that "Babblers that establish status by demonstrating ability to bear the short-term costs of cooperative behavior, rather than through direct aggression toward rivals, are likely to forge collaborative relationships with other group members" (p. 339), which are of evolutionary value, especially in the harsh environment that these birds inhabit. This resonates with our previous discussion of increasing group members' evolutionary fitness by adopting a normative structure based on indirect reciprocity – i.e. helping regardless of whether or not they had been helped.

*

To conclude, the evolutionary explanations of helping echo the belongingness and hierarchical aspects in helping relations. Although genetic relatedness is not synonymous with psychological belongingness, both underscore the commonality between helper and recipient as the precursor of helpfulness. At the same time, giving to others advertises the helper's relative advantage and receiving from them the recipient's relative disadvantage. These two evolutionary explanations are united in viewing helpfulness as enhancing the altruist's evolutionary fitness and the transfer of one's genes into the future, and constitute *distal* explanations of helping and altruism. These explanations represent multiple levels of abstraction and methodological and theoretical tools relevant for the understanding of helping relations. As the holder of a colored cube gains greater knowledge of what he or she holds if they view it from different angles, so is the student of social behavior more knowledgeable about helping relations after viewing it from different disciplinary perspectives. In the next sections, we move to a social psychological perspective on helping relations.

The rest of this book is devoted to the social psychological research focused on the *proximal* determinants of helping relations. These include the characteristics of the situation, the helper, and the person in need. We begin by providing the reader with an overview of the themes that have dominated social psychological research on helping since its inception in the mid-twentieth century. In contrast to the foregoing section, that focused on the long past of helping – the philosophical and early psychological theorizing on the "nature of man" – this section focuses on the short history of social psychological research on helping. It begins with research on help-giving, continues to research on the consequences of giving and receiving help for helper and recipient, and concludes with research on intergroup helping relations. The interplay between helping as expressing people's need for belongingness to others and the wish to be independent of them will be the scarlet thread running through this review. Before moving to a detailed examination of social psychological research on helping relations, the final subsection in this part draws a broad view of the themes of this research from the mid-twentieth century up to the present.

2.3 Overview of Social Psychological Research

Dating the first empirical psychological study on helping is difficult, if not impossible. Yet one early study stands out. In the latter part of the 1920s, two researchers from Columbia University sought to identify and measure the ingredients that make up "human character," of which generosity was conceptualized as an important one. The main goals of this research were to establish whether the qualities that make up people's character (e.g. persistence, honesty, helpfulness) constitute personality traits or are situationally determined (Hartshorne and

May 1928; Hartshorne et al. 1929, 1930). To measure children's generosity, they gave some 11 000 elementary and high school students 33 different tests that measured helpfulness, which they labeled "service tendency". For example, they assessed whether boys would be willing give up building a car model and make toys for hospital children instead, or distribute money given to them between themselves and a charitable cause. In this large-scale and sophisticated research project, they also examined the relationships between children's actual helping behavior and the way it was perceived by peers and teachers.

Some viewed the findings as substantiating the *situational approach* to helpfulness (i.e. that it is determined by the specific situation; e.g. Mischel 1968), and others as supporting the *personality approach* (i.e. that helpfulness is a generalized trait observable across situations; e.g. Eysenck 1970; Rushton et al. 1981). We will revisit these two sides of the personality-situation argument in a subsequent section, but for our present purposes, note the Hartshorne and May's research as an impressive example of early research interest in helping that developed, 40 years later, into an independent field of social psychological research.

A search in the PsycNet database for papers that include as keywords any of the three most commonly used terms in this research context – "helping behavior," "prosocial behavior" or "altruistic behavior/altruism" – retrieved only 363 papers until 1965, compared to 13 878 papers published between 1965 and 2015. These numbers reflect the development of helping research into an independent field of inquiry. Also, during the 50 years that ended in 2015, textbooks in social psychology have devoted about 10% of their overall space to research on helping (e.g. Baron and Byrne 1987; Baron et al. 2006; Myers 2012); numerous reviews have summarized advances in this field (see Batson 1998; Keltner et al. 2014; Nadler 2018 for a sample of these reviews in the last two decades); and a number of recent books provide social psychologists with broad and detailed reviews (e.g. Bierhoff 2002; Dovidio et al. 2006a; Schroeder and Graziano 2015).

Modern social psychological research on helping began with Latané and Darley's (1970) study on the unresponsive bystander problem. Why then? One answer is the sociocultural change that the Western world underwent during the 1960s. Young people marched in the streets calling for greater spontaneity and caring in social life, and many saw social psychology as the scientific discipline that could promote such a social change. Thus, since its beginnings, research on helping has been driven by two motivations: to gain better understanding of social behavior, and to contribute to the creation of a more caring society. This dual emphasis has remained with the field and will, in all likelihood, impact on its development in the future.

The question that "ignited" the field was the puzzle of the unresponsive bystander. It is emblematized by the story of Kitty Genovese, who was murdered near her home in Queens, New York, in 1964, while dozens of people calmly watched and did nothing to help. As detailed in a subsequent section a more thorough examination of the facts of that night in 1964 reveals that not all bystanders had watched apathetically as their neighbor had been murdered. Regardless, the Kitty Genovese murder being used as a metaphor for bystander apathy during an emergency, Latané and Darley (1970) proceeded to address the question of bystander apathy in the social psychological laboratory, and research on the unresponsive bystander dominated much of the attention of social psychologists in those early years.

This and subsequent research on help giving was guided by three questions: When, Who and Why help (Dovidio et al. 2006a). The "When" question focused on identifying the situational conditions under which people were more or less likely to help others in need. The "Who" question inquired whether some people were characteristically more helpful than others and sought to identify the personality dimensions and developmental antecedents that could explain these differences. The "Why" question focused on uncovering the motivational and cognitive dynamics that explained the reasons that motivated people to help others. Similar to the dilemmas that dominated philosophical discussions centuries before, the motivational question asked whether people helped others because they cared, were motivated to gain personal benefits, or were compelled to do so by social norms. With the development of experimental paradigms that allowed examining these questions empirically, the answers moved from scholars' libraries to the social psychology laboratory.

Beyond the emphasis on understanding human generosity, research in the field has broadened in three major respects: (i) focus on seeking and receiving help, (ii) intergroup helping relations, and (iii) moving beyond the help/no-help dichotomy to consider different kinds of help. Research on receiving and seeking help has indicated that being dependent may imply the recipient's relative inferiority and constitute a self-threatening experience (Nadler and Fisher 1986). Because of this, individuals in need may refrain from seeking help and respond negatively to help offers (Wills and DePaulo 1991).

Second, while much of the research in the field has centered on interpersonal helping interactions, more recent investigations have analyzed helping interactions across group boundaries. Developments in social identity and self-categorization theory tell us that when individuals' collective identity is salient, what seems like an interpersonal interaction needs to be analyzed as an intergroup interaction (e.g. when an African-American receives help from a European-American; Saucier 2015). Oftentimes intergroup helping relations are relationships between unequal social entities and the dynamics of intergroup helping relations reflect groups' desire to maintain or challenge their group's position in the social hierarchy. Advantaged groups may use the giving of help strategically to ascertain their privileged position (Nadler et al. 2009), while the disadvantaged may decline offers of assistance to signal their independence and their quest for greater equality with the more advantaged outgroup (Nadler and Halabi 2006).

Finally, recent research has departed from the dichotomous distinction between help and no-help to consider the *kinds* of help that is being transacted. Some helping interactions aim to solve the problem for the recipient, while others aim to provide the recipient with the tools that will enable them to solve the problem on their own (i.e. dependency-oriented and autonomy-oriented helping, respectively) (Nadler 1997, 2015). In general, autonomy-oriented help, where the recipient retains a sense of self-reliance, is preferable for the recipient. Its merits have been noted, 800 years ago, by Maimonides, a Jewish physician and philosopher, who wrote about eight steps of generosity in an ascending order of benefit for the recipient, where the highest form of helping is when one gives the needy assistance that teaches them a skill or collaborating with them in a way that will reduce their future dependence on help (Maimonides 1998). For the most part, social psychological research has focused on help that aims to solve the recipient's current sufferings or difficulties, i.e. dependency-oriented help, rather than on assistance that promotes future self-reliance, i.e. autonomy-oriented help. In the present book, we will depart from this tradition and consider the different antecedents and consequences of autonomy- and dependency-oriented helping relations.

In recent years, researchers have taken the wealth of knowledge accumulated during these 50 years of research and applied it to real-life social contexts. Throughout the book, the social relevance of social psychological research is interwoven into the description of findings regarding basic social psychological processes in helping relations. This reminds us of the two feet on which the study of helping stands: to accumulate basic knowledge on human social behavior and to contribute to a human society built on caring and respect for others' needs.

3

Social Psychology of Help-Giving

The When, Who, and Why of Help-Giving

Most, if not all social psychology textbooks begin their coverage of research on helping by telling readers the story of the murder of Kitty Genovese in Queens, New York, in 1964. In fact, over the years this tragic story has gained the status of a metaphor for people's apathy to the sufferings of fellow human beings. Although recent reexaminations of the actual events have cast grave doubts on the facts as told and retold, we will begin by telling the story as generations of students have read it in their textbooks or heard it in lecture halls. In a following section, I will set the record straight and point out the inaccuracies that have turned the story into an iconic symbol of bystander apathy.

The story began in a *New York Times* news report by Martin Gansberg, two weeks after the event, which was titled: "37 who saw murder and didn't call the police." The report went on to say that on the night of March 13, 1964, a young woman named Kitty Genovese returned to her Queens apartment from her work as a bartender at around 3:00 a.m. As she left her car, she was attacked, raped and robbed by a man named Winston Moseley. The news story went on to tell the readers that although she screamed for help, no one in the apartments overlooking the parking lot where the attack took place came to her rescue. Even worse, no witness called the police. The story was popularized by A.M. Rosenthal, the *New York Times*' city editor, who wrote a book about the incident titled *Thirty-Eight Witnesses.*

Social Psychology of Helping Relations: Solidarity and Hierarchy, First Edition. Arie Nadler.

Before considering how this metaphor of bystander apathy has shaped social psychological research on helping, note that recent examinations of what really happened that night reveal a different story than the one familiar to generations of social psychology students. Academic research (Manning et al. 2007), newspaper articles (e.g. a 2004 article by Jim Rasenberger in the *New York Times*), and a 2016 research-based documentary (*The Witness* by James Solomon) all pointed to inaccuracies in the original story. Apparently, some eyewitnesses did call the police, the number of "apathetic bystanders" was neither 37 as reported in the news story nor 38 as in the title of Rosenthal's book, and Kitty Genovese did not die alone without human comfort – a neighbor came down and stayed with her until the ambulance arrived. Genovese passed away on her way to the hospital. The discrepancy between what we came to believe about the event and the facts says something important about the power of the media in creating images that unify public opinion around an issue. The journalists who dramatized the murder unintentionally spurred the development of research in social psychology.

The story of Kitty Genovese, and similar reports about rampant crime in big cities where bystanders do not intervene to help their fellow humans, were especially relevant in the sociocultural context of the 1960s. On the one hand, this period was close enough to the horrors of the Second World War, when evil triumphed because good people did nothing when Jews, Gypsies, homosexuals and dissidents were taken away and killed. On the other hand, as already noted, the 1960s were a time of cultural change, when many in Western societies challenged the then prevailing values of conservatism and conformity and advocated social change in the direction of greater interpersonal intimacy, spontaneity, and caring in personal relationships (Chalmers 2013). These winds of political and cultural change blew in major university campuses and in the streets of Paris, New York, and London. The juxtaposition of the relatively recent inaction in the face of atrocity and inhumanity, and the cultural change that called for greater responsiveness to others' plight was the historical background for the emergence of scientific interest in the question of bystander apathy, and helping more generally. The definition of social psychology as the science of social behavior made it the natural candidate to uncover when and why people would help others in need.

Although isolated studies such as Hartshorne and May (1928) had considered the question of helpfulness before the mid-twentieth century, the first program of social psychological research on helpfulness appeared in the 1960s and was guided by the question, *The Unresponsive Bystander: Why Doesn't He Help?* (Latané and Darley 1970). To study the reasons behind the bystanders' apparent apathy to Genovese's plight, and similar incidents, Darley and Latané (1968) sought to simulate the conditions that had prevailed in the crime scene in their social psychological laboratory. This pioneering research opened the door to the development of an entire field of social psychological study on the determinants of human helpfulness and the psychological processes that explain people's decisions whether to intervene to help others in need.

3.1 The "When" of Help-Giving: Characteristics of the Situation

3.1.1 Bystander Intervention

3.1.1.1 The Beginning Latané and Darley (1970) proposed a four-stage decision-making model that describes the process bystanders go through when deciding whether to intervene. First, the bystanders need to *notice* that something out of the ordinary has taken place – an event. If they do not notice, they will go on their daily business and intervention will not occur. Once they notice something has happened, e.g. an individual lies on the lawn with their eyes closed, they need to *interpret* the event as an emergency that requires intervention. If the bystanders think the person lying on the lawn is just soaking up the summer sun, this is not interpreted as an emergency, and the bystanders will do nothing. Yet if the event is interpreted as requiring intervention, e.g. that the person lying on the lawn needs medical attention, the bystanders must decide whether it is their *responsibility* to intervene. If, for any reason, they do not see themselves as responsible they will not intervene. Finally, after the event had been noticed, interpreted as an emergency, and the bystanders assumed responsibility to intervene, they must decide *how*. Should they help directly by approaching the victim, or indirectly by calling an ambulance, for example?

This progression of decisions that culminates in intervention is depicted below. The positive answers to noticing an event, interpreting it as an emergency, and assuming responsibility to intervene are the stages that culminate in an intervention decision. If at any step in the process the answer is negative, intervention will not occur.

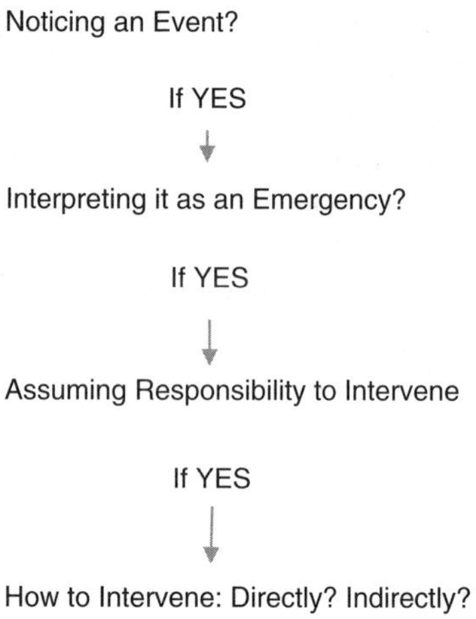

Noticing an Event?

If YES

↓

Interpreting it as an Emergency?

If YES

↓

Assuming Responsibility to Intervene

If YES

↓

How to Intervene: Directly? Indirectly?

This stage model serves us as a convenient conceptual framework for reviewing subsequent research on bystander intervention.

Noticing an event. The importance of noticing an event is demonstrated in that participants whose attention had been distracted by a loud "white noise" were subsequently less likely to help another person who had accidentally dropped their belongings (36% helped), compared to those who had not been distracted (72.2% and 66.7% helped in the no-noise and low-level noise conditions, respectively) (Mathews and Canon 1975).

Lower attentiveness to others is one explanation for the finding that people living in big cities are relatively less helpful than their counterparts in smaller communities. Levine et al. (1994) compared readiness to help across 36 American communities varying in size from a megalopolis like New York to small towns. On diverse measures of helping (e.g. returning a pen to its owner, helping a person with an injured leg, or helping a blind person cross the street), the larger the bystanders' place of residence the lower their readiness to intervene to help. Similarly, in their pioneering study on bystander intervention, Darley and Latané (1968) reported that out of 16 personality and demographic variables, the only one that predicted likelihood of intervention was the size of the community in which the participant grew up.

One explanation for the negative relationship between community size and readiness to help is that in small communities, the number of other people around us is relatively small and unchanging. In such communities, people tend to know others by name and meet each other frequently. This is not the case in the large city, where the number of individuals one encounters is much larger. In these environments, people develop selective attention to cope with the stimulus overload that the mass of people around them presents. They pay attention to the few they know, and disregard the many they do not. Therefore, the likelihood that bystander attention would be diverted to a mishap that had befallen another is higher in the small town (Milgram 1970). Thus, it is not that people in the big city are inherently less caring than people in small towns. In both social environments, people attend to what is happening to others they know, others with whom they feel solidarity. In the big city, the likelihood that the person needing our help is someone we know and feel shared belongingness with is simply lower.Therefore bystanders in the big city are less likely to **notice** an event that may be interpreted as an emergency than their counterparts in small towns.

Interpreting the event as an emergency. After the bystander had noticed the event, they need to interpret it as an emergency if helping is to occur. Yet, many life situations that require us to intervene are ambiguous and clear interpretation is difficult. For example, we may find ourselves standing in a very long line to buy tickets to a show when someone in front of us moves out of the line, and sits on a fence with their hands on their chest. Why is he or she doing this? Are they simply tired? Maybe they have chest pain and need immediate medical assistance? We are not sure and therefore we often do not move. Such misinterpretations have been shown to contribute to people's delayed responses to a fire in an office or restaurant (Canter et al. 1980).

The reactions of other bystanders may help disambiguate the situation and facilitate its interpretation as an emergency. Because friends' spontaneous reactions to an unexpected situation are more readily understood, people in a group of friends who sat facing each other intervened faster in an emergency than when they were with strangers, or with friends whose faces they did not see (Dovidio et al. 2006). A simple way to reduce misinterpretation is simply telling bystanders that this is an emergency. When a confederate said in response to hearing the sound of a crash in an adjoining room, "this sounds serious," all participants intervened, as opposed to only 25% when the confederate did not make this comment (Staub 1974). The importance of disambiguating an emergency to increase the likelihood of intervention was also highlighted in a meta-analysis of 40 years of research on bystander intervention, which found that one is less affected by others' reactions in situations that are consensually dangerous, where the interpretation of the event as an emergency that requires intervention is faster and clearer (Fischer et al. 2011).

Assuming responsibility to intervene. After an event had been noticed and interpreted as an emergency, people must assume responsibility to intervene if helping is to occur. In their pioneering study that "jumpstarted" the social psychology of helping, Darley and Latané (1968) demonstrated that whether or not other bystanders are present affects the willingness of the individual to assume responsibility and intervene. Participants in their experiment who were under the impression that they were alone in witnessing an emergency situation (i.e. a supposed epileptic seizure experienced by a person in an adjoining cubicle) intervened more frequently and three times faster than if they thought that other four bystanders were present (85% vs. 65%, respectively). Post-experimental interviews suggested that a witness to an emergency is caught up in a dilemma: should I risk making a fool of myself by overreacting, or should I stay put and run the risk of feeling guilty because I did nothing in a situation that called for action?

Why should the presence of others have such a strong effect on resolving this intervention dilemma? Darley and Latané (1968) suggested that just as witnesses to the Kitty Genovese murder – who had been separated from their neighbors by their apartment walls – might have thought that someone else had already intervened, participants in their experiment who were under the impression that they were alone and were secluded in their cubicle told themselves that someone else would or had already intervened. Put differently, the responsibility to do the right thing tends to be distributed across the "unseen others." This effect on bystander intervention was labeled the *diffusion of responsibility effect* and demonstrated in numerous studies conducted over the years (cf. Fischer et al. 2011).

The diffusion of responsibility effect occurs even when one does not think that others are present but just imagines him- or herself in a large group (Garcia et al. 2002). People who had imagined themselves in a large group (i.e. having dinner with 30 others) gave less to charity than those who had imagined themselves as being with only one other person in the same situation (Study 1). Moreover, the negative effect of others' presence on willingness to help was evident even when the imagined group was completely unrelated to the helping context. Participants who had been asked to imagine a group of strangers in a movie theater were later relatively less willing to donate to an annual alumni campaign (Study 2). This finding seems to refute the diffusion of responsibility explanation: after all, the others in this study could not be presumed to have had already helped. To account for this inconsistency, Garcia et al. (2002) proposed a broader cognitive conception of the effect that went beyond the immediate situation. They suggested that "people who imagine group situations have notions of unaccountability triggered, and this leads them to see the situation as one that does not call for their personal help" (p. 851).

How to intervene? After the bystander had noticed that something had happened, interpreted it as an emergency requiring intervention, and assumed responsibility to intervene, how should this be done? In the Kitty Genovese case, bystanders could have helped directly by going down to confront the attacker, or indirectly by calling the police. A conceptually driven answer to this question of "how to help" is suggested by the *cost-reward model of helping* that tells us that when bystanders contemplate how to intervene in an emergency, they weigh the costs of helping against the costs of not helping (Piliavin et al. 1975). Costs of helping may consist of the physical danger associated with direct intervention (e.g. a violent fight) and costs of not helping may consist of guilt feelings the person anticipates if he or she decided to do nothing. The model suggests that when the costs of helping are low and the costs of not helping are high (e.g. an adult witnessing young children in a violent fight), direct intervention is likely. When both costs are high (e.g. the violent fight is between two muscular adults), indirect intervention is more likely (e.g. calling the police). When the costs of helping are high (e.g. the fight between muscular adults), but the costs of not helping are low (e.g. the persons hitting each seem drunk and therefore less guilt for doing nothing is expected) intervention will not occur. Finally, when both costs are low (e.g. a beggar asking for a handout) prediction is difficult. Help will depend on personal preferences and momentary influences.

The costs of helping and not helping may be determined by variables that define the need situation, and by variables that are not directly relevant to it. Variables of the first group may include the bystander's relevant skills, resources or knowledge (e.g. physical strength or professional skill needed to cope with the situation). The second group includes variables that affect the bystander's evaluations of the needy, such as their skin color, religion or some other marker of stigmatised group. Thus, although people are not likely to admit that the needy's physical appearance weighs into their decision to help, bystanders were less likely to help when the individual in need suffered from a facial disfigurement than when not (i.e. "port-wine stain" birthmark) (Piliavin et al. 1975). Physical disfigurement may unconsciously increase the costs of interacting with the person in need, thereby lowering the willingness to help him or her. Also, when people are viewed as responsible for their plight, guilt feelings associated with not helping are relatively low and intervention is less likely (Weiner 1980). Such judgements are often determined by the other's group affiliation. For example, when we have a stereotype of members of a certain group as being lazy we are likely to view them as responsible for their predicament and be less willing to help them.

These processes are of great social relevance. They indicate that the stereotypes and prejudices we hold about outgroup members affect the costs of helping and of not helping, which translate into lower or higher likelihood of intervention. Thus, for example, the stereotype that members of a certain outgroup are violent may mean that intervention to help one of them would be costly, discouraging bystanders from direct intervention. By the same token, if a teacher perceives a certain minority group as nurturing values of dependence on others, children from that group may be blamed for their difficulties, which will reduce the costs of not helping them, and lead to lesser willingness to intervene on their behalf. Obviously, these are not conscious processes. Rather, they may reflect general perceptions about outgroups that people carry with them across multiple situations and life domains, and that affect interpersonal helpfulness. This underscores the role of ***intergroup relations*** in interpersonal interventions. We now turn to this aspect in bystander intervention, and expand on it later in this book.

3.1.1.2 Bystander Intervention: The Social Identity Perspective If the reader was to stop here, they would have probably concluded that the presence of others discourages intervention. Yet research on intra- and intergroup processes situated within the social identity framework does not warrant such a whole-hog conclusion (Turner and Reynolds 2001). Briefly stated, the social identity perspective holds that an important part of one's sense of self includes is based on the individual's collective identity that is anchored in his or her affiliation with psychologically relevant social groups (e.g. tribal or national affiliation). In addition, the social identity perspective asserts that self-categorization of collective identity is malleable and situationally determined. To illustrate, when I am in a football stadium cheering my favorite team, my categorization as a fan of that team is dominant. When, however, the game is an international match between my country's national team and another country, my national identity is the situationally dominant self-categorization that affects my feelings, cognitions and behaviors.

The shared belongingness between bystanders and people in need who have the same collective identity translates to increased bystander readiness to help members of the ingroup. Social identity theory asserts, and research indicates, that humans give more to the ingroup than to outgroups (Levine and Manning 2013). This tendency for ingroup favoritism occurs even when the criterion that differentiates the groups has no psychological importance or meaning. For example, based on a dot-estimation task, people in my group are labeled as "specific" or "global" perceivers. This inconsequential group distinction is enough to engender a sense of ingroup belongingness (Jetten et al. 1997). Also, bystanders and people in need who have shared the same traumatic event often become part of the same category of trauma victims that facilitates within-group helpfulness. Thus, in the days and weeks following 9/11, people were more willing to donate blood and money, and help victims of the same trauma that they had experienced (e.g. Schuster et al. 2001). Similarly, the shared traumatic experiences by victims and bystanders in the 2005 London bombings led to a sense of common identity, which manifested itself in high levels of mutual helpfulness (e.g. Drury et al. 2009). A more recent disaster underscores how the sharing of a traumatic event can induce a feeling of shared identity that facilitates helping members of outgroups who had shared the same traumatic event as oneself: native Italian children who had experienced the 2013 earthquake in northern Italy together with immigrant children viewed the latter as Italians like themselves, and this perceived commonality mediated their willingness to assist them (Vezzali et al. 2015).

The role of the ingroup-outgroup distinction in helpfulness has been demonstrated experimentally among research participants who were all Manchester United fans (Levine et al. 2005). Being a fan of a certain football team is a significant source of self-categorization in many countries, certainly in England where the game was born. Capitalizing on the fans' love for the game, the study examined how the role of people's perceived group identity affects their willingness to help others in distress. The experimenter asked participants to walk to an adjacent building. On their way there, each participant encountered a confederate, who had supposedly suffered an injury and needed their help. The victim's group identity varied. In the first condition, he wore a T-shirt identifying him as a Manchester United fan, and in a second condition, the T-shirt identified him as a Liverpool fan. In a third, control condition the victim wore a blank T-shirt. When the victim shared group belongingness with the helper, 12 out of 13 participants stopped to help. When, however, he was identified as a member of the outgroup only 3 out of 10 participants stopped to help. In the control condition, 4 out of 13 participants helped. These findings demonstrate the critical role of shared belongingness in promoting helpfulness. The similar pattern of findings observed in the outgroup and control conditions indicates that it is not the "animosity" toward the outgroup that decreases helpfulness, but the shared belongingness with the victim that increases it.

In a second experiment, Levine et al. (2005) demonstrated how bystander intervention may be shaped by changes in the outgroup's categorization. As in the first experiment, all participants were Manchester United fans. Yet their social identity as Manchester United fans was replaced by a more inclusive category of lovers of the "beautiful game of football." This extended categorization created a common identity with fans of the rival team Liverpool. Based on the common identity model (Gaertner and dovidio 2009), it was expected that as "football lovers," participants would show similar rates of intervention when the victim was a member of the ingroup and outgroup. In terms of the present analysis, such a cognitive redrawing of group boundaries would extend shared belongingness and solidarity beyond the ingroup's limits. As expected, participants helped a person in need similarly regardless of whether he wore a T-shirt identifying him as a Manchester United or Liverpool fan (8 and 7 participants out of 10, respectively, stopped to help the person in need). Under these conditions, the person in need in the control condition who wore a blank T-shirt and thus out of the boundaries of the participants' extended identity as football lovers, was helped significantly less (only 2 out of 9 participants stopped to help).

A real-life demonstration of the effects of shared belongingness on helpfulness was provided by Reicher et al.'s (2006) analysis of the saving of Bulgarian Jews from Nazi extermination in 1943. To a large degree, this heroic rescue was due to that the Bulgarian leadership of the time, i.e., the Bulgarian National Assembly and the Bulgarian King Boris III, induced the perception that Jews and Non-Jews share the same overarching identity of Bulgarians. This is born out by analysis of speeches and documents of the time collected by Todorov (1999, 2001). One example of this inclusive message was a speech by communist parliamentarian Todor Polyakov, who declared to the National Assembly: "Bulgarian Jews ... speak Bulgarian.... They sing Bulgarian songs and tell Bulgarian stories" (cited by Reicher et al. 2006, p. 58). These dramatic events demonstrate how the induction of shared belongingness by cognitively redrawing group boundaries can save lives.

3.1.1.3 Bystander Intervention: Concluding Comments Beyond opening the door to research on the social psychology of helping, bystander intervention research has had an important role in shifting the focus of explanations for bystander apathy. Originally, events such as the presumed bystander inaction during the murder of Kitty Genovese were said to represent "moral decay," "dehumanization," a state of "social anomie," and "existential despair" in modern Western cities (Darley and Latané, 1968, p. 371). The pioneering research on bystander intervention has shifted the limelight of explanation from these general sociological and cultural explanations to the characteristics of the specific situation (number of others present, whether they are communicating with each other, etc.). To a large extent, whether or not people would help depends on relatively mundane situational variables. Increase the clarity of the situation or reduce the costs of intervention, and "dehumanization" and "existential despair" miraculously disappear.

The message regarding the effects of the situation as construed by the bystander on willingness to intervene is echoed in the research on the effects of social identity on helping. Shared collective identity encourages intervention. The malleability of the boundaries of one's social identity sends a hopeful message regarding the possibility for creating human solidarity across group boundaries. In fact, the induction of common identity between strangers who may belong to rival groups increases feelings of shared belongingness and the resultant willingness to intervene and help others in need. This emphasis on the effects of group-related variables on helping constitutes leads us to the following section that focuses on the way the content of group norms affects group members' readiness to help others.

3.1.2 Social Norms and Helping: Sharing, Social Responsibility, Reciprocity

Norms represent social expectations about what should and should not be done in a particular situation without law enforcement intervention (Cialdini and Trost 1998). Norms can be situation specific, personal or general (Nadler 2018). A *situation-specific* norm tells people what is expected of them in a particular situation. Thus, if children are asked by an adult to wait in a room, the situation-specific expectation is that they would not leave the room unless permitted to do so. Demonstrating the effects of situation-specific norms on helping, children who had been told that they could leave the room to obtain a pencil were twice as likely to intervene in an emergency outside the room as those who had not been given permission to leave the room (Staub 1971).

A *personal norm* reflects a person's values and preferences and guides behavior in relevant situations. Thus, a person who cares about the environment would contribute to the common good by recycling, but not necessarily by being more willing to donate blood (Schwartz and Howard 1982). The situational salience of a norm affects norm-related helpfulness. To use the previous example, the environmentally sensitive person would be more likely to promote the cause of a clean environment if he or she had just been exposed to a televised story about the dangers of a polluted world. The situational effects of personal norms were also demonstrated in a study where players in a Prisoner's Dilemma game who had been primed with belongingness-related words (e.g. "together") were more cooperative than those exposed to individuality-related words (e.g. "independence") (Utz 2004).

Finally, a *general norm* guides behavior across a wide range of situations. Examples are the norm to show consideration toward older people, take care of young children, and help those in need. These norms serve as behavioral guides for all members of society. The present discussion on the effects of social norms on helping focuses on three general norms: sharing with others, social responsibility, and reciprocity.

3.1.2.1 Sharing with Others Social norms that tell group members to be sensitive to others' needs and be ready to help them exist in most, if not all, human societies. The universality of this normative expectation is reflected in research on values, which indicates that the value of benevolence is found across all societies in the cultural atlas (Schwartz 2012). One behavioral expression of this universal emphasis is that people share their resources with others who lack resources even when they are not compelled to do so. A series of studies across 15 different societies revealed that in an ultimatum game, where the player determined how much of available resources he or she would share with others, people gave an average of 39% of their resources to strangers, despite of the fact that they could keep all to themselves (Henrich et al. 2005).

Sharing with others by giving them what one has and others lack does not represent a single one-sided event, but an interaction where the recipients may accept, reject, or negotiate what and how much they are given. The interactive nature of normative helping relations is reflected by the fact that other social norms shape the course of the sharing interaction. Thus, the norm of fair distribution between the haves and the have-nots affects recipients' reactions to givers' benevolence. In experimental games where one player is free to offer any amount of their resources to the other player, offers that fall below 25% of the giver's resources are generally rejected (Fehr and Fischbacher 2003). Thus, one would rather get nothing than accept less than a quarter of the giver's resources. Although it is not written in stone, it seems that the norm for what constitutes fair sharing hovers around 25%, with anything less viewed as demeaning. The stability of harmonious interactions within the group is predicated on people's readiness to use such norms as behavioral guides.

3.1.2.2 The Norm of Social Responsibility Social responsibility means that people are responsible for the well-being of those who are dependent on them and should therefore help them (Berkowitz and Daniels 1964). The clearest example of how the norm of social responsibility shapes our care for others are relations between adults and young children. Because children are dependent on adults, there is a clear expectation that adults would be responsible for their well-being and help them when needed.

The situational salience of this norm determines whether it would guide behavior. For example, the norm is salient if we have previously been helped by others in overcoming our own predicament. In support of this, Berkowitz and Daniels (1963) demonstrated that people who had been helped in completing a task later helped another individual who was highly dependent on them, more than they helped an individual less dependent on them. Gender relations and the masculine or feminine nature of the social context can also affect the salience of the norm of social responsibility. Thus, in a predominantly masculine environment, i.e. a prison for men, male correction officers perceived female correction officers as dependent on them and evidenced greater responsibility to help them (Bowersox 1981).

Before we move on to discuss the general norm of reciprocity, a word of caution regarding the potentially negative consequences of the norm of social responsibility is in order. As we will see in subsequent chapters, the other side of social responsibility is paternalism. By keeping those who depend on us dependent on our help we may, intentionally or not, help them stay where they are, i.e. dependent on our assistance (Nadler and Chernyak-Hai 2014). For example, by being helpful and protective toward women, men are said to demonstrate "benevolent sexism" as a way of solidifying gender inequality (Jackman 1994; Shnabel et al. 2016).

3.1.2.3 Reciprocity In the previous discussion on evolutionary bases of helpfulness, we noted that reciprocal altruism explained the seemingly evolutionarily illogical behavior of helping genetically unrelated strangers that is prevalent in the animal world. To recap briefly, this principle says that "if I help you today you'll do the same for me when I need your help." The reciprocity norm expresses this principle in human interactions. In his seminal contribution, Gouldner (1960) showed that the norm of reciprocity exists in all human societies and guides people to help those who had helped them and retaliate against those who had hurt them. One reason for the cross-cultural prevalence of this norm is that in the long run, a quid-pro-quo strategy is the most profitable in social dilemma situations, as simulated by experimental games such as the prisoner's dilemma (Axelrod and Hamilton 1981; Hoffman 2000). The difference between the evolutionary principle of reciprocal altruism and the norm of reciprocity is that the former reflects an instinctive behavioral pattern that has developed over millions of years, while the latter is a cognitively knowable principle that people can formulate and decide to abide by, or not (Nadler 2018).

From a bird's-eye view, the norm of reciprocity reigns in all social relations across time and cultures (Gouldner 1960). Yet the more proximal perspective offered by social psychological research indicates that how this norm governing helping interactions varies in different kinds of social relations. Based on Goffman's (1961) distinction between social and economic relationships, Clark and Mills (1993) distinguished between communal and exchange relations. *Communal relations* exist within what Fiske (1991) labeled a "communal-sharing" relational model, which "organizes relationships in terms of collective belongingness and solidarity" (Haslam and Fiske 1999, p. 242). The paradigmatic example of communal relations are relations between family members or close friends, where people's helping is based on others' needs and not on whether the others had helped them in the past. Because the norm in such social settings obligates members to help each other based on need, there is no expectation that the recipient will reciprocate in kind. For example, I may need my brother to lend me his car today, and he may need me to help him install his new computer sometime in the future. In communal relations, people do not worry about when and what the other would reciprocate.

Exchange relations are relations between peers that are not based on shared belongingness but on rules of fairness and equality. Such relations characterize social interactions in "equality matching" relational systems (Fiske 1991), which "organize relations with reference to their degree of balance or imbalance… manifested in turn-taking, reciprocity … and tit for tat" (Haslam and Fiske 1999, p. 242). Examples include relationships between coworkers or neighbors. Here, giving is not based on the other's need for help, but on whether they had helped one in the past. In exchange relations, there is also an expectation of comparability of return. The recipient is expected to reciprocate in kind, and within a relatively short time. For example, if while standing in line for lunch at the workplace cafeteria I discover that I am without my wallet, and a coworker pays for my lunch, the expectation is that I pay back the money at an early opportunity.

Recent work by exchange theorists extended the dichotomy between exchange and communal relations to a tripartite distinction between negotiated, reciprocal, and communal exchange (Molm 2010; Molm et al. 2012). Social norms of *negotiated exchange* are based on rules of rigid reciprocity where recipients are expected to return in kind and at a certain time. The former example of paying back the person who saved me in the line for lunch is an example of rigid exchange. I am expected to get back to my office, pick up my wallet, look for the person and pay back the exact amount. Such an exchange rule characterizes relationships marked by low felt shared belongingness.

Social norms of *reciprocal exchange* are based on rules of soft reciprocity where it is not specified what needs to be reciprocated and when. A delay in returning a favor is not only acceptable but expected, and unlike the expectation in rigid reciprocity, here return need not be in kind. Rather, reciprocity consists of a symbolic gesture that reinforces the positive and trustworthy relations between helper and recipient (e.g. a bouquet of flowers or a dinner invitation). Here relationships are characterized by a medium level of shared belongingness. To use the previous example, if the person who saved me during lunchtime is a close work colleague, a norm of soft reciprocity may apply and instead of rushing to his office with the money, I may leave him a thank you note with a chocolate bar.

Finally, relations of *communal exchange* parallel communal relationships as defined by Clark and Mills (2012). In these relationships, helping is based on the other's need and not on whether or not they had helped in the past. These relationships reflect high shared belongingness, as between intimate friends and close family members.

Relationships dominated by communal norms and soft reciprocity are similar in that people are not expected to return what they received at a specific time, as in relationships dominated by rigid reciprocity (i.e. negotiated and reciprocal exchange in Molm et al., 2012 terminology, respectively). Yet communal and soft reciprocity relationships differ in one major aspect. In relational systems based on soft exchange, there is an expectation for symbolic return even if the other person has no need for help. In communal relations, help is given only when the other person needs it. Therefore, if the recipient in a relationship governed by soft reciprocity fails to return a favor with a symbolic gesture, the relationship may suffer.

In general, when behavior deviates from these unwritten rules it may damage the relationship. For example, if in a communal relationship the recipient hastens to reciprocate what he or she received, the giver may interpret this as a signal that recipient does not view the relationship as communal and reevaluate the relationship accordingly. Mutual conforming to the norms that govern reciprocity in a particular kind of relationship is a key to its stability.

Whether a given kind of relationship is governed by communal, soft, or rigid exchange norms varies across cultures. A comparison of reciprocity rules among friends in India and the US – a collectivistic and individualistic society, respectively – indicated that although in neither society relations between friends were governed by norms of rigid exchange, in India friendships were governed by communal norms, while in the US they were dominated by soft exchange norms. American participants reported that they reciprocated to a friend through symbolic gestures (e.g. inviting a generous friend to dinner), while Indian participants viewed mutual responsiveness, i.e. giving to the friend who had helped whenever they needed assistance, as the more appropriate response (Miller et al. 2014). A subsequent section is devoted to considering cross-cultural differences in helping in greater detail.

3.1.2.4 Socioeconomic Determinants of Social Responsibility and Reciprocity The relative salience of the norms of reciprocity and social responsibility as determinants of helping behavior are also affected by socioeconomic variables such as the person's socioeconomic status and their entrepreneurial, or bureaucratic, familial background. Regarding socioeconomic status, early theory (Simmel 1950) and research (Muir and Weinstein 1962) indicate that because people in the middle class have more experience with monetary-financial matters that are based on principles of quid pro quo, their help-giving is governed by the norm of reciprocity. On the other hand, low-class individuals are affected to a greater extent by the norm of social responsibility that leads them to give to others when they need help. This analysis is supported by more recent research showing that, in different situations, relative to people in higher social class, those in lower social class behave more generously (e.g. Piff et al. 2010). We return in greater detail to the role of socioeconomic status as a determinant of helpfulness in a later section.

Another variable associated with a person's experience with monetary-financial issues that affect their help-giving is whether the person grew up in an entrepreneurial or bureaucratic family (Miller and Swanson 1958). Young adults from entrepreneurial families where the wage earner was self-employed and concerned with the exchange of money and services helped others who had helped them (i.e. reciprocity). Conversely, those from bureaucratic families, where the wage earner was employed by someone else and was concerned with following organizational norms, followed the general norm of social responsibility: they helped others in need who were dependent on them regardless of whether they had helped them before (Berkowitz and Friedman 1967).

The general norms of sharing, reciprocity, and social responsibility affect giving to others across different social contexts. Yet their specific effects on helping depend on characteristics of interpersonal relationships, and on cultural differences, and the person's socioeconomic background. Thus, the way in which reciprocity affects giving to others varies between relational systems of low, medium, and high shared belongingness between interaction partners or group members, individualistic and collectivistic cultures, and socioeconomic status. The next section proceeds to consider the role of norms in helping relationships by focusing on what may be the oldest and most influential normative system in human societies: religion.

3.1.3 Religiosity and Helpfulness

For many, religion is a source of norms that tell them how to behave toward others. All major religions put the compassionate and helpful person on a pedestal. Judaism exhorts believers to "love thy neighbor as yourself"; in Christianity, the parable of the "good Samaritan" shows believers the path for being a good Christian; the Quran views the virtuous person as one who gives his wealth to orphans and the needy; and Buddhism regards compassion as a central characteristic of the enlightened.

These emphases suggest that, regardless of the specific religion, people who define themselves as religious would be more generous than non-religious persons. Yet the empirical picture in this regard is mixed. Some studies report that religious people are more generous in donations to charity, volunteering, and helping strangers; Regnerus et al. 1998; Saroglou 2013), while others have not found such an effect (e.g. Darley and Batson 1973). Research using economic games, e.g. the dictator game and prisoner's dilemma, to assess people's readiness for sharing and cooperation paints a similar mixed picture. Some studies report that religious individuals are more cooperative (e.g. Ahmed 2009; Tan and Vogel 2008), while others find no such differences (e.g. Ahmed and Salas 2011; Shariff and Norenzaryan 2007). One explanation for this empirical inconsistency is that religious people are more or less helpful depending on the target of their generosity. Religious people are said to be more helpful than their non-religious counterparts toward other ingroup members but not toward outgroup members (Ben-Ner et al. 2009; Saroglou 2006). According to this explanation, for religious people solidarity tend to stop at the border of the group.

Another explanation for the empirical inconsistency regarding the religiosity-helping relationship is the multifaceted nature of religiosity itself (Stavrova and Siegers 2014). Religiosity can be extrinsic or intrinsic. *Extrinsic* religiosity is motivated by the individual's desire to satisfy personal goals that are not included in the religious belief system (e.g. be in the company of like-minded churchgoers). For the *intrinsically* religious, religiosity is an end in itself based on a decision to adopt a particular value system. Because the intrinsically religious are more likely to follow religion's imperative to help all other beings regardless of their identity than are extrinsically religious individuals, the link between religiosity and generosity is expected to be stronger among the former. This hypothesis was supported in a large cross-cultural study in 70 countries. People's agreement with a survey item stating that "politicians who do not believe in God are unfit for office" was taken as a marker of extrinsic religiosity (Stavrova and Siegers 2014). In support of the prediction that intrinsic religiosity would be a better predictor of generosity, the positive effect of an overall level of religiosity within a society and doing charity work was significantly stronger in countries where more people disagreed with the statement that "only religious people are fit for political office" (i.e. low level of extrinsic religiosity).

A recent meta-analysis based on experiments that examined the effects of primed religiosity on prosociality supports the link between religiosity and helpfulness (Shariff, Willard, Andersen and Norenzaryan, 2016). These experiments primed religiosity explicitly (e.g. asking participants to read biblical passages, Carpenter and Marshall 2009) or implicitly (e.g. subliminal presentation of religious concepts, Johnson et al. 2010), and assessed various expressions of prosociality (e.g. sharing resources with another person, contributing to a common pool, and willingness to volunteer). The analysis yielded a significant effect size of primed religiosity on helpfulness, which was higher among religious than among non-religious individuals (effect sizes were 0.27 and 0.18 for religious individuals and the general population, respectively).

Although these analyses tilt the balance in favor of the association between religiosity and prosociality, caution needs to be exercised before concluding that religious people are "better" than secular individuals. Religiosity has a dark side as far as social behavior is concerned, and emphasizing religious concepts can encourage negative social phenomena such as racism (Hall et al. 2010). This resonates with the previously noted findings that religiosity increases helpfulness only toward ingroup members. Further, belief in religious concepts is one, but not the only, expression of people's commitment to moral values. In fact, highlighting secular systems of morality, i.e. the justice system, increased readiness to share resources in the dictator game (Shariff and Norenzayan 2007).

In summary, religion seems to send a double message regarding helpfulness. One is that we should extend a helping hand to the needy, and the other is that solidarity is restricted to one's group. Intrinsically religious people tend to follow the universal implication of the imperative that we should help our neighbor regardless of who he or she is. Extrinsically religious people tend to emphasize the more particularistic implication of religion's exhortation that we should help our neighbor, and take neighbor to mean people like them. The next section examines another broad aspect of the effects of normative context on helping: cross-cultural differences.

3.1.4 Cross-Cultural Differences in Help-Giving

Even in this day and age of navigational aids and GPS, I often find myself needing to ask local residents for directions. My experience has been different in different countries. In some places, I would be greeted with a smile, a detailed explanation and even an insistence to show me to the street I am looking for. Elsewhere, the responses are much colder. The passerby may not establish eye contact, continue hurriedly on his or her way and blurt out an "I don't know." Such anecdotal cross-cultural differences reflect how the universal norm that we should help those in need varies across cultures.

Cultural comparisons in the context of helping (and many others contexts of social behavior) have tended to focus on the individualism–collectivism construct (Hofstede 1991; Triandis 1995). Individualistic societies tend to be relatively modern and industrialized, secular and open, while collectivistic societies are traditional, religious and less open. This cultural tendency affects the borders of shared belongingness, solidarity and helpfulness. However, the exact implications of these cultural differences are not straightforward. On the one hand, in collectivistic societies, the borders of solidarity are relatively narrow and rigid and therefore more help may be given only to those considered within one's ingroup, whereas in individualistic societies the permeability of intergroup borders may lead to a relatively high helpfulness toward strangers. On the other hand, relying on the previously discussed finding that people in small communities are more helpful than those in the large city suggests that the pressures of living in the individualistic modern city may result in lesser helpfulness in individualistic-modern societies than in more traditional-collectivistic societies.

Research on cross-cultural differences in helping has attempted to provide empirically-based answers to this question by pursuing two lines of distinct, yet related, traditions of research. The first line of research has used experimental games (prisoner's dilemma, ultimatum, dictator, etc.) in comparing people's willingness to give to strangers in different places across the globe (Feygina and Henry 2015). The second line of study has been conducted within mainstream social psychology using more traditional measures of helping. Among these are measures of spontaneous helping (e.g. helping a blind person cross the street); sustained helping such as volunteering; and willingness to make financial contributions. Beyond these methodological differences, the two traditions differ in their conceptual emphases. The experimental economic-games tradition has tended to focus on macro-level socioeconomic explanations for cross-cultural differences (e.g. the need to cooperate with others to grow food), while the social psychological tradition has focused on the individual person's individualistic or collectivistic value orientation.

3.1.4.1 Experimental Games In an extensive program of research, Henrich and his colleagues examined cross-cultural variations in people's willingness to share their resources with strangers as reflected in their choices in experimental games. This research demonstrates both the universality and the cross-cultural variability of people's willingness to share with strangers. In their research, the investigators used the ultimatum and dictator games, which are similar but differ in one important respect. In both, the first player needs to divide a certain resource with the second player. However, in the dictator game, the recipient of an offer cannot reject it, while in the ultimatum game the recipient may reject what they had been offered, in which case neither of the two players gets anything. Therefore, in the dictator game the recipient cannot affect the giver, while in the ultimatum game they can. Accordingly, in the ultimatum game, both helpfulness (voluntary offering) and "altruistic punishment" (rejecting an offer thereby reducing own and the other's outcomes) can be assessed.

Although players in different societies have offered others a substantial share of their resources voluntarily (an average of 39%), there has been large variability across societies. For example, the Machiguenga people in South America offered only 26% of own resources, while the Lamalera in Polynesia offered 58% (Henrich et al. 2005). These differences are explained by the different levels of economic interdependence necessary to meet basic needs in different societies. The Lamalera, the most generous society in Henrich's study, depend on each other to grow their food, while the Machiguenga, the least generous, tend to grow their food on their own. Thus, habitual tendencies for interdependence or independence in economic life translate into a social norm that affects the general level of sharing with others.

Similar cross-cultural differences in voluntary sharing exist between societies in today's industrialized world. In one study, Chinese players, members of a collectivistic society, offered more on the ultimatum game than did their relatively more individualistic British counterparts (Chuah et al. 2009). Although growing food is not as relevant in industrialized as in pre-industrialized societies, social norms shaped centuries ago seem to be manifested in current individualistic or collectivistic cultural orientations, affecting willingness to share with strangers. Moreover, the fact that the degree of generosity observed in each society was predicted, with a large degree of accuracy, by other members of the community supports the idea that the sharing in experimental games reflects a general social norm (Gurven et al. 2008). Finally, generosity in collectivistic societies tends to stop at the group's border with ingroup helped more than outgroup members. In a study that supported this generalization, children in the Philippines were more helpful than were American children toward family members, but the opposite was true with strangers (de Guzman et al. 2008).

The differences between traditional and modern cultures in giving to an ingroup member or a stranger were supported in another experiment that actively induced people's feelings of affiliation with participants' individualistic or collectivistic ingroup (Wong and Hong 2005). The researchers examined the behavior of Chinese-Americans under conditions where identification with either of these two cultures had been primed. In the Chinese-culture priming condition, participants playing an experimental game were exposed to an image of a dragon placed in the corner of their computer screen, while in the American-culture conditions they were exposed to an image of the Stars and Stripes. The findings indicated that when the other player was a friend, participants in the "Chinese condition" displayed more cooperative choices than those in the in the "American condition"; this difference disappeared when the other player was a stranger.

From an overall perspective this research tradition suggests greater helpfulness by members of collectivistic than individualistic societies. However, this difference may disappear, or be reversed, when outgroup members are the targets of one's benevolence.

3.1.4.2 Social Psychological Research Research within the social psychological tradition corroborates the main conclusions of the previously described findings from the experimental game tradition of research. A study of spontaneous helping conducted in 23 different societies worldwide provides a clear demonstration of cross-cultural differences in helping strangers (Levine et al. 2001). The indicators of helping consisted of (i) returning a pen that had been accidentally dropped by a passerby, (ii) helping a person wearing a visible leg bracelet who had fallen, and (iii) helping a blind person cross the street. All observations were made in large metropolitan areas (e.g. Rio de Janeiro, Calcutta, Tel Aviv, Bangkok, New York). The findings revealed significant variability on a composite measure of helpfulness. For example, 93% of passersby helped in Rio de Janeiro, but only 45% in New York. People in rich countries helped less than those in poor countries, but this was not true across the board. Some economically strong cities like Vienna and Madrid were among the six most helpful cities, while Calcutta, Bangkok and Kuala Lumpur were at the bottom of the helpfulness list.

A possible explanation for the overall greater helpfulness in poorer countries is that poorer societies have a more collectivistic value orientation. Consistent with this explanation, children in cultures characterized by extended families and low specialization at work (i.e. collectivistic-traditional cultures) were more helpful than those in cultures with smaller families and high level of work specialization (i.e. individualistic-modern cultures) on a variety of indices (e.g. sharing food and toys) (Whiting and Whiting 1975). The collectivism–helpfulness nexus was also demonstrated in a study in which Israeli children in a kibbutz (a highly collective form of community life) were found to be more generous than children from an individualistically-oriented urban environment (Nadler et al. 1979).

Beyond the effects of the general individualistic or collectivistic societal orientation, the emphasis on a specific generosity-related value also affects cross-cultural differences in helping. Thus, people living in Latin American and Spanish cities behaved in a relatively more helpful manner than those living in comparable cities elsewhere in Europe and in North America (Levine et al. 2001). The authors attributed this to the prevalence of the cultural value of *simpatico/simpático* (Spanish and Portuguese, respectively) in these countries that puts a high premium on behaving amicably toward strangers (Triandis et al. 1984).

Another interesting demonstration of the link between collectivism–individualism and helping relates to the way in which the *singularity effect* is manifested differently in these societies. The singularity effect is our tendency to be moved more by the plight of a single individual than by that of the many. An example is the way in which the American public reacted to the photograph of a single napalm-burned girl running toward the photographer while remaining relatively unmoved by the knowledge that thousands of Vietnamese people suffered a similar fate. A more recent illustration of the singularity effect was the alarmed response of the Western world to the photo of a dead Syrian toddler lying on the shores of a Greek island in 2015, despite the fact that the same public opinion has remained relatively indifferent to media reports of the death of thousands of other Syrian children. One explanation for this is that a single identifiable person is more psychologically coherent than the anonymous many, eliciting more intense feelings that drive action (Kogut and Ritov 2005).

It appears, however, that this greater responsiveness to the plight of the individual than to that of the anonymous group prevails mainly in individualistic societies (Kogut et al. 2015). For example, while Westernized Israelis were more willing to help a single identifiable sick child than to help a group of similarly sick unidentified children, Bedouin Arab participants, representing a collectivistic culture, did not show this difference. Moreover, in a randomly selected sample of people with collectivistic values as assessed by the Schwartz Value Survey (SVS; Schwartz 1992) or experimentally primed, the singularity effect was more evident than among those with individualistic values (Kogut et al. 2015, Studies 2 and 3, respectively).

As this section on cross-cultural effects draws to a close, it is tempting to argue that when we say "individualistic society" we all understand what we mean. Yet individualism and collectivism do not necessarily imply selfishness and caring, respectively. Kemmelmeier et al.(2006) suggest that in modern social contexts, individualism is not a "selfish orientation that is inherently opposed to community" but rather a position of "personal responsibility paired with the desire to live one's life as an ethical actor" (p. 338). From this perspective, it is expected that individualism would be positively associated with readiness to help strangers. Supporting this possibility is the finding about the high rates of volunteering and donating in the US and Canada, which are among the most individualistic countries in the world (Dovidio et al. 2006). To examine this more benevolent meaning of individualism, Kemmelmeier et al. (2006) assessed societal individualism and collectivism in 40 states in the US as and found that consistent with the more benign interpretation of individualism, people in more modern and individualistically oriented states were more likely to be involved in volunteering and made more donations than those in collectivistic states. Importantly, these differences existed after the effects of other relevant variables (e.g. economic wealth) had been statistically controlled. As in the case with the concept of religiosity, here too the findings portray a multifaceted picture of the concept of individualism and its links to helpfulness.

In conclusion, the distinction between collectivistic and individualistic societies subsumes many of the normative differences relevant to helping. In general, compared to people in individualistic societies people in collectivistic cultures display more helpfulness. Yet helpfulness is affected by specific cultural values (e.g. "sympatico"), and individualism as personal commitment to moral values results in greater volunteering of one's time and resources in individualistic societies, than in collectivistic societies. These findings, coupled with the fact that much of social psychological research on helping has been conducted within individualistic Western cultures, call for caution when making general conclusions.

This concludes the review of research on the "When" question – the situational variables that affect willingness to help others. We began by considering the variables that affect noticing, interpreting, assuming responsibility to help, that translate into a bystander's decision whether to intervene in a particular manner. Then we considered how intervention differs in contexts of high and low shared belongingness (i.e. ingroup and outgroup victims, respectively). In a subsequent section on the effects of social norms, we addressed the effects of the norms of "sharing," "social responsibility" and "reciprocity" and considered these effects in the context of different relational systems (e.g. "communal" and "exchange"). Finally, we reviewed research on the effects of broad value systems on helping (i.e. religiosity and individualism vs. collectivism). In the next section, we move to the second help-giving question: Who is more likely to help?

3.2 Who Helps: Characteristics of the Helper

This section begins with research on the developmental antecedents of helping (e.g. socialization practices), continues to personality differences between more and less helpful individuals, and concludes by examining the role of gender and socioeconomic status in helpfulness.

3.2.1 Developmental Antecedents

The nature–nurture controversy has been a dominant theme in much of the research on developmental antecedents of social behavior (Plomin 1994). The nature side of the argument tells us that people are more aggressive and hostile or considerate and helpful because they were born this way, while the nurture side of the argument suggests that these variations are the outcome of environmental influences; chief among these influences are parental socialization practices. The answer to the question whether nature or nurture are more important in shaping helpfulness is, as is true of most if not all social behaviors, "both": people's differential willingness to help others in need is the result of both genetic and environmental antecedents (Keltner et al. 2014).

Supporting the nature side of the argument is the finding that day-old newborns responded to the audiotaped crying of another baby in what appeared like an empathic distress. This suggests that we are genetically hardwired for empathy even before any environmental influences can shape our social behavior (Martin and Clark 1982). Further support for the role of innate influence comes from an identical twin study that demonstrated that a significant proportion of the variance in helpfulness was genetically determined (Knafo-Noam et al. 2015).

Although both the psychological and biological levels of explanation are important to gain a full picture on the development of helping, our focus here is on the psychological level. We begin by describing the development of people's capacity for empathy and continue to research and theory on parental behavior (i.e. rewarding and modeling helpfulness) and socialization practices (e.g. parental emotional warmth) on children's helpfulness.

3.2.1.1 The Development of Empathy: from "Global Empathic Distress" to "Adult Empathy" Exposure to the suffering of others results in two different emotional reactions: empathy with another's pain, and personal distress resulting from witnessing it (Batson 2011). The very young child is overwhelmed by feelings of personal distress. Only when he or she grows older, can they experience empathy with another's distress without being overwhelmed by it. Such adult empathy enables helpfulness that is guided by the needy's perspective.

This developmental process, predicated on the child's developing cognitive skills, is described in Hoffman's *developmental model of empathy* (2000). The model suggests that in the first year of life, children do not differentiate between themselves and others. In this first stage, the child's reaction to another's predicament is one of *global empathic distress,* and when the child encounters another person's distress, they respond as if it were their own. Thus, upon seeing another child crying the young child will begin to cry as if he or she were suffering. The second stage, *egocentric empathic distress*, occurs around age one, when the child begins to differentiate between him or herself and others. At this stage, the child's reaction to the suffering of others is similar to that in the previous stage, but instead of responding with signs of personal distress, the young child will try to comfort him- or herself. For example, upon viewing another child being hurt the child may try to comfort him- or herself by putting their head in their mother's lap. In the second year of life, as children gain a clearer distinction between themselves and others, they enter the third stage: *quasi-egocentric empathy*. They exhibit awareness that when someone else suffers, it is the other who needs to be comforted; the comfort they provide, however, is based on things they do to comfort themselves. For example, if an adult had been hurt and was visibly aching, the young child may try to comfort him or her by giving them their favorite toy. Finally, around age three, the child enters the stage of *veridical empathy*, in which he or she comforts the other in ways appropriate to them. For example, upon seeing his sister crying the young child will hand her her favorite toy.

The cause for these age differences is said to be intra-psychological cognitive processes of maturation. This position has been aptly summarized by Graziano and Habashi (2015): "the primary reason young human children [...] appear to be selfish and less prosocial than older children is due to limitations in cognitive processes like perspective taking" (p. 233). Other scholars, however, note that cognitive development is not the only explanation and that the child's social environment (e.g. awareness of social norms) also plays a role in shaping the different facets of empathy in different ages (Hay and Cook 2007).

In later years, empathy develops and is felt not only in reaction to witnessing a concrete episode, but is extended to less concrete suffering that emanates from knowledge about the other's life conditions. *Adult empathy* can be felt toward others whom one has not seen, but had read about. Such abstract empathy is key for social action which is predicated on the ability to empathize with the pains experienced by the injustice committed against a class of victims (e.g. the underprivileged), rather than a concrete, specific victim.

Empirically, the principle that as children grow up they become more attentive to the needs of other people and tailor their help accordingly was supported in studies that examined help-giving in different age groups in controlled laboratory settings. In one such investigation, Svetlova et al. (2010) studied the responsiveness of 18- and 30-month-old children to others' need for instrumental and emotion-based support. Instrumental support is defined as helping others overcome a visible and concrete difficulty (e.g. handing them an object they cannot reach), and emotion-based support as interpreting and trying to eliminate the cause of the other's negative emotion. In the instrumental help condition, the child could help the experimenter by handing her a nearby blanket needed to wrap up an object. In the emotional-based condition, the experimenter sitting next to the child showed signs of distress because she was feeling cold (e.g. shivering, saying "brrr..." while rubbing her arms). To help her, the child, who had been previously exposed to the warming function of the blanket, needed to correctly interpret her emotional distress and hand her the blanket. The findings showed that children at both ages helped readily in the instrumental condition, but emotion-based helping was relatively more difficult for the younger children who required an explicit and direct communication from the experimenter telling them that she was cold and needed a blanket. These findings demonstrate the developmental nature of children's helpfulness. At a younger age, their help-giving depends on concrete information, and as they grow up it is prompted by less concrete cues that are relatively detached from the specific situation.

Another indication that only at an older age do children rely on abstract cues beyond the immediate need situation is the finding that only after age three did children base their helping decisions on social norms and abstract principles, e.g. deservedness. By that point in their development, children's readiness to help was affected by the needy's prior behavior and their intentions, i.e. they were less helpful if the needy had previously harmed another individual or intended to do so, than toward a "neutral" or previously helpful individual (Vaish et al. 2010).

3.2.1.2 Socialization Practices In addition to inborn tendencies and cognitive and emotional maturation, helpfulness is also shaped by care takers' behavior and disciplinary practices. We turn to these in this section, which begins with the effects of directly rewarding generosity, continues to consider the effects of modeling helpfulness, and concludes with considering the effects of disciplinary practices on the child's helpfulness.

3.2.1.2.1 Rewarding Helpfulness How can parents encourage their children to grow into generous adults? Based on learning theory's principles the obvious answer would be to reward them when they act generously. Research indicates that the effects of direct rewarding of helpfulness are less straightforward than the principles of operant conditioning would have us predict. In fact, while children as young as 14–18 months old readily help others regardless of whether they have been directly rewarded for doing so (Warneken et al. 2007), rewarding them for helping seems to actually reduce their subsequent helpfulness (Warneken and Tomasello 2008). In this study, 20-month-old children who had received a toy from the experimenter as a reward for helping her retrieve an object were subsequently less helpful in similar circumstances than were children who had been verbally rewarded for helping or who had not been rewarded at all. Receiving a toy for helping is likely to have led children to misattribute their generosity to external causes rather than to their internal motivation ("I helped because I wanted to get a toy and not because I wanted to help") (i.e. "overjustification effect"; Lepper et al. 1973). Verbal praise, on the other hand, "typically endorses intrinsic motivation rather than supplying an alternative external motivation" (Warneken and Tomasello 2008, p. 1787).

In support of the role of intrinsic motivation as a driver of helpfulness, adults who had helped a shoppers, i.e. complying with their request to keep an eye on their bag until they returned, because of a compelling reason (i.e. the person needed to retrieve their lost wallet), later intervened less by helping another shopper than those who had had helped because of a less compelling reason (i.e. needed to retrieve a $1 bill) (Uranowitz 1975). These findings suggest that the person who had helped because of a trivial reason attributed their action to their being a helpful person. People who help because of a compelling external reason (e.g. reward or an extreme state of need) attribute their helpfulness to an extrinsic reason, leading to lesser subsequent helpfulness.

3.2.1.2.2 Modeling Helpfulness Parental modeling of helpfulness leads children to become generous. Thus, parents' volunteering for prosocial causes was found to significantly affect children's readiness to volunteer for a first aid organization (McGinley et al. 2010). Similarly, social activists who volunteered during the 1960s to further the goals of the civil rights movement remember their parents as having been similarly committed to help others by being involved in anti-fascist activities in the 1930s (Rosenhan 1970).

Similarly, parents' considerate and caring behaviors toward their children models concern for others within the parent–child interaction, which has positive effects on the child's generosity toward others. Thus, mothers' level of sensitivity for their children's needs at the age of ten months predicted their reactions of sympathy to a display of an adult's distress six months later (Spinrad and Stifter 2006).

An important source of modeling of social behaviors is children's exposure to pro- and antisocial behaviors in TV shows and computer games. In one early study, six-year-old children watched scenes from the movie *Lassie* depicting the canine heroine as coming to the rescue of her puppies. In one control condition, children were exposed to a scene that did not involve rescue, and in a second control condition, they were exposed to an excerpt of similar length from a "neutral" film. Following this exposure, children in all groups played a game during which they heard the whining of a nearby hungry puppy. They had the choice of continuing to play the game, with the possibility of winning an attractive reward, or stopping to help the puppy. Children who had previously been exposed to the rescue scene were more likely to stop playing and help the puppy than were children in the two control groups (Sprafkin et al. 1975).

The positive effects of "benevolent" TV programs (e.g. *Mister Rogers' Neighborhood*) on children's later prosociality was also supported in two meta-analytic studies (Hearold 1986; Mares and Woodard 2005). In a more recent demonstration of the effects of symbolic modeling on helpfulness, Gentile et al. (2009) similarly found that Japanese children who had reported playing video games with prosocial content were more likely to agree with statements expressing helpfulness and to behave more generously toward others (i.e. give them easy questions on an award-winning task) than were those who had played a neutral or violent game.

Finally, note that the effect of prosocial modeling on helpfulness is not limited to children. The likelihood that adults would donate money to a worthy cause increased when they had been previously exposed to others doing so (Macaulay 1970), and people were more likely to stop to assist a stranded motorist if they had been previously exposed to someone else doing the same thing (Bryan and Test 1967).

Several psychological mechanisms have been proposed to account for the positive effects of modeling on subsequent helpfulness. Greitemeyer's (2009a) application of the general learning model (GLM; Buckley and Anderson 2006) suggests that exposure to prosocial content activates prosocial cognitions and feelings that channel the arousal generated by being exposed to others' misfortune to helping them. This suggests that exposure to *any* prosocial content, not necessarily others' helpful behavior, would increase readiness to help others. In support of this idea, participants who had listened to prosocial songs (e.g. "Help" by the Beatles) had more prosocial thoughts, experienced more interpersonal empathy and behaved more prosocially than those who had listened to comparable "neutral" songs (Grietemeyer 2009a). Related research indicates that the effects of listening to prosocial songs on subsequent helping was mediated by an increase in the listeners' prosocial empathy (Grietemeyer 2009b).

Another emotional consequence of observing others behaving generously are observers' feelings of elevation (Haidt 2003), described as the "subjective experience when observing others perform act of moral excellence such as kindness or heroism" (Schnall and Roper 2012, p. 374). When experiencing elevation people describe themselves as having an urge to do good (Algoe and Haidt 2009), which is translated into greater helpfulness (Schnall and Roper 2012; Schnall et al. 2010). This research suggests that the affective route, i.e. empathy or elevation, mediates between witnessing generosity by watching a prosocial model or listening to prosocial contents in songs and subsequent generous acts.

3.2.1.2.3 Explaining Helpfulness Having discussed the mixed benefits of directly rewarding children's prosocial behavior and the clear-cut benefits of modeling such behavior, how should parents react to children's failure to empathize with or help others in need? Is punishment an effective way to eradicate such negative behavior? To illustrate, let us imagine the parents and their young child in a restaurant when the child points at someone in a wheelchair and cries out: "Look at that funny man, he has wheels instead of legs!" By frowning at the child and telling them: "This is bad, you are not allowed to …," the parent is using a power-assertive disciplinary tactic to eradicate this undesirable display of the child's lack of sensitivity to others. This approach, however, is unlikely to facilitate prosociality because it arouses anxiety, which interferes with the child's ability to internalize the value of "being nice to others" (Eisenberg et al. 2015).

In support of this logic, research indicates that the frequent use of assertive socialization tactics was associated with weaker prosocial tendencies (Bar-Tal et al. 1980). A more effective practice is inductive socialization, which consists of explaining the situation to the child from the victim's perspective. Using the previous example, inductive socialization would consist of telling the child: "Imagine that you were sitting in a wheelchair and someone was laughing at you, how would that make you feel?" Using such a disciplinary tactic, the parent trains the child in taking the perspective of the person who needs help. Consistent with this idea, there is a positive relationship between parental use of induction and children's empathy (Eisenberg and Miller 1987).

Parental emphasis on prosociality through word and deed (i.e. verbal inductions and modeling of prosociality, as described in the previous subsection) is not enough. These values will be internalized by the child as guides for future social behavior when expressed by an emotionally warm parent. In fact, by behaving in a consistently warm manner toward their children parents model sensitivity to others' needs. Moreover, an open and warm emotional environment facilitates the internalization of the prosocial values that are expressed and modeled by the parent. Consistent with this emphasis on warmth and expressivity in parent–child relationships, mothers who had discussed their own sadness with their children had more prosocially oriented children than those who had not (Denham and Grout 1992). Similarly, mothers' conversations about their feelings after viewing an empathy inducing film were associated with high levels of empathy in their children (Eisenberg et al. 1992).

Thus, the socialization of helpfulness stands on a cognitive leg of prosocial values transmitted through inductive socialization practices, as well as on an affective leg of emotional warmth and sensitivity to the child's needs. Consistent with this, heroic rescuers of Jews in Nazi-occupied Europe during the Second World War remember their parents both as having emphasized moral values as guidelines for future behavior and as being emotionally warm and caring individuals. Compared to people who had not saved Jews under similar circumstances, rescuers also had higher scores on "extensivity," i.e. greater degree of perceived similarity between themselves and other groups (Oliner and Oliner 1988). Put differently, their feelings of shared belongingness transcended ingroup boundaries and led the rescuers to perform "extreme altruism" across group boundaries. We have already noted how a cognitive restructuring of ingroup boundaries to include the outgroup increases cross-group helping (p. 42), a topic that will be revisited in greater detail in our subsequent section on intergroup helping relations.

In the next section, we turn to the consequences of the developmental processes and antecedents of helpfulness reviewed here: Personality characteristics and their links to different levels of helpfulness.

3.2.2 Characteristics of the Helpful Person's Personality

Samuel and Pearl Oliner titled their study of rescuers of Jews in Nazi-occupied Europe *The Altruistic Personality* (Oliner and Oliner 1988). The term altruistic personality suggests that some people are consistently more generous and helpful than others across time and situations. This means that the dispositionally helpful person will be so across different situations: he or she will rescue others who face mortal danger, donate money to a worthy cause, and help a blind person cross the street, etc. more than will a person who does not possess the ingredients that make up the altruistic personality. Generalization across time implies that the dispositionally helpful will be more responsive to others' needs today, tomorrow and years from now.

Early research on helping held a generally skeptical attitude toward the role of personality differences in explaining helpfulness. This research sought to improve social life by identifying *situational* variables that prompt most people to help others. This situational emphasis was reinforced by research that found no support for the role of dispositional tendencies in the bystander paradigm (Darley and Latané 1968), and was consistent with the general critical view of personality variables as predictors of social behavior, held by social psychologists during the 1970s and 1980s. This situational emphasis rendered the goal of uncovering the personality antecedents of helpfulness less pressing, at least during those years.

Echoing the emphasis on situational antecedents of social behavior, Mischel (1969) argued that the evidence did not support the utility of using personality dispositions in psychological research, arguing we needed to "go beyond the conventional definition of stable and broad enduring individual differences in behavioral dispositions" (p. 1017). In a similar emphasis on "the power of the situation" Ross and Nisbett (1991) suggested the principle of "situationism" as one of the three pillars that make up the proverbial tripod on which social psychological research and theory stand (the other two are "tension systems" and the principle of "active construal").

More recently, however, the negative appraisal of the role of personality in helpfulness has been revised. It is now commonly accepted that an optimal account of helping and social behavior results from a joint consideration of personality characteristics and the situation. In fact, in certain extreme situations almost everyone will, or will not, help. Interpersonal differences in helpfulness are likely to appear in more ambiguous situations. For example, everyone is likely to help a close family member, but if the target is a stranger, those with higher dispositional empathy are more likely to help (Graziano et al. 2007).

Finally, the distinction between personality and situation is neither clear-cut nor mutually exclusive. In fact, situational variations can cause personal experiences that parallel a certain personality dimension. For example, a person's secure attachment can be primed by exposing him or her to words that have a connotation of relational security (e.g. love, concern, togetherness, etc.) (Gillath et al. 2005). Another example for the empirical similarity between a situationally induced feeling and a parallel personal disposition comes from recent findings on the effects of feelings of awe on helpfulness. Exposing people to awe-inspiring natural phenomena (e.g. a gushing waterfall) causes them to feel "small and insignificant," and this diminished self-centeredness leads them to behave generously. Similarly, high scorers on a dispositional measure of tendency to feel awe were more helpful than those who had scored low on this scale (Piff et al. 2015). With these comments in mind, we turn to review the search for the helpful personality.

An early study failed to support the idea of a generalized personality characteristic that is related to helpfulness across different times and situations (Gergen et al. 1972). In this study, undergraduates filled out a number of personality scales and were then asked to volunteer to help in different projects (counseling a male or female high school student, helping with an experiment on deductive reasoning, or helping with a project on states of consciousness). The findings indicate that different personality characteristics were related to willingness to help in different situations. Thus, the personality characteristic of need for nurturance was positively associated with willingness to counsel a high school student, while the personality dimension of sensation seeking was positively related to willingness to help in the states-of-consciousness project, and negatively related to readiness to help in a deductive reasoning experiment. These findings suggest that helping is not determined by a fixed set of personality characteristics but by the situational payoffs helping has for different people. For example, while the project title "states of consciousness" was potentially satisfying for people characterized as high sensation seekers, a project titled "deductive reasoning" was not.

3.2.2.1 The ABC of the Helpful Personality More recent research designed to answer the question "Who helps?" suggests that a helpful person is someone who characteristically evidences a high level of *empathy* when confronted with others' sufferings, regards him- or herself as *responsible* to ease these sufferings, and is able to *behave* in an effective manner to do so. These three elements parallel the ABC social-psychological analysis of the antecedents of behavior: affective, behavioral, and cognitive processes and variables.

In support of the role of the dispositional element of empathy, people high on a dispositional measure of empathy (i.e. the Interpersonal Reactivity Index, IRI; Davis 1994) indicated a commitment to volunteer to help others in need (Davis et al. 1999) and were readier to donate money to worthy causes (Otten et al. 1991). A meta-analysis that examined the links between empathy and helping indicated an overall positive relationship between dispositional empathy and helpfulness and cooperation. This relationship was evident on a number of helping measures, such as teacher and peer ratings of one's helpfulness, readiness to share with friends, and volunteering (Eisenberg and Miller 1987).

Further support for the role of dispositional empathy comes from studies that related people's scores on the Big Five Personality Factors (5PF; McCrae and Costa 1987) to helpfulness. These five factors emerge when analyzing people's descriptions of their and others' common personality characteristics and include "openness to experience" (curious vs. cautious), "consciousness" (well organized vs. disorganized), "agreeableness" (compassionate vs. detached), "extroversion" (outgoing vs. preferring solitude) and "neuroticism" (confident vs. unsure of him- or herself). Research has consistently indicated that people's scores on the "agreeableness" dimension are positively associated with their dispositional empathy (Graziano and Tobin 2002), helpfulness in laboratory studies (Graziano and Habashi 2015), and readiness to volunteer (Carlo et al. 2005). Given that the "agreeableness" factor describes people's dispositional tendency to maintain harmonious relations with others and have friendly and compassionate relations with them, this relationship is not surprising. Yet, under certain conditions where everyone is expected to help, the interpersonal variance due to "agreeableness" will not predict helping. Thus, while high and low scorers on agreeableness showed similar readiness to help socially close others (e.g. siblings and close friends) high scorers were more willing to help strangers than were low scorers (Graziano et al. 2007, Study 1). This suggests that in social contexts governed by salient normative expectations social behavior is relatively uniform. Interpersonal differences associated with personality characteristics are manifested in situations that allow greater variability in interpersonal behavior (i.e. helping strangers).

Feelings of empathy translate into helping action when the would-be helper perceives him- or herself as *responsible* to alleviate the needy's predicament, and as *able* to do so effectively. The pivotal role of perceived responsibility was highlighted, as seen above, in the research on bystander intervention where it was noted that intervention in an emergency is unlikely when the responsibility to act falls on the shoulders of many (Latané and Darley, 1970).

In a similar vein, adherence to the norm of social responsibility is an important normative antecedent of helping and is a Cognitive in the ABC tripartite characteristics of helpfulness. As may be recalled, this norm expresses the would-be helper's belief that "it is my responsibility to help those who depend on me." However, not everyone has internalized the norm of social responsibility to the same degree. Those who score high on the Attitudes of Social Responsibility scale (ASR; Harris 1957) view themselves as responsible to help others more than do those who score relatively low (Midlarsky and Bryan 1972). The links between dispositional adherence to the norm of social responsibility and helpfulness have also been demonstrated on measures of actual helping behavior. Children who scored higher on this scale gave more of their hard-won valuable prizes of color pens to poor children, described as having no toys, than did low-scorers (Nadler et al. 1979).

Finally, helpfulness depends on the person's view of him or herself as dispositionally efficacious, and therefore able to plan Behavior that will ameliorate others' suffering in an efficient manner. Past research has highlighted the importance of this, the third element in the ABC (i.e. the Behavioral element) of the helpful personality. Beginning with extreme altruism, rescuing Jews during the Second World War required people who could plan their actions carefully (Oliner and Oliner 1988). In order to help under such extreme circumstances, rescuers must have had an enduring sense of self-efficacy that enabled them to believe that they could successfully manage the complexities and dangers involved. In support of this, an early study that interviewed rescuers reported that rescuers expressed more willingness to take behavioral risks as evidenced in their relatively high involvement in risky sports (London 1970). In a similar vein, more recent research found that in addition to having high scores on dispositional empathy and social responsibility measures, rescuers of Jews had a high level of perceived control over their lives (Midlarsky et al. 2005). Although perceived control is not synonymous with one's ability to plan behavior effectively, it is likely to be associated with it.

Research on volunteers also points to the importance of people's ability for planned and controlled behavior as key element defining the helpful person. Penner et al. (1995) measured the "prosocial personality" by an especially built "prosocial battery." Analyses on this 56-item scale resulted in two independent factors: an emotional factor that measured "other-oriented empathy" and a behavioral factor of "helpfulness" that reflected acting on one's feelings of empathy in the past by actually helping others. One's experiences of successfully helping others in the past translate to his or her perception that they can do so also in the present. Importantly, people who volunteered to help the homeless (Penner and Fritzsche 1993), and people whose volunteering was lengthy, i.e. more than six months (Penner and Finkelstein 1998), were characterized by high scores on both factors. Finally, people's helpfulness was found to be associated with both the "agreeableness" and "consciousness" factors on the 5PF (King et al. 2005). While agreeableness describes a person as compassionate and friendly and is associated with dispositional empathy, consciousness reflects their dispositional tendency to behave efficiently, with well-organized, goal-directed behavior.

The research reviewed hitherto has not revealed a single personality characteristic that can be said to be the personality marker of the helpful person. Rather, it indicates that the helpful personality consists of the stable and enduring tendencies to *feel*, *think* and *act* in a way that benefits others in distress (Penner and Finkelstein 1998). More specifically, individuals who are dispositionally empathic, have internalized the norm of social responsibility, and have perceptions of efficacy and control are more likely than others to be helpful across time and situations.

3.2.2.2 Attachment and Helpfulness Before we abandon the idea of a relatively basic and unitary personality dimension that translates into helpfulness, research within the framework of attachment theory raises the possibility that secure attachment may be such a parsimonious marker of helpfulness. Attachment theory holds that young children's experience of their caregivers as being available to them in times of need, or not, turns into adult working models of interpersonal relationships (Bowlby 1973). These working models consist of people's scores on the relational dimensions of anxiety and avoidance (Mikulincer and Shaver 2007). A high score on avoidance defines the *avoidantly attached* person and indicates distrust of others' availability and goodwill in times of need, and is expressed in a motivation to maintain independence and emotional distance from others. The *anxiously attached* person (i.e. high score on anxiety) is anxious as to whether others would be available for them in times of need, an anxiety related to uncertainty about others' love and concern for them. The *securely attached* person scores low on both dimensions, while the *insecurely attached* person scores high on these dimensions.

While this theory has stimulated voluminous research on interpersonal relations, it is reviewed below only in terms of its implications for help-giving. The logic of attachment theory suggests that compared to insecurely attached people who are preoccupied with their own vulnerabilities and therefore do not attend to others, securely attached individuals are more attentive to others' needs and will be therefore more helpful to them. Beyond the idea that there needs to be a basic level of felt security for one to attend to others, securely and insecurely attached people are expected to be differentially helpful because of their different levels of comfort with being close to others (Hazan and Shaver 1987). Securely attached people experience greater comfort with emotional closeness to others and are therefore likely to reach out and help them more than those who are insecurely attached. Avoidant individuals experience a need to retain their independence and maintain their distance from others, which is expected to cause them to back away from others in need. Anxiously attached people are said to be preoccupied with their insecurities and therefore unlikely to have the psychological energy to consider others' needs; if they do help, their intense need for emotional closeness with others may cause them to provide "suffocating" help, rendering them ineffective helpers. In terms of the previously suggested distinction between autonomy- and dependency-oriented help (p. 25), such "suffocating help" will be expressed in giving dependency-oriented assistance (i.e. solving the problem for the needy) even when the other requires autonomy-oriented assistance that will allow him or her to help themselves (e.g. guidance, hints, or general directions).

Research on the links between attachment and helpfulness has provided empirical support for the effects of attachment security on willingness to help. Avoidant attachment is associated with lower reports of empathic concern for others in need (Wayment 2006), a lesser willingness to volunteer, and giving "selfish" rather than "other-centered" reasons when they had given help (e.g., gaining positive reputation in one's community and alleviating others' sufferings, respectively). Such selfish giving is motivated by one's desire to be perceived positively (Gillath et al. 2005). Because they are relatively overwhelmed by others' predicament, anxiously attached individuals report relatively more distress when they encounter others in need (Joireman et al. 2002).

Finally, a study that explored the effects of attachment security on empathy and helping indicates that securely attached people are more empathic and helpful toward others (Mikulincer et al. 2005). In this study, attachment security was examined both as a person's score on an attachment questionnaire, and as experimentally induced by exposing participants subliminally to names of people whom they had previously identified as providing them with a sense of security. Following the measurement or induction of attachment security, participants were exposed to a woman who was distressed because of the task she was working on. Participants could help her by trading places with her. The findings indicated that securely attached people, identified by their score on an attachment scale and those who had been experimentally induced to feel securely attached, were relatively more empathic toward the person in distress and more willing to relieve her distress by trading places. Summarizing the link between attachment security and helpfulness, Mikulincer and Shaver wrote, "Attachment security, whether established in a person's long history of close relationships or induced experimentally [...] makes compassion and altruism more likely" (2015, p. 221).

Beyond the decision to help or not, the conceptual logic underlying the attachment-helping link suggests that different attachment styles would also predict dependency- or autonomy-oriented helping differently. As noted previously, the anxiously attached helper will tend to provide dependency-oriented help even when autonomy-oriented help is more situationally appropriate. Avoidants who wish to maintain their distance from others are expected to give autonomy-oriented assistance even when dependency-oriented help is more situationally appropriate. Finally, securely attached people who are relatively more attuned and sensitive to others' needs are likely to base the autonomy/dependency nature of the help on the other's actual need. These hypotheses go beyond the narrow help-no help distinction to focus on the kind of help given and need to be addressed by future research.

3.2.2.3 Beyond Empathy and Attachment: Metaphors, Awe, and Vagal Activity Recent research has gone beyond the personality dispositions commonly studied in the helping context: dispositional empathy, 5PF, attachment. In this section, we address three such approaches. The first is based on the idea that people use *taste metaphors* to describe others' dispositional tendencies. We describe others as sweet or bitter to capture their characteristically friendly and compassionate, or more distant and hostile attitude. In everyday interactions, in many languages, describing someone as a "sweet person" implies that the person is nice and kind (Meier et al. 2012). Consistent with the association between a metaphoric description of sweetness and helpfulness, research results indicate that people described as preferring sweet foods were judged as considerate individuals; that actual preference for sweet foods predicted volunteering; and that people who had consumed sweet foods were readier to help (Meier et al. 2012). Summarizing their findings, the authors write that "metaphors constitute a rich largely untapped source of potential insights [...] concerning person perception and individual differences" (p. 171).

Another recent approach centers on the suggestion that people's feelings of *awe* are associated with their readiness to help others. As mentioned previously, we experience a sense of awe when witnessing grand phenomena that make us feel humble (e.g. a snow-capped mountain). What is the rationale for the hypothesis that a sense of awe would facilitate helpfulness? Piff et al. (2015) suggest that feeling awe in the face of magnanimous events causes the person to have a sense of "smaller self," which leaves more room to attend to others' needs. Therefore, a sense of awe was expected to be positively associated with helpfulness. In support of this hypothesis, a dispositional tendency to experience awe and an experimental induction of awe (i.e. looking at the canopies of tall and large trees) led to greater helpfulness on a number of indices (economic games, giving to strangers, and endorsing prosocial values).

The third approach represents the growing use of physiological concepts to explain prosocial behavior. Kogan et al. (2014) studied the link between a person's characteristic level of *vagal activity* and helping. The activity of the vagus nerve is a physiological proximate of emotional control. At very low levels, the person is likely to be overwhelmed with emotion when witnessing another's plight; at high levels, they may not even notice the other's predicament. At intermediate levels, vagal activity is associated with "social connection and emotional expressivity" and the ability to regulate one's "negative emotion in response to intense stress" (Kogan et al. 2014, p. 1052). Consistent with the idea that helping others requires a balance between social sensitivity and emotion control, Kogan et al. found a quadratic relationship between vagal activity and indices of pro-sociality (i.e. prosocial traits and emotions, and helpfulness as rated by strangers).

*

In summary, the personality-helping relationship stands on a tripod of empathy, responsibility and efficacy. Although each of these variables predicts help-giving separately, their combination approximates the essence of the altruistic personality. People who are dispositionally empathic to others' predicaments, believe they are responsible to assist them, *and* see themselves as able to do so effectively are those who are likely to be helpful across time and situations. Research on attachment and helping portrays secure attachment as a broad personality characteristic that encapsulates this tripod. Yet, the effects of personality dimensions, separately or in combination, on help-giving depend on situational variables. For example, as noted, dispositional empathy does not differentiate between helpers and non-helpers when the target of help is a close friend or family member (Graziano et al. 2007). This section has also discussed the importance of going beyond the help/no help decision to consider personality dispositions associated with providing dependency/autonomy oriented assistance. Finally, we closed this section by describing recent research that identified dispositional dimensions beyond traditional characteristics directly relevant to helping.

In the next section, we turn to the third category of the answer to "Who helps?": demographic determinants of help-giving, with particular focus on the roles of gender and social status in helpfulness.

3.2.3 The Demographics of the Helpful Person: Who Helps More: Men? Women? Rich? Poor?

3.2.3.1 Gender Differences in Helping Are women generally more helpful than are men, or vice versa? The answer provided by social psychological research is that neither women nor men can be labeled the "helpful gender." Men and women help, more than the opposite sex, in different ways and under different circumstances. Partly, at least, gender differences in helping are attributable to physical differences between the average man and woman. Men are more likely to intervene in situations where physical strength matters. Yet, social psychological research on gender differences in helping has gone beyond physical differences to consider the effects of gender role expectations on men and women's readiness to help in different situations. At the center of this approach is the role perspective on social behavior (Eagly et al. 2000).

Role theory is premised on the idea that people's social behavior is determined to a large extent by the roles they play in society. Social roles can be relatively specific or general, and constitute social categories that are associated with people's expectations of themselves and others. Individuals occupy several social roles, the expectations of which may or may not be consistent. Social behavior is shaped by the situational salience of a particular role, and the behavioral expectations associated with it. For example, a police officer who is also a mother is expected to behave in a certain way when on the job chasing criminals, and in a diametrically opposite way when at home raising her children.

Gender is a general social role that shapes behavior in all societies across many situations. The expectations that men and women have of themselves, and of each other, are perhaps best subsumed under the differences between "communal" and "agentic" orientations to social life (Bakan 1966). Agency is used to describe "the existence of an organism as an individual, and communion for the participation of the individual in some larger organism of which the individual is part"; agency manifests itself "in the urge to master" and communion in "non-contractual cooperation" (Bakan 1966; pp. 14–15). Applied to the present context, the communal orientation is marked by caring, nurturance and sensitivity for the needs of close others whom we see as part of the "we," and the agentic orientation by a more selfish focus, and the person's need for efficacy and "getting things done." Parallel to our conceptualization of people's needs for belongingness and independence as universal, here, too, the communion and agency modalities of existence represent social orientations that are experienced by all.

Yet women and men are said to be characterized by relatively strong emphasis on communal and agentic orientations, respectively (Archer and Lloyd 2002; Diekman and Clark 2015). Evolutionary theory and role theory account for the affinity between one's gender and communal vs. agentic orientation. From an evolutionary perspective, reproductive success is promoted by males' agentic-aggressive orientation, and by females' communal-nurturing orientation. In the animal world, a male that impregnates a large number of females increases the likelihood that its genes would be transferred to the next generation. On the other hand, nurturing females who take good care of the young increase their genes' survivability. In human societies, the parallel difference between the sexes appears in the division of labor between child-rearing mothers and breadwinner fathers, which has reinforced the agentic and communal gender-role orientations. It should be noted, however, that the differences between men and women are much less rigid than between males and females in the animal world and are becoming even less so in modern times.

The association of the feminine gender role with a communal orientation and the male role with an agentic one is reflected in research findings on women and men's self-reports of values and traits relevant to helpfulness, and actual helping behaviors. Regarding values and traits, women endorse social responsibility and concern for others more than do men (Schwartz and Rubel 2005), and rate communal goals as more important than agentic goals (Diekman et al. 2010). Importantly, relative to men, women not only hold prosocial values but also believe in their ability to act upon them. Self-efficacy reflects people's beliefs of their competence in particular domains and predicts their performance in these areas (e.g. people's perceived academic self-efficacy predicts their academic performance; Eccles 1994). Although ratings of empathic self-efficacy predict self-reports of prosocial behavior by both genders, women score higher on empathic self-efficacy than do men (Bandura et al. 2003). Women also report possessing traits of warmth, tender mindedness and altruism more than do men (Costa and McCrae 2009) and although there is a substantial overlap in the distribution of empathy scores between genders, women score consistently higher than men on various measures of caring and altruism (Pursell et al. 2008). Based on these and other findings, Baron-Cohen (2003) suggested that brain differences between men and women were responsible for women's greater empathy: "The female brain is predominantly hard-wired for empathy. The male brain [...] for understanding and building systems" (p. 1).

These attitudinal gender differences translate into actual differences in helping behavior. In general, both women and men are more likely to help in situations that draw on traditional gender roles. In situations that are more gender-role neutral, we should expect no differences between men and women. In support of this hypothesis, there is no difference between men and women in prosocial behavior when they interact in the context of economic games (Balliet et al. 2011). Yet because men are expected to take more risks than women are, people think that men are more likely to rescue others in emergencies (Eagly 2009), and they indeed help more when situations are unfamiliar and involve strangers (Eagly and Crowley 1986). The link between rescuing others in danger situations and the content of the masculine gender role is exemplified by the finding that 91.1% of recipients of the Carnegie Medal in 2003 were men (Becker and Eagly 2004). When one considers that the medal is awarded for stereotypically masculine behaviors, i.e. saving another's life while placing one's own life on the line, the high percentage of male recipients is not surprising. Conversely, in altruistic activities that are more gender neutral (e.g. joining organizations like Doctors Without Borders or donating a kidney) there is either no gender difference or one that favors women (Cross and Madson 1997).

Finally, although much progress has been made in past decades toward greater gender equality, relative to women, men still represent an advantaged group in many societies. To a large extent, this is because men, more than women, occupy the more socially valued agentic positions (e.g. leadership roles) while women tend to specialize in less valued roles that amplify communal characteristics (e.g. teachers, nurses) (Eagly et al. 2000).

Over the years, the line that represents this gender role division has been blurring, but it is still a dominant feature of the division of labor in many societies, and deviations from it are "punished." Thus, for example, highly competent female leaders were seen as masculine, cold and unlikeable (Eagly and Karau 2002). A more implicit mechanism that helps maintain the gender-role division is what Mary Jackman (1994) calls the "velvet glove" – the replacement of explicit, often forceful means to maintain inequality by paternalistic ideologies that give the disadvantaged protection and assistance in exchange for their tacit agreement to adopt the existing unequal hierarchy and accept their disadvantaged place within it. In fact, the stability of an unequal hierarchy where the disadvantaged coexist with the advantaged is often based on a "deal" where the former accept their inferiority in exchange for care and protection by the latter (Nadler 2015; Tajfel and Turner 2004; Zahavi and Zahavi 1999). This deal is reflected in personal ideologies held by both the advantaged and the disadvantaged that serve to justify the unequal hierarchy (Jost and Hunyady 2005; Sidanius and Pratto 1999).

In the context of gendered helping, paternalistic attitudes and behaviors of men toward women constitute an implicit means to maintain their social advantage. Past research has explored this phenomenon using the concepts of benevolent sexism (Glick and Fiske 2001), defined as a "set of interrelated attitudes towards women [...] viewing women stereotypically and in restricted roles [...] but also tend to elicit behaviors typically characterized as prosocial" (Glick and Fiske 1996, p. 491). Similarly, chivalrous sexism is a "chivalrous yet subtly oppressive view of women" (Shnabel et al. 2016, p. 55). Such a restrictive view of women reinforces their assumed weakness relative to men, and the expectation that men should support them.

Chivalrous helping is most likely when male and female gender roles are salient. Such salience may be dispositionally determined (i.e. a person's long-held beliefs in gender role stereotypes; Bem 1974) or situationally induced. An experimental demonstration of the effects of situational salience of gender-role stereotypes on chivalrous helping is that after being primed to such stereotypes by memories of romantic love, men helped a woman collect objects she had dropped more than when gender-role stereotypes had not been primed (Lamy et al. 2009).

Importantly for our purposes, chivalrous helping is reflected not only in whether men help women more, but also in whether they provide them with *autonomy-* or *dependency-oriented help* (Shnabel et al. 2016). How are these two kinds of help related to chivalrous helping? As elaborated in the section on intergroup helping relations, giving dependency-oriented help may be a seemingly prosocial yet subtly oppressive behavior designed to maintain the helper's social advantage (Nadler et al. 2009). Women's scores on a scale measuring their beliefs in benevolent sexism – the Ambivalent Sexism Inventory (ASI; Glick and Fiske 1996) – was positively related to their seeking of dependency- but not autonomy-oriented help from a male helper (Shnabel et al. 2016, Study 1). Also, women who worked on a difficult task and scored high on the ASI sought more dependency-oriented help from a male than from a female instructor; and male instructors who scored high on the ASI gave women working on a difficult task more dependency-oriented help than they gave to men working on the same task (Shnabel et al. 2016, Studies 3 and 4, respectively). These findings demonstrate how benevolence can be used to maintain the helper's superiority. A subsequent section on helping relations between structurally unequal groups will address these social mechanisms in greater detail and discuss the variables and psychological processes that can be used to untie the knot between helping and inequality.

3.2.3.2 Socioeconomic Differences: Helpfulness of the Rich and the Poor Interpersonal and intergroup relations often involve interactions between unequal actors. One dominant marker of such inequality is wealth. This difference exists in smaller and larger communities, in tribal societies and in modern nation-states, and is often associated with other social indicators, such as educational attainment and professional prestige.

There are two equally compelling, and opposite, answers to the question who helps more, the poor or the rich. On the one hand, because the poor have fewer resources they may be expected to give less. On the other hand, one important way for people in the lower rungs of the socioeconomic ladder to cope with the more stressful and threatening environments they live in is to develop relatively stronger cooperative networks. In support of this logic, research shows that the poor are comparatively more attentive to others in their environment and are more dependent on them to achieve their goals (Kraus and Keltner 2009). This in turn suggests that the poor would be generally more helpful than would the rich. Indeed, large-scale surveys indicate that lower-class individuals donate a relatively higher proportion of their income to charitable causes than do people in higher classes (Greve 2009). The tendency of poorer people to be relatively more compassionate is congruent with the findings that members of collectivistic cultures are more helpful than their counterparts in individualistic cultures (pp. 45–51). In general, collectivistic societies tend to be less resourceful than individualistic societies. We turn now to consider research that centered on difference in helpfulness between people in high and low socioeconomic classes within the same society.

In their research program on social class and generosity, Piff et al. (2010) asked people to rate themselves on a 10-point scale ranging from the lowest to the highest socioeconomic class, and then asked them to play the dictator game, in which they could give an anonymous stranger as many of the 10 points at their disposal as they saw fit. The findings indicate that the lower the self-rated status the higher the generosity (Study 1). A subsequent experiment (Study 2) replicated this finding using a different operationalization of status and helping measure: people's social status was manipulated by asking participants to place themselves on a 10-point status scale, and then to imagine others in social classes above or below theirs. Participants who had been induced to imagine others above their socioeconomic class (i.e. induced relatively low class) recommended that a higher proportion of people's annual salary go to charitable donations than those who had been induced to experience themselves in a higher social class, i.e. imagine others below their socioeconomic status.

Consistent with the previous reasoning, the antecedents of this link between social class and helpfulness are the different patterns of social relationships that are dominant in each group. Because they need to face more daily challenges, lower-class individuals live in more affiliative social environments than do their richer counterparts. Two variables have been identified as the psychological mediators of the link between socioeconomic status and generosity. First, the relative greater generosity of poorer participants in an economic game was mediated by their beliefs in egalitarian social values (Piff et al. 2010, Study 3). Second, lower-class individuals were found to be more compassionate than those in a higher social class. Lower social class individuals scored higher on dispositional tendency for compassion, reported feeling more compassionate when watching children suffering from cancer, and were judged as more compassionate toward a conversation partner in distress than high social class individuals (Stellar et al. 2012).

Research on the effects of power on compassion reinforces this argument. Van Kleef et al. (2008) had people, who had previously filled out the Sense of Power Scale (Anderson and Galinsky 2006), listen to another person who described a sad event they had experienced in the past five years. In addition, participants' vagal activity level was assessed. As noted previously, high vagal activity is associated with emotion control. High scorers on the the "Sense of Power" scale felt less distress and less compassion, and evidenced higher levels of vagal activity when listening to the sad story than did low scorers. The finding regarding vagal activity is important because it indicates, on an unobtrusive measure, that individuals with a high sense of power exerted efforts to regulate their emotion in the face of the other's predicament. Finally, the data indicate that high power individuals were not less attentive to the other's story about their adversity, but that they were simply motivated to keep distance from them.

Findings on class differences in utilitarian decision-making support the idea that compared to low social class, high social class individuals exert efforts to control their emotions and keep their distance from others in need. A utilitarian judgment represents ignoring the plight of an immediately present individual in favor of future benefits for the many (Baron and Ritov 2009; Bentham 1948). An example is when a person ignores the dangers for an individual who is administered an experimental drug in the hope it would benefit many in the future.

Based on the findings on class differences in helping, Côté et al. (2013) reasoned that in situations involving utilitarian dilemmas, low social class individuals would feel greater empathy toward the immediately present suffering person and be more helpful toward them. Conversely, high social class people would be expected to make utilitarian decisions and ignore the sufferings of the one present in favor of the many who are not immediately present.

To test this hypothesis, high and low social class participants faced dilemmas that represented high and low levels of moral conflict. In the high conflict condition, participants were faced with the "footbridge dilemma," that instructed them to imagine themselves standing on a bridge with another person next to them while five people sat on the train tracks below. According to the story, they then suddenly saw a trolley rushing down on the tracks, certain to kill the five sitters if not stopped, with the only way to stop the trolley being to throw the person next to them to block its movement. More high social class than low social class individuals made that utilitarian decision. No social class differences emerged, on the other hand, in a low-conflict moral dilemma where participants needed to push a lever to the right, thereby causing the trolley to kill three workers, or to the left, thereby saving three while killing one. On this dilemma, all participants chose to save three at the cost of killing one. The main difference between the high and low moral conflict situations was that the latter did not involve empathizing with a person who was supposedly standing next to you. The finding that empathy, measured or induced, mediated the lesser willingness of lower social class individuals to make the utilitarian decision in the high-conflict moral dilemma (Côté et al. 2013, Studies 2 and 3) supports the idea that higher-class individuals tended to exert emotional control to suppress their empathy, and distanced themselves from the person standing next to them. This facilitated their willingness to make a utilitarian decision.

The overall conclusion from the research reviewed in the preceding sections is that people who are positioned lower in the social hierarchy are more compassionate. This conclusion is based on different operationalizations of social class, including a subjective measure of social status (Piff et al. 2010, Study 1); objective assessment of status (family income and parental education level; Stellar et al. 2012, Study 2); and experimentally induced social status (Piff et al. 2010, Study 2). Measures of helpfulness and compassion were also multifaceted and included generosity in experimental games (Piff et al. 2010, Study 1); willingness to donate (Piff et al. 2010, Study 2); helping someone in distress (Piff et al. 2010, Study 4); and various indices of compassion when viewing another's predicament (Stellar et al. 2012). Moreover, the link between social status and prosociality was observed when other conceptually relevant variables (e.g. ethnic group, religiosity) had been controlled (Stellar et al. 2012, Study 3).

The validity of the status-prosociality nexus is further enhanced by the fact that the same pattern emerges when people with high and low sense of personal power are compared (e.g. Van Kleef et al. 2008). Although the concepts used here have different meanings (e.g. socio-economic status, subjective sense of power), they all share a common denominator of an individual's or group's hierarchical standing relative to others. A likely explanation for the finding that those in the relatively lower place on the hierarchy are more generous than their high counterparts is that being, or feeling, relatively powerless or with lower resources lead people to develop a culture that emphasizes values of cooperation and shared belongingness that allows them to cope with their lack of resources. Those higher on the hierarchy who are, or feel themselves to be resourceful have a lower need to rely on others to cope, and "shut themselves" to others' sufferings by exercising emotional control.

Before concluding, note that the findings linking lower hierarchical position and helpfulness have not considered the distinction between dependency- and autonomy-oriented help. Yet, if given the opportunity, people who are higher on the social hierarchy and likely to value personal success would give more autonomy-oriented help than would those who are placed lower on the hierarchy. For the latter, the goal of helping may be the alleviation of the other's immediate suffering, while for the former, it may be the goal of increasing the other's future self-reliance. Phrased in the language of the present book's emphasis on belongingness and independence, the helpfulness of those low on the social hierarchy may be dominated by considerations of belongingness and solidarity, while that of those high on the hierarchy by considerations of independence and individual achievement. This perspective on the link between social class and helpfulness through the prism of autonomy- and dependency-oriented help needs to be addressed in future research.

*

In summary, the research in the preceding sections indicates that both gender and socioeconomic status affect helpfulness. Regarding gender, the answer to the question of who helps more, men or women, is "it depends." It depends on the congruity between the person's gender and relatedness of the help to the assumed masculine or feminine gender role. Men will help more in need situations that call on the helper to exercise agentic skills and women in situations that call for communal skills. Men help more than do women in risky situations that demand a significant amount of physical exertion, such as short-term rescue effort.

Women on the other hand are likely be more involved than men are in long-term caring. Further, research on chivalrous helping demonstrates the Janus face of help-giving. It is frequently motivated by genuine care for the recipient, but when helper and recipient are in hierarchical relationships helping may constitute a subtle oppressive mechanism.

Regarding socioeconomic status, the answer to the question of who helps more, the "rich" or the "poor," seems more clear-cut: those in lower socioeconomic classes are more helpful and compassionate than their higher socioeconomic class counterparts. The findings suggest that people in higher socioeconomic classes distance themselves psychologically from the situation and are therefore relatively less compassionate and helpful. Yet these findings are based on the "help/no help" dichotomy, and the effects of social class may be different if a more nuanced perspective on helpfulness is presented (i.e. autonomy vs. dependency-oriented help). Finally, these two lines of research on the effects of the demographic variables of gender and social class are united in their emphases on the role of helpfulness between socially unequal groups. This perspective on helping relations within contexts of social inequality is analyzed at greater depth in the subsequent section on intergroup helping relations.

In the preceding sections, we focused on variables that sought to predict the giving of help. Answers to the question "When help?" included variables that characterized the social context (e.g. number of bystanders); relations between helper and recipient (e.g. communal or exchange relations); the normative and cultural context within which helping occurs; and group differences (e.g. cross-cultural differences). Answers to the question "Who helps?" addressed developmental processes and personal characteristics of the helper (i.e. personality dispositions and demographic characteristics). Drawing on the view of helping relations as expressing people's needs for belongingness and independence, this research has examined the situational, relational, cultural, personality and demographic-structural variables that affect shared belongingness within a particular context, which in turn is expressed in their willingness to help others in need. In the next section on "Why Help" we center on the *motivation* that underlies helping others in need.

3.3 "Why Help?": Empathy, Attribution and Prestige

The section begins by considering whether helpfulness is an expression of caring for others or a veiled expression of the desire to increase own well-being. Subsequently we address cognitive processes that explain why people help or do not help others. A final section examines how the helper's motivation to gain prestige in the group drives help-giving. This discussion will take us to the other side of the Janus-faced helping relations: from helping as an expression of shared belongingness between helper and recipient to helping as an expression of one's desire to gain prestige by giving.

3.3.1 *Empathy: Altruism or Selfishness*

If we were to ask a random sample of people why people help others, the most likely answer would probably be something along the lines of "People help because they care." This response constitutes the essence of the *empathy-altruism hypothesis* that holds that helping is motivated by genuine concern with the other's welfare and not by the helper's desire for self-gain (Batson 2011). The feeling of empathy that drives helpfulness is defined as an "other-oriented emotional response elicited and congruent with the perceived welfare of others in need" (Batson 2011, p. 11). The finding that empathy is a precursor of helping is well established in psychological research (Keltner et al. 2014), and has been attributed to the evolutionary-based instinct of parents to care for their vulnerable offspring when they show signs of distress. This instinct is said to generalize to other social relations and lead the empathically aroused observer to help those they empathize with even when they are not bound to them by bonds of family or friendship (Keltner 2009).

However, this view of helping has been challenged by alternative approaches that attribute helping to selfish motivations. One such early alternative to the empathy-altruism hypothesis is the *aversive arousal reduction hypothesis.* It suggests that because people who empathize with the needy feel distressed when exposed to their predicament they seek to ameliorate their own distress by helping the needy (Cialdini et al. 1973). In other words, the higher helpfulness of the emphatically aroused bystanders reflects their motivation to help themselves.

In order to counter this explanation and demonstrate that empathically aroused helping is altruistically motivated, Batson et al. (1981) employed the "physical escape" paradigm. This pioneering study consisted of a 2 (high vs. low empathy) × 2 (difficult vs. easy escape) experimental design. All participants watched through a one-way mirror another person who displayed signs of anxiety because they were about to experience an electric shock. Consistent with research showing that we empathize more with people similar to us (Batson et al. 1995), participants were under the impression that the protagonist was similar or dissimilar to them (i.e. high and low empathy conditions, respectively). In the "difficult escape" condition, participants had been told that they would have to watch the suffering protagonist for many "shock trials," whereas in the "easy escape" condition they expected to watch her only for one trial. The participants' willingness to trade places with the suffering protagonist served as the dependent measure of helping. Batson and his colleagues reasoned that if the other's welfare is what drives the observer's willingness to help, participants in the high empathy condition would help regardless of ease of escape. If, however egoistic motivation propels helping, people in the easy escape condition would be unwilling to help despite feeling empathy toward a similar other. The results indicate that in the high empathy condition, people volunteered to help regardless of ease of escape, supporting the assertion that when one feels empathy helping is altruistically motivated. The same pattern of findings was observed with experimentally induced and dispositional empathy: when empathically aroused, people help because they are motivated to ease the other's pains rather than to increase their own well-being (Batson 2011).

Over the years, other non-altruistic explanations for the empathy-helpfulness link were proposed. One such explanation relies on the principles of classical conditioning and suggests that from an early age infants learn to associate the relief of other's distress with own joy. Aronfreed (1968) suggested that relief from empathic distress that young children experience when the caretaker is distressed and the prospect of feeling empathic joy by helping them is an important precursor of their helpfulness. Thus, the vicarious joy that the infant experiences when they relieve their mother's distress by smiling at her forms the basis for adult helping that is motivated by helpers' anticipated vicarious joy.

The idea that empathically aroused observers help more because they wish to share, vicariously, in the good feelings of the recipient was labeled as the *emphatic joy hypothesis* (Smith et al. 1989). Based on this logic, it was predicted that empathically aroused individuals would provide more help than the non-empathically aroused only when they expect to receive feedback about the recipient's response. In the experiment designed to test this prediction, participants viewed an interview with a distressed female student and could help her relieve her distress and do better on a subsequent interview by giving her structured and effective advice. To manipulate high and low levels of empathy, participants in the high empathy condition had been instructed to imagine how the interviewee felt during the stressful interview and those in the low empathy condition had been instructed to observe her bodily gestures (e.g. head movements). Further, half the participants were told that if they decided to help they would be able to see the interviewee on a second interview (feedback condition). The findings support the empathic joy hypothesis: participants in the high empathy–feedback condition helped the most, while participants' helpfulness in the high empathy–no feedback condition was similar to that of participants in the low empathy condition. Summarizing their findings, Smith et al. (1989) write that "personal distress reflects a predominance of the distress relief motive and empathic concern a predominance of the joy motive" (p. 648). This suggests that helping is based on the selfish motivation of reducing empathic distress through the experience of vicarious joy.

The ping-pong between the egoistic and the altruistic motivational explanations of helping by the empathically aroused bystander has been central to helping research since the 1980s. Some suggested and tested other egoistic alternatives, while others sought to demonstrate that under certain conditions egoism could not explain help-giving. On the egoistic side of the debate, Maner et al. (2002) added to the stress relief and empathic joy explanations the idea that high empathy resulted in feeling of "oneness" between the observer and the person in need, such that helping the other is akin to helping oneself. Therefore, empathy-based helpfulness cannot be viewed as driven by the desire to increase the other's well-being. Based on experimental findings that supported the hypothesis that feeling of "oneness" propels helpfulness, Maner et al. (2002) expressed the skeptical position that "evidence for true altruism remains elusive" (p. 1601).

Others supported the empathy-altruism hypothesis. Participants watched an interview with a young woman talking about her difficulties and had been induced, or not, to empathise with her by placing themselves in her shoes. They were later given the opportunity to help her on the problem she described, or on another unrelated problem (Dovidio et al., 1990). The results indicate that high empathy participants helped more than low empathy participants only on the problem to which they had previously listened. There was nod difference between the high and low empathy conditions in helping on another unrelated problem. Also, only a measure of empathic concern associated with the specific problem they had listened to, was related to helping. General feelings of empathic concern did not predict helpfulness. The specificity of the effects of empathy on helping supports the empathy-altruism hypothesis. We feel empathy with a specific person who experiences a specific difficulty, and are driven to ameliorate it by helping. Had we been motivated, for example, to ameliorate our own distress occasioned by witnessing another's difficulty we would have taken the opportunity to relieve our distress by helping also on an unrelated problem.

In another study, participants induced to feel high or low empathy for a sick woman received updates on her improvement, and were told there was a 20%, 50% or 80% chance for her recovery (Batson et al. 1991). The empathic joy interpretation of the empathy-helping link would suggest that the higher the chances for improvement, the more the high empathy individuals would want to receive updated information. It was found that participants in the high empathy condition expressed a stronger wish for updates, and that this wish was not affected by the probability of recovery, supporting the empathic concern-altruism hypothesis. In a recent review of this and other related research, Daniel Batson, who as we have seen had played a pivotal role in the initiation and development of research on the empathy-altruism hypothesis, cautiously wrote: "Pending new evidence [...] the empathy-altruism hypothesis appears true" (2015, p. 271). This understated wording reminds us of the multicausal nature of helpfulness. In this spirit, it appears that all we can say for now is that under certain conditions people's helping is driven by their desire to increase others' welfare.

Thus, the debate concerning the motivation that drives the empathically aroused person to help cannot remain limited to an "either/or" question. Posing the question in this binary form obscures the fact that benefitting oneself and the needy need not be mutually exclusive. A more constructive way to pose the question regarding the egoistic or altruistic motivational basis of helping is to ask whether altruism or egoism is the *ultimate goal* of prosocial behavior, rather than an instrumental goal designed to achieve another, higher order goal (Lewin 1951). When the ultimate goal is the other's welfare, helping is altruistically motivated, even though it may be associated with significant personal benefits (e.g. feeling good about oneself, being praised for one's generosity). If, however, one's well-being is the ultimate goal (e.g. one seeks status in the group) then helping is egoistically motivated even though it leads to significant benefits for the needy. Moreover, a key difference between these two positions is that while helping others can be instrumental, the opposite is not true. When the helper's ultimate goal is to increase others' well-being, it is hard to imagine how selfish goals can be an instrumental stepping-stone to getting there. These are byproducts associated with the ultimate altruistic goal.

Research on the motivational antecedents of help-giving demonstrates how a continuous empirical and conceptual effort around a single basic question affects the development of the entire field. The ongoing altruism-egoism debate has led to the development of new conceptual insights and experimental methodologies. It also points at other, yet unstudied, research questions. One such question is what we mean when we say that the empathically aroused helper is motivated by care and concern for the needy's well-being. Is it alleviating the needy's current difficulties or increasing the probability that he or she would not face a similar predicament in the future? Employing the distinction between dependency- and autonomy-oriented helping, most, if not all, past research has focused on help-giving as alleviating the other's present predicament, which often meant giving them dependency-oriented help. Yet, sometimes a more significant form of help is not to provide the complete solution but provide the kind of help that would enable the needy to overcome similar difficulties in the future. How is empathic concern related to these two forms of help? When does empathy translate into dependency- or autonomy-oriented help? The importance of going beyond the dichotomy of help/no help is discussed throughout the book. Yet these and other open questions that need to be addressed by future research could not have been raised without the theoretical and experimental work described in this section.

3.3.2 *The Quest for Prestige*

As noted previously, helping expresses people's belongingness as well as the inequality between them. The previous section centered on the social belongingness aspect of help-giving. The present section on giving motivated by prestige centers on aspects of inequality in helping relations.

Prestige, relative self-worth and status are three concepts relevant to considering dimensions of inequality in social relationships in general, and helping relations in particular. *Prestige* refers to an individual's image in the eyes of others. *Relative self-worth* refers to one's view of oneself as able and worthwhile relative to others and is markedly different from prestige in that it reflects the individual's self-perceptions of him or herself, whereas prestige refers to others' perceptions. *Status* has a dual meaning. *Situational status* is close in meaning to prestige and defined as "the prestige, respect and esteem that a party has in the eyes of others" (Blader and Chen 2012, p. 995). *Structural status* is defined by the hierarchical position of one's ingroup; for example, if in a certain society men are more privileged than women, being a man means that one has higher status (Nadler et al. 2009). Although all three concepts share an emphasis on hierarchical relations, they are relevant to different aspects of helping relations. Because the desire for high prestige may motivate generosity, prestige is relevant to the present concern with the motivation for giving help. Relative self-worth is a central concept in considering the consequences of giving and receiving help and will be the focuse of subsequent sections. Finally, structural status is most relevant for helping interactions between structurally unequal groups and will be the conceptual anchor of a later section on intergroup helping relations.

Previous sections described the evolutionary and anthropological analyses of the links between help-giving and prestige (pp.15, 20–22). To reconnect with these discussions, we begin by reminding the reader of the main themes. The handicapping principle (Zahavi and Zahavi 1999) refers to the evolutionary logic that explains an organism's motivation to handicap itself: the peacock's tail is a prime example, as it advertises the peacock's desirability as a mate and ally that flourishes despite this self-imposed handicap. Similarly, the evolutionary irrational behavior of a bird that gives food to genetically unrelated chicks signals to onlooking birds that it is resourceful enough to feed its own and strangers – a prestige-gaining mechanism also described in premodern human societies (Mauss 1954). Summarizing these observations Boone (1998) suggests that giving to others constitutes "costly signaling" that tells the recipient and others that the helper is resourceful enough to bear the short-term costs of helping others; thus, "self-sacrifice might actually be self-presentation" (Van Vugt and Hardy 2010, p. 108).

The costly signal transmitted by helpfulness translates into viewing the helper as a caring and/or resourceful group member, resulting in either case in higher prestige, i.e. situational status. In organizational settings, team members assigned more prestige to helpful than to less helpful colleagues, and less to those habitually dependent on others' help (Blau 1963; Flynn 2003). Based on these observations, Van Vugt and Hardy (2006) proposed the *competitive altruism hypothesis:* to gain prestige, people compete over who will be more generous, given that the helpful act is visible or knowable to other group members. To examine this hypothesis, participants played an experimental game where they could give some of their earnings to other players. The participants were under the impression that their generous behavior would be either known or unknown to others. Consistent with the competitive altruism hypothesis, participants displayed more generosity in the public than the private condition. This visible generosity was associated with short-term costs and long-term benefits: the most altruistic individuals earned less in the experimental game, yet they were more respected and likely to be selected as group leaders.

In further support for the prestige-seeking motivation for helping, participants helped more when their generosity was visible, even when they knew that their helping was superfluous (Van Vugt and Hardy 2010). People helped more not because they were motivated to relieve the other's predicament, but because they sought to aggrandize themselves in the eyes of others. Also, the finding that self-monitoring, i.e. a dispositional tendency for positive self-presentation (Gangestad and Snyder 2000), moderated the relationship between visible helpfulness and help-giving is another demonstration of the prestige-seeking motivation for helping: under conditions of visible generosity, high self-monitors behaved more generously than did low self-monitors (Flynn et al. 2006).

Another finding suggestive of that motivation is that intuitive and fast allocation decisions are more prosocial and cooperative than deliberate and slow decisions. Rand et al. (2012) conducted three experiments where participants were asked to allocate funds to a common pool. The first found that faster allocation decisions made in under 10 seconds were more generous than slower decisions. The second study showed that when people had been under time pressure to make an allocation decision, i.e. "you have to decide in 10 seconds," they were more generous than when they had been instructed to take some time to deliberate. Finally, participants who had been instructed to remember a past successful intuition-based decision contributed significantly more to the common pool than those who had been asked to remember a successful decision following deliberation. Taken together, these findings imply that people are intuitively cooperative and become self-interested only after reflection. Why are we intuitively prosocial and cooperative? The authors suggest that this is because we are rewarded with prestige for cooperation and punished for being egoistic. Consequently, cooperation with others becomes the first automatic response.

These findings resonate with the previous discussion of the group selection approach as the evolutionary basis of helpfulness (pp. 19–20). They suggest that positive social behaviors are intuitive because they increase the group's evolutionary fitness. A group that is made up of people whose instincts are to help, cooperate, and trust each other has higher prospects for success in the evolutionary struggle. This is why such behaviors are rewarded with higher prestige. This conclusion is consistent with the observation that individuals and groups that commit antisocial and morally dubious behaviors (e.g. killing or torturing others) do so after they had invested cognitive efforts to restructure or reframe the destructive behavior as being morally acceptable (e.g.

dehumanizing the other; blaming "them" for own aggression) (Bandura 2000).

Another social mechanism people use to gain prestige is conspicuous consumption. This term was coined by Thorstein Veblen (1994 [1899]), an economist and sociologist vocally critical of capitalism, who suggested that in their quest for prestige people engage in public philanthropy and spend resources on goods they do not really need. For example, although any pen will do as a writing instrument, any watch will show the time reliably, and most cars will take us from one point to another, people spend large sums of money to buy expensive and branded pens, watches, and cars. Also, those who can afford it make public donations to let others know how caring and resourceful they are – the name plaques in universities and hospitals tell this story, and are akin to the bird feeding chicks not its own. Using the distinction between economic (resources), political (influence), and social (prestige and respect) dimensions of status (Sorokin 1927), such displays of generosity constitute a tradeoff between short-term loss of economic status and long-term gains of political and social status.

The pressure for costly signaling by conspicuous consumption or helping is situationally dependent. In some situations, we care about what other people think of us more than in others. The context of romantic relations, for one, increases the pressure for conspicuous displays of oneself as resourceful and caring. Like peacocks, romantically aroused men and women want to present themselves in their best light to potential partners. Based on this rationale, it was expected that romantically aroused people would engage in more conspicuous consumption and helping than those in a control condition. This hypothesis was supported for both men and women, albeit with different patterns (Griskevicius et al. 2007). Romantically aroused men (shown photos of attractive women) indicated that they would spend more money on expansive, highly branded items than those in a control condition. They were also more willing to engage in heroic helping (e.g. rescue someone from a burning house), but not in non-heroic helping (e.g. helping a disadvantaged child). Unlike men, women who had been romantically aroused (having imagined meeting an attractive man and spending the afternoon with him) did not indicate more conspicuous consumption than those in the control condition, yet were readier to behave in a conspicuously prosocial manner in situations that called for more nurturant behavior (e.g. volunteering in a publicly visible organization). Beyond demonstrating that one answer to the "Why help?" is that people are motivated to gain prestige by costly signaling, these findings alert us to the specificity of this phenomenon for different people in different situations. Conspicuous helping is not a universal or unidimensional phenomenon. It is more prevalent in situations where the motivation for positive self-presentation is high, and its specific expression is affected by demographic (e.g. gender) and personality (e.g. self-monitoring) variables.

3.3.3 Attributional Answers to Why Help

3.3.3.1 Do they Deserve It? In the preceding sections, reasons offered for "why help-giving" centered on the help giver's motivation. The empathic concern-altruism hypothesis asserted that people help because they are motivated to increase the other's well-being. Alternative interpretations for the empathy-helping link (e.g. the state-relief hypothesis), together with research showing that people help to gain prestige, posited that helping is motivated by the helpers' desire to increase their own well-being.

The present section provides a cognitive-attributional rather than motivational answer to the question of "Why help." This perspective asserts that would-be helpers base their decision to help on whether or not they view the needy as responsible for their need in help. If the state of need is viewed as controllable or avoidable, the person in need is viewed as responsible for his or her plight and therefore as not deserving help. If the predicament is perceived as uncontrollable, the person in need is judged as not responsible for their plight and therefore deserving help. Weiner writes about this attributional or judgmental view of help-giving that "like God,..." helpers "...regard themselves as having the right or legitimacy to judge others as [...] responsible or not responsible for an event or a personal plight" (1993, p. 957).

In an early study that tested this idea, a confederate collapsed in a New York subway car (Piliavin et al. 1969). In half the cases, he was visibly drunk, and in the other half visibly ill. Fellow passengers helped the ill person but not the drunkard. Why? Consistent with the above reasoning, when bystanders asked themselves why the drunkard needed their help, they answered that he was to blame for needing and therefore not as deserving. Conversely, the ill person's need was perceived as beyond their control and therefore the innocent victim as deserving help.

Weiner's *attribution-affect model* provides a conceptual framework for the effects of perceived controllability of the need for help on help-giving (Weiner et al. 2011). The attribution-affect model of help-giving suggests that bystanders' affect mediates the effects of perceived controllability on helping. The attribution of the predicament to controllable causes (e.g. the person is negligent or lazy) leads helpers to view others as *responsible for their need* for help, which results in feelings of *anger* toward them, which in turn leads potential helpers to judge them as *"sinners" not worthy of help*. When, however, the would-be helpers attribute the needy's predicament to *reasons beyond their control* (e.g. *illness)* they experience feelings of *sympathy* toward them, judge them as *deserving help*, and help them.

Note that the attribution-affect model represents a general framework of people's social behavior. For example, if someone is 45 minutes late to a meeting we had scheduled with them, we immediately ask ourselves why. Is this offensive tardiness attributable to a controllable or uncontrollable cause? In the first case, we are likely experience anger and respond punitively toward the late person, but if the same tardiness is attributed to causes beyond the person's control, such as a traffic jam, sympathy rather than anger is likely to be felt (Weiner 2006).

To turn back to helping, personal predicaments are often categorized into problems of a physical or mental-behavioral nature. When one needs help because of an illness or a handicap, the need is viewed as uncontrollable, while a need associated with destructive life style (e.g. drug abuse) is viewed as being under the person's volitional control (Weiner 1993). When confronting a need state in the second category, bystanders are less likely to help. This is demonstrated by research that compared people's reactions to the need for help of those suffering from physical versus mental-behavioral problems (e.g. Alzheimer's and alcoholism, respectively). Consistent with the attribution-affect model, those needing help because of physical problems were viewed as not responsible for their predicament, were liked and pitied, and evoked high readiness to help. On the other hand, individuals needing help because of a mental-behavioral problem were viewed as responsible for their predicament, were less liked, and evoked anger and lesser willingness to help (Weiner et al. 1988).

Yet the same need situation, whether physical or mental-behavioral, can be attributed to controllable or uncontrollable causes. For example, heart failure may be described as due to controllable (e.g., excessive smoking) or uncontrollable reasons (e.g., hereditary factors). Similarly, drug abuse may be the result of long-term recreational use or the use of prescription painkillers after a car accident. Experimental findings indicate that the *perceived controllability* of the cause for the problem, rather than its physical as opposed to mental-behavioral nature, determines readiness to help. Compared to the presentation of a physical problem such as AIDS as resulting from uncontrollable causes (e.g. faulty blood transfusion), its presentation as due to controllable causes (e.g. promiscuous sexual behavior) led to more blaming, anger, lesser liking, and lesser readiness to help (Weiner 2006). Finally, a meta-analysis of 39 studies supported the link between perceived controllability, affect and subsequent positive (helping) and negative (aggressive) social behavior (Rudolph et al. 2004).

On the societal level, this applies to perceived causes of poverty and readiness to help the poor (Weiner et al. 2011). People who hold a liberal ideology view poverty as due to uncontrollable causes, primarily government policies, and the poor are therefore deserving of assistance. A conservative ideology, on the other hand, views the poor as personally responsible for their plight (e.g. laziness), and therefore not deserving. Consequently, liberals endorse more help and public assistance for the poor than do conservatives (e.g. Applebaum 2001; Feather and McKee 2009; Janoff-Bulman et al. 2008).

Research assessing the prevalence of "blaming" and "compassionate" response profiles toward the poor found that about one fifth of a sample of undergraduate students in New Zealand viewed poverty through the "compassionate" lens and expressed willingness to help them. Another fifth blamed the poor for their predicament, and the scores of the remaining three fifths fell between the compassionate and blaming profiles (Osborne and Weiner 2015). The willingness of these ambivalent individuals to help is likely to be affected by situational variables. For example, they will assist when poverty-related needs are extreme (e.g. children with malnutrition) but will be less likely to help children go to see a movie.

In summary, this approach to answering the question "Why help?" holds that people distance themselves from those they regard as "guilty" of their predicament. This "wall of perceived guilt" is reinforced by feelings of anger toward the needy that allow bystanders to look the other way. The separation between oneself and the needy is less likely when people in need are regarded as innocent victims. These processes describe benevolent attitudes and behavior on the interpersonal and societal levels of analysis. Framed within the present emphasis on shared belongingness as a precursor of helping, belongingness is predicated on viewing the needy as a victim. Exonerating the needy from blame is not a sufficient, but a necessary condition for helpfulness to occur.

Finally, these findings resonate with the previous observation that, relative to individuals in low socioeconomic classes, those in higher social classes tend to distance themselves from others in need and are less likely to help them (pp. 70–75). Taken together with the present attributional analysis this suggests that, relative to those in lower social class, people of higher socioeconomic status tend to a generalized view of others being responsible and in control of their fate. This may lead them to adopt a blaming attitude toward others in need of help, distance themselves from them, and evidence lower readiness to help them.

3.3.3.2 Models of Helping and Coping In an attempt to paint a more complete picture of the conditions for helpfulness, Brickman et al. (1982) proposed that would-be helpers' decision to help is based on their answers to two questions: "Do they *deserve* to be helped?" and "Is it *effective* to help them?," rather than only to the question of "Do they deserve?" Consistent with the previous attributional analysis of helping, when the needy are seen as responsible for their plight they are viewed as undeserving of help. When, however, the need for help is attributed to causes beyond their control they will be regarded as deserving. The answer to the effectiveness question is determined by whether the person in need is viewed as able enough to be part of the solution. If the answer is "yes," help is more likely to promote a long-term solution, rather than just ameliorating the experienced difficulty. Integrating this with the recent emphasis on differences between dependency- and autonomy-oriented help (pp. 25) suggests that when viewed as able to contribute to the solution the needy will receive autonomy-oriented assistance that will promote future self-reliance. Conversely, when the needy are viewed as unable to be part of the solution help is likely to be dependency-oriented and promote future chronic dependency.

Importantly, Brickman et al. (1982) suggest that judgments about deservedness and effectiveness of help are negatively related to each other: it is ineffective to help those who deserve help, and effective to help those who do not deserve it. For example, when a student's failure on an important test is attributed to controllable reasons (e.g. laziness) he or she is not deserving of help. Yet, because if they invest efforts to prepare for an upcoming test they may achieve success, it is effective to help them. When, however, the student is known to have studied hard and failed, they deserve to be helped but apparently, they are viewed as having low abilities and it is therefore ineffective to help them.

Models of helping and coping. By contrasting the answers to whether or not the needy is responsible for the problem and if he or she are viewed as part of the solution, four models of helping and coping emerge (Brickman et al. 1982). These models differ, among other things, in the emphasis on the kind of help given, its duration, and the most appropriate helper.

In the *moral model*, the needy is viewed as responsible for both the problem and its solution (viewed as guilty and strong). The title "moral model" reflects the idea that because the needy is guilty, it is their moral responsibility to solve the problem. In this case, help is likely to consist of exhortations intended to motivate the person to do so. Such exhortations are likely to be more effective when they are delivered by a figure of authority (e.g., a teacher) and the duration of helping is short. It lasts as long as moralizing the other may take.

In the *medical model*, people are exonerated from responsibility for the problem and are not viewed as responsible to solve it (viewed as not guilty and weak). Here assistance will be given by an expert who has skills and knowledge to ameliorate the needy's difficulties (e.g., a physician). The duration of helping will be the time it takes to solve the problem.

In the *compensatory model*, the needy is viewed as not responsible for the predicament they are in, yet competent enough to be part of the solution (not guilty and strong). The name implies that the helper needs to compensate the person in need for the predicament, which is not of their making, by giving them tools, or teaching them skills, with which they can solve the problem on their own (i.e. autonomy-oriented help). The duration of help will be a predetermined period that allows the recipient to master the skills they need to solve the problem

Finally, in the *enlightenment model*, the needy is regarded as responsible for the problem, but not for its solution (i.e. guilty and weak). The name reflects a view of the needy as requiring enlightenment about the true nature of their problem, and submit to an authority who will show him or her the proverbial light. Alcoholics Anonymous (AA) is an example for a highly effective helping organization that adopts the enlightenment model (Moos and Moos 2004). When joining AA, people declare themselves guilty of alcoholism and because they cannot cope on their own, they commit themselves to belonging to the AA community for an indefinite period. Other, more sinister organizations adopt this helping model. For example, many cults tell their followers that their previous way of life is the source of their suffering, which they can remedy only by lifelong commitment to the cult and its leader. Cult followers are told that they are guilty of the problems they experience but weak and therefore not able to part of the solution. In order to 'heal' they must depend on a higher authority that will show them the 'light' for the rest of their lives.

These four models of helping and coping are presented in Table 3.1.

The question of interest in this context is what causes helpers to pigeonhole a person in need into any of these four models. Why do people view some individuals in need as not guilty for their predicament,

Table 3.1 Models of helping and coping based on Brickman et al. (1982).

	Needy Responsible for Problem	*Needy NOT Responsible for Problem*
Needy Responsible for Solution	MORAL model	COMPENSATORY model
Needy NOT Responsible for Solution	ENLIGHTENMENT model	MEDICAL model

yet strong enough to be part of its solution (the compensatory model) and therefore give them autonomy-oriented assistance? Why are others with the same problem viewed as not guilty of their predicament yet unable to be part of the solution (the medical model) and therefore receive dependency-oriented help?

One answer is the needy's group affiliation. For example, it is likely that relative to younger people, older people tend to be assigned to the medical model. Commenting about staff-patient relationships in old people's nursing homes, Timko and Rodin (1985) write that the resident of nursing homes "is generally stereotyped as more passive, sickly, dependent and helpless than younger populations" (p. 96). The tendency to assign the elderly to the medical model is detrimental to them because it deprives them of control and has them rely on dependency-oriented help. However, giving nursing home residents control over the solution of everyday problems resulted in higher feelings of well-being (Langer and Rodin 1976), and viewing them as responsible for solving daily problems was associated with higher life satisfaction and overall health (Zevon et al. 1982). Although it is objectively true that due to deteriorating skills older people are not responsible for many of the difficulties they experience, beliefs about their responsibility for the solution are more malleable. Adopting a compensatory model in helping the elderly is likely to result in autonomy-oriented assistance that will contribute to their overall well-being more than the dependency-oriented assistance associated with the medical model.

Another social characteristic that causes helpers to assign people in need to one or the other models is the needy's socioeconomic status (Nadler and Chernyak-Hai 2014). As discussed later at greater length at pp. 164–166), a poorer person in need was expected to be less able to be part of the solution and was therefore given dependency-oriented help. A high-status person was viewed as competent and able to participate in the solution, and was therefore given autonomy-oriented assistance. These and related findings to be reviewed in subsequent sections on intergroup helping suggest that the kind of help we give to others may reinforce the dependency associated with their disadvantaged social positions.

In several ways, Brickman et al.'s (1982) theorizing connects the first and second parts of the book. The first part focused on the "when," "who" and "why" of help-giving, while the second addresses a broader range of questions regarding helping relations. This is evidenced in three aspects. First, like the forthcoming sections Brickman et al.'s theorizing draws attention to the effects of help on the recipient. Second, unlike the previous sections that focused on the distinction between giving and not giving help, Brickman et al.'s theorizing considers different *kinds* of help. This is consistent with the present emphasis on the distinction between autonomy- and dependency-oriented help, which is pivotal in the forthcoming discussion of intergroup helping relations. Third, the emphasis on recipients' deservedness of help and its effectiveness in promoting recipient's long-term self-reliance resonates with the focus in the next sections on the short- and long-term consequences of receiving help.

4

From Help-Giving to Helping Relations

Consequences of Giving and Receiving Help

In this part of the book, we cross the line between research on *help-giving to* research on *helping relations* and consider the short- and long-term consequences of helping for the helper, the recipient, and their relationship. The section begins by considering the short-term effects of giving to others and the long-term consequences of sustained helping. Subsequently, the limelight shifts onto the recipient of help and highlights the fact that being at the receiving end of help is a mixed blessing.

4.1 Short- and Long-term Consequences of Giving

An early study titled "Helping the Needy Helps the Self" (Fisher et al. 1981) represents the focus of the present section. Participants in the experimental condition had been exposed to a woman confederate, who upon entering the room they were in dropped a stack of 50 uncollated pages crying out loud: "Oh no! It's my thesis!" Half the participants were exposed to a person with a high need for help, and the other half to one with a relatively low need. In the high need condition, the woman's arm was bandaged and in a sling and in the low need condition, it was not. In the control condition, the confederate entered the room and put the stack of papers on the table in front of her. Almost all the participants helped the fellow student. Subsequently, in a different context, participants were asked to rate themselves on

Social Psychology of Helping Relations: Solidarity and Hierarchy, First Edition. Arie Nadler.

bipolar adjectives that constituted a measure situational self-esteem (e.g. warm–cold, competent–incompetent, liked–disliked). The findings indicated that people who had helped in the high need condition had higher self-esteem scores than those in the control condition. There was no significant difference between those who had helped in the low need condition compared to the control condition. Thus, echoing the title, meaningful helpfulness benefits helpers by positively affecting their self-esteem.

Recent experimental research has similarly demonstrated the positive effects of helping on the helper's feelings and psychological and physical well-being. In one experiment, people were given either 5 or 10 dollars and asked to spend them during the day, on themselves or on others. At the end of the day they filled out an affect scale, and regardless of the amount spent, those who had spent the money on others were happier than those who had spent it on themselves (Dunn et al. 2008). The positive relationship between giving to others and feeling good about oneself held in 120 countries, rich and poor (Aknin et al. 2013). Aknin et al. (2012) also discovered that the joy of giving is not limited to adults. Analysis of facial expressions of two-year-olds who gave a treat to a puppet indicates that they felt happier than a comparison sample of toddlers who had received the treat themselves (Aknin et al. 2012). In another example, employees in Google who could recommend a bonus for a co-worker (i.e., prosocial spending) evidenced greater job satisfaction and better job performance. Finally, employees who had given their bonuses to charities experienced higher job satisfaction, (Anik et al. 2013). Summarizing these findings, Dunn et al. (2014) write that "the capacity to derive joy from giving might be a universal feature of human psychology" (p. 42).

While these findings provide impressive support for the "joy of giving" thesis, and demonstrate the conditions under which it is more likely (e.g. the other experiences high need for help), they do not tell us *why* people report being happier after behaving prosocially. One answer is proposed by *self-determination theory* (SDT; Ryan and Deci 2000). According to SDT, by acting prosocially, people fulfill three basic psychological needs that are the foundation of psychological well-being: to be competent, autonomous, and related to others. The need for *competence* is fulfilled when it is clear that one's prosocial action makes a difference. This is supported by the abovementioned finding that helping the high-need person who is unable to help herself because of an injured arm is more impactful than helping a person who could easily pick up the scattered pages. In a similar vein, people who had donated to a project that provided them with concrete information on the effectiveness of their assistance (e.g. mosquito nets to protect against malaria) felt happier than those who had contributed to a general cause with no such information about concrete benefits (i.e. UNICEF) (Aknin et al. 2013). Giving to others also fulfills people's need for *autonomy*. People felt happier after giving to others, but only when they had decided on the amount to be given (Weinstein and Ryan 2010). Finally, and consistent with the present emphasis on helping as expressing people's belongingness, giving to others fulfills the need for *relatedness*. The finding that people felt happier when giving to close others than to acquaintances supports this. It indicates that when helpfulness is directed at others who share belongingness with oneself it constitutes an especially uplifting experience (Aknin et al. 2011). Echoing this, Dunn et al. (2014) write that "individuals get the biggest happiness bang for their buck when they spend money on close others rather than on acquaintances, perhaps because close relationships are especially critical for satisfying the need to belong" (p. 44). Finally, the suggestion that giving to others is a psychologically positive experience because it fulfills the needs suggested by SDT is corroborated in that the effect of giving on the helper's positive feelings was mediated by the fulfillment of those needs (Weinstein and Ryan 2010).

The experimental research on the consequences of helping for the helper has focused on relatively short-term helping interactions. Another source of evidence for the beneficial effects of helping on the helper comes from studies on the effects of sustained help-giving on the helper's well-being. Sustained helpfulness consists of volunteering to help needy populations (e.g. the aged) and support given to close others over a long period (e.g. caring for a bedridden family member). Such sustained helpfulness incurs significant costs for the helper, yet its positive consequences can be quite dramatic.

Thoits and Hewitt (2001) examined the relationships between volunteering and well-being in a sample of 3617 adult respondents interviewed in two waves three years apart (750 respondents dropped out between the first and second waves). Respondents were administered measures of psychological and physical well-being consisting of self-ratings of happiness, life satisfaction, self-esteem, sense of control and physical health. Forty percent reported having been involved in volunteer activity during the 12 months prior to the interview. This rate of volunteerism is slightly lower, yet similar to the 45–55% rate reported in national surveys for adults in the US at the period when the data were collected (Hodginson and Weitzman (1994). The findings indicated that the higher the number of hours spent in volunteer activity in the past 12 months, the higher the well-being on all indices. Yet, the reverse was also true. People who were high on indices of well-being to begin with were also likely to spend more time volunteering. It is not clear whether this is because volunteering organizations welcome people higher on well-being, or because these individuals are more likely to join volunteer organizations (self-selection). The profile of the volunteer as an individual with relatively ample social and psychological resources who enjoys a sense of well-being suggests a "positive loop of volunteering": people with relatively more resources are more likely to volunteer, which further increases their well-being, and so on.

Another study assessed the effects of volunteering to help aged people on high and low socioeconomic status (SES) volunteers. The effects of volunteering were measured three times over a seven-year period (Krause and Shaw 2000). The findings indicated that in the first wave of measurement, soon after the beginning of volunteering, both the high- and low-SES groups gained similarly from the volunteering. Yet, in the third wave, the positive consequences of volunteering were limited to the high-SES volunteers. One explanation for this finding is that the low-SES volunteers lacked the necessary social skills and resources to cope with the difficulties associated with sustained volunteering, and the experience turned out to be a frustrating one for them. From a societal perspective, the moderating effects of SES on the effects of volunteering on the volunteers represent the danger of leaving out from the positive cycle of volunteering those who most need to enjoy its gains: the weaker segments of society whose well-being is relatively low to begin with.

The positive effects of sustained helping on well-being are explained by the self-transcendent nature of volunteering. Sustained helping contributes to a "sense of mattering" to others (Piliavin 2009). It goes beyond positive effects on the helper's feelings, as short-term helpfulness has been shown to have, and contributes to one's sense of meaning in life (hedonic and eudaemonic well-being, respectively; Piliavin 2009). These observations resonate with Viktor Frankl's insight, based on his experiences as a prisoner in a Nazi concentration camp, that finding existential meaning enables people to increase their well-being and consequent chances of survival even in the darkest of circumstances (Frankel 1984).

The positive consequences of sustained helping have also been documented in a study of people who had lost their spouse at an advanced age (Brown et al. 2008). The loss of one's spouse is one the most stressful life events (Lund et al. 1985) and is associated with increased risk for the onset of depression (Silverstein and Bengtson 1994). Yet, helping others seems to buffer against the negative consequences of this extremely stressful life event. Widowers who reported having helped others in the six months following the loss of their spouse were less likely to suffer from depression. The buffering effects of helping have also been documented in research showing that social isolation is associated with increased mortality (House et al. 1988), where "the magnitude of the association [...] was comparable to that of high blood pressure, smoking, [...]" (Poulin et al. 2013, p. 1649).

Sustained helping through volunteering also increases the helper's feelings of social connectedness (Omoto and Snyder 2009). Therefore, volunteering in times of stress may buffer against effects of stress and its detrimental physiological effects. Thus, people involved in helping others during stressful times were expected to be less likely to suffer from ill health and die. To examine this hypothesis, Poulin et al. (2013), asked a sample of 846 older adults (65–100 years old) to indicate major stressful life events in the preceding 12 months (e.g. job loss, death in the family), and whether they were involved in helping others during that period. In addition, indices of SES, overall health and psychological well-being were collected and used as control variables. In the five years following the collection of these measures, stressful life events predicted the mortality rate of those who *had not* been involved in sustained helping. Among them, exposure to stressful events was associated with a 30% increase in mortality risk. Among those who had reported having been involved in sustained helping, there was *no* association between exposure to stressful life events and mortality.

The relationship between sustained helping, in the form of volunteering, and reduced mortality has been corroborated in a meta-analysis of 11 studies (Okun et al. 2013). The explanation for this fairly dramatic finding suggests that stress increases inflammatory tendencies that are associated with increased risk of cardiovascular disease (Steptoe et al. 2007), and helping releases hormones like oxytocin into the bloodstream that "regulate stress and down-regulate inflammation" (Okun et al. 2013, p. 475).

In summary, helping benefits the helper. People are emotionally uplifted by giving to others, and sustained helpfulness increases the helper's psychological and physical well-being. Sustained helpfulness also buffers against the life-threatening effects of prolonged and acute stress. The explanations for these beneficial consequences of helping range from the micro-biochemical, through the meso-psychological, to the macro community level of analysis. The common conceptual ground for all is subsumed in their emphasis on the importance of feelings of shared belongingness between helpers and recipients. This applies to the description of oxytocin as a hormonal agent related to increased trust and cooperation in humans (Bartz et al. 2011), satisfaction of the basic human need for relatedness, and the increased communal feeling that webs of volunteering create.

4.2 Receiving Help: Gratitude and Threat to Self-Esteem

What about the reactions of those at the receiving end of helping? I would like to share with you a personal memory from my days as graduate student in social psychology. One afternoon I listened to a lecture on reactions to receiving American foreign aid by Kenneth Gergen. Then, as now, I was fascinated by research on helping and its potential to contribute to caring in social life. Yet the lecture I listened to flipped the question on its head. It did not ask the commonly studied question of when people are more willing to give a helping hand to others, but rather centered on how recipients of aid reacted to receiving it. A major finding was that reactions to receiving of American aid were determined by the receiving society's prior perceptions of the US. When it was perceived as an imperialist world power, recipients viewed the assistance as a manipulative ploy intended to reinforce American world dominance, and receiving help resulted in a negative view of the helper (Gergen and Gergen 1974). This opposite perspective on the helping question fascinated the eager and excitable young graduate student that I was.

My training as an experimental social psychologist led me to try to phrase the question of reactions to American aid more abstractly, in a way that would allow its further study in the laboratory. This I did together with my lifelong friend and then fellow student Jeff Fisher. Being students of Donn Byrne, author of *The Attraction Paradigm* (1971), which argued that similarity bred liking, we designed an experiment where participants had received help to overcome a task-related difficulty from an attitudinally similar or dissimilar other. Participants' feelings and self-perceptions were then compared to those of participants in a control condition who had not received such help. Based on the logic of the attraction paradigm and Gergen's findings, we expected that receiving help from an attitudinally similar helper would result in better feelings and self-perceptions. To our surprise, the findings did not conform to this logic. People who had been helped by a similar other felt *worse* and had lower ratings of self-worth than those who had not received help. These findings, to be reviewed and explained in subsequent sections, were later corroborated and extended by other studies that suggested that although giving to others in need is regarded as a uniformly virtuous behavior, receiving it is a mixed blessing.

A similar sentiment about the duality of giving and receiving help was captured by Gordon's (1893) poem "Ye Wearie Wayfarer," quoted in the beginning of this book, that admonishes people to display "kindness in another's trouble, courage in your own." This message encapsulates norms, values, and expectations that govern helping relations in human societies. To overcome people's selfish tendencies, society tells them that they should show "kindness in another's trouble" but be courageous and cope independently when they are the ones experiencing difficulty. This contradictory message amplifies the previously made suggestion that human helping relations constitute a stage on which two basic and often conflicting psychological needs play out. The first is the need to belong to others, which finds expression in relying on others' help when in need and giving them a helping hand when they are in need, and the second is to be independent. In fact, except for the very early and very late stages in life, people are expected to be self-reliant (Nadler 2018).

The threat-to-self-esteem model of reactions to receiving help describes the processes and variables that render the receipt of help a mixed blessing (Fisher et al. 1982; Nadler and Fisher 1986). On the positive side, help has the instrumental benefit of ameliorating the recipient's difficulties and it can also be a psychologically supportive experience that constitutes a sign of the helper's genuine care for one's well-being. When these elements predominate, recipients are likely to feel gratitude toward their benefactors and perceive them, and the help they had provided, in a favorable light. Yet, under other conditions, receiving help may be experienced as a self-threatening experience. People desire individual achievements (McClelland 1967), and depending on others to overcome one's difficulties can be experienced as threatening to recipients' feelings of self-worth. Moreover, being helped causes recipients to be indebted to their benefactors (Greenberg 1980), which may result in loss of freedom and the aversive emotion of reactance (Brehm 1989). Receiving help is therefore a double-edged sword: a potentially positive and gratifying self-supportive experience that expresses one's solidarity with others, or a self-threatening one that amplifies one's need to be dependent on others to cope. The threat-to-self-esteem model and related research has sought to elucidate the characteristics of the helper, the recipient, and the help that tilt the balance of receiving help in the direction of either self-support or self-threat (Fisher et al. 1982).

This section on reactions to receiving help begins by addressing the "sunnier" side of dependency: the antecedents and consequences of gratitude. Subsequently, attention will turn to the "darker" side of receiving help and consider research that informs us about the conditions under which dependency is experienced as threatening, thereby leading people in need to avoid seeking much-needed help and respond negatively to its receipt.

4.2.1 Receiving Help as a Self-Supportive Experience: Gratitude

In her theorizing on human development, Melanie Klein held that gratitude was a necessary condition for the formation of close social relationships in adult life. She reasoned that the joy the infant experiences when her needs are met is transformed to feelings of gratitude toward one's benefactor later in life (Klein 1950). She wrote that "one major derivative of the capacity for love is the feeling of gratitude" (p. 187), and that because gratitude encourages repaying in kind to the person who has helped us, it constitutes the emotional basis of generosity. Accordingly, an individual who grew up in the presence of a non-giving caretaker would be ungrateful when receiving from others later in life and unresponsive to their need for help. Thus, gratitude is viewed as the emotional glue that connects people in meaningful social relationships. Georg Simmel, one of the founders of sociology, viewed feelings of gratitude as the invisible emotional strings that tie people together, and because it underlies recipients' giving to those who had helped them Simmel regarded gratitude as "the moral memory of mankind" (Simmel 1950/1908, p. 388). These two early discussions of the feeling of gratitude underscore its dual function in building and maintaining close interpersonal relations, and as the emotional basis of reciprocity in helping interactions.

More recently, and under the influence of the developing field of positive psychology (Seligman et al. 2005), social psychologists have devoted increasing attention to the study of the antecedents and consequences of gratitude. Research has distinguished between three major conceptualizations of gratitude: (i) Benefit-triggered/situational gratitude felt toward a helper (e.g. Algoe et al. 2008); (ii) Generalized gratefulness for what is valuable and cherished in life (McCullough et al. 2002); and (iii) Trait gratitude that reflects people's enduring tendency to appreciate benevolent others and positive things in life (e.g. Ma et al. 2017; Wood et al. 2010).

The particular conceptualization of gratitude has shaped the way it has been studied. Studies of benefit-triggered or situational gratitude have induced gratitude experimentally; for example, Lyubomirsky and Layous (2013) induced feelings of gratitude by asking participants to write letters expressing gratitude to people who had helped them. Trait gratitude has measured people's scores on a scale made of items that assessed their generalized gratefulness for good things in their lives (e.g. "I have so much in life to be thankful for"), and toward others who had helped them "I am grateful to a wide variety of people, respectively") (McCullough et al. 2002).

Regardless of the particular conceptualization of gratitude and its measurement, research has corroborated its positive effects on recipients' well-being (Wood et al. 2010), and relationships with the helper (e.g. Joel et al. 2013). The next section delves deeper into research on benefit-triggered/situational gratitude.

4.2.1.1 Benefit-Triggered/Situational Gratitude: Antecedents and Consequences

4.2.1.1.1 Antecedents Present-day research has viewed gratitude as emanating from either the economic value of the gift for the recipient or its meaning for the relationship with the helper. The *economic* perspective suggests that the higher the benefit of the assistance for the recipient, the stronger the feeling of gratitude which drives subsequent reciprocity. This view was expressed by Trivers, who wrote that "the emotion of gratitude has been selected to regulate human response to altruistic acts and the emotion is sensitive to the cost/benefit ratio of such acts" (1971, p. 49). The economic view of gratitude is supported by research showing that feelings of gratitude are more likely when the perceived cost of the benefit to the helper and its value to the recipient are high (Tesser et al. 1968). It was also noted by research that demonstrated an association between the benefit of the help for the recipient and feelings of gratitude (the "benefit function" of gratitude; McCullough et al. 2008).

Yet, already in their pioneering research, Tesser et al. (1968) noted that beyond the economic variables of perceived cost to the helper and utility to recipient, the relationship-related variable of the perceived benevolent intention of the helper was also positively related to feelings of gratitude. This came to be known as the *relationship-centered* view of the antecedents of gratitude. Support for this perspective on gratitude was provided by research showing that people felt gratitude to the degree that the assistance they had received was experienced as a marker of the helper's genuine care, or of his or her being responsive to their needs and preferences. This approach is also labeled the "find-remind-bind" theory of gratitude, and suggests that when the helper is viewed as responsive, the recipient has found, or has been reminded of a valuable interaction partner, and the feeling of gratitude binds both in meaningful social relations (Algoe 2012). The role of responsiveness of a gift to the recipient's need or desire as an antecedent of gratitude was demonstrated in a field study conducted in college, where freshwomen received gifts from veteran members of their sorority. The results indicate that although both the value of the gift and its responsiveness predicted gratitude, perceived responsiveness contributed more to feeling grateful than did the perceived value of the gift (Algoe et al. 2008). When the other's gift/help is viewed by the recipient as responsive to his or herwishes/needs it is likely to seen as more reflective of the helper's genuine care and consideration for oneself than when it is not so perceived.

Similar emphasis on the role of perceived genuine care as an antecedent of gratitude is echoed in research that examined the effects of help seen as driven by the helper's autonomous or controlled motivations (Weinstein et al. 2010). Autonomous motivation for help is said to exist when the helper is seen as having helped because they genuinely care for the recipient and controlled motivation exists when the giving of help is perceived as due to internal or external pressures. In Weinstein et al.'s (2010) study, participants read a vignette describing a tourist who had lost the way to their hotel and were helped by a local resident. In the autonomous motivation condition, help was attributed to the helper's wish to ameliorate the tourist's predicament, while in the controlled motivation condition the helper was said to have helped because they did not want to feel bad about themselves. Similar to the findings about the effects of recipient perceived responsiveness, here, too, recipients felt more gratitude toward helpers who were seen as driven by autonomous rather than controlled motivation. Importantly, feelings of gratitude mediated the effects of autonomous help on the recipient's positive reactions to receiving it. Another demonstration of the importance of helper's autonomous decision to help (i.e. a decision reflecting genuine concern) on gratitude comes from research showing that feelings of gratitude are higher for people who believe in free will than those who do not. It is suggested that recipients who view others' behavior as reflecting their free will would view their helpfulness as driven by an autonomous motivation and therefore feel more gratitude (Mackenzie et al. 2014).

Taken together, these findings tell a similar story about the relationship-based antecedents of gratitude. When help is attributed by the recipient to the helper's positive intentions (Tesser et al. 1968), the helper's autonomous decision (Mackenzie et al. 2014; Weinstein et al. 2010) reflects the helper's free will (MacKenzie et al. 2014), and is viewed as responsive to the recipient's needs (Algoe 2012), receiving help is self-supportive. Under these conditions, it constitutes a signal of shared belongingness between helper and recipient and elicits feelings of gratitude that further strengthen the social bond between helper and recipient.

As noted above, real-world research on the reactions to American foreign aid also underscores the importance of perceived helper's intentionality in generating gratitude (Gergen et al. 1973). Gratitude for such aid was the more prevailing response in countries who had been a-priori positively disposed toward the US. A more recent example of the same phenomenon are the reactions of African societies, hard hit by the AIDS epidemic, toward the American President's Emergency Plan for AIDS Relief (PEPFAR). Although this program saved lives, it was viewed by many in the receiving African societies as driven by the American wish to extend its influence rather than as altruistically motivated (Fisher et al. 2008).

Gergen et al.'s (1973) findings were replicated and extended in an experiment that simulated receiving aid from a friendly or unfriendly helper in the context of a simulated intergroup conflict (Nadler et al. 1974). Relative to help received from a friendly helper, help from an unfriendly helper was regarded as driven by ulterior motives and assessed as being less useful. More recently, the links between perceived intentionality and gratitude were further supported by findings on people's reactions to another form of prosocial behavior: apology. When distrust dominates in conflictual interpersonal or intergroup relations the perpetrator's apology is viewed as insincere and does not contribute to the recipient's willingness to solve the conflict (Darby and Schlenker 1989; Nadler and Liviatan 2006).

As we conclude this subsection on the antecedents of benefit-triggered, or situational, gratitude it should be reemphasized that both the relational and economic aspects of receiving help trigger gratitude. The value of help for the recipient constitutes the economic aspect in receiving help, while viewing help as a marker of the helper's genuine care constitutes the relational aspect of self-supportive help. The nature of the helper-recipient relationships may determine the relative weight of instrumental (economic) and psychological (relational) self-supportive elements in help leading to gratitude. For example, in communal relationships based on mutual care the psychological aspects of self-support in help, i.e. receiving help as an indication of the helper's genuine care, are likely to dominate and lead to feelings of gratitude more than in exchange relationships where helping relations are dominated by the norm that if one has been helped they should return the favor (i.e. reciprocity) (Clark and Mills 2012).

Before we proceed to the consequences of gratitude for recipients' well-being and for their relationships with the helper, a distinction needs to be drawn between two related yet different emotions: *gratitude* and *indebtedness*. Although both represent an affective reaction to receiving help and are both precursors of reciprocal interactions, they constitute two opposite emotional states. Indebtedness is a negative emotion that is a source of tension and uneasiness in one's relationship with the helper. It is associated with the recipient's desire to erase a debt that he or she owes the benefactor. Until this debt had been repaid, recipients seek to keep their distance from the helper (Greenberg 1980). Gratitude, on the other hand, is a positive emotion of thankful appreciation associated with a wish for a close relationship with the helper (Salovey et al. 1991). Supporting this distinction, participants felt more grateful when the helper had been described as having benevolent intentions toward them, but felt similarly indebted to the helper regardless of whether or not the helper's intention had been described as benevolent (Tsang 2006a). Also, the feeling of gratitude, but not indebtedness, results in giving that is motivated by care and concern for the other rather than simply repaying a debt (Tsang 2006b).

Consistent with this, in his seminal analysis of interpersonal relations Heider (1958) suggested that to the degree that the benefactor obliged the recipient to be grateful, less gratitude was to be expected. In empirical support of this insight, the more recipients perceived the helper as expecting them to return a favor the lesser their gratefulness, and the higher their indebtedness (Watkins et al. 2006). Thus, while indebtedness remains high regardless of the attributed reason for the helper's benevolence, gratitude increases when help is attributed to genuine care and decreases when attributed to ulterior motives.

4.2.1.1.2 Consequences of Gratitude Research on gratitude has been pursued from the three perspectives: (i) The consequences of feelings of gratitude for the grateful recipient, (ii) the effects of expressions of gratitude (i.e. its expression to the helper) on the thanked helper, and (iii) the quality of relationships between helper and recipient. These three perspectives are used in this section to consider social psychological research on the consequences of gratitude.

CONSEQUENCES FOR THE GRATEFUL RECIPIENT In one study on the consequences of gratitude for recipients' well-being participants had been asked to think back on the past week and write about five things in their life they were grateful for, five hassles that occurred in their life, or five daily events that had an impact on them (i.e. the gratitude induction, daily hassles, and daily events conditions, respectively) (Emmons and McCullough 2003, Study 1). In the second and third studies, the daily hassles control condition was replaced with an upward comparison control condition, where participants were asked to list ways in which they were better off than others or just fill out the dependent measures. This was to be done weekly over a 10-week period. The findings demonstrated the positive consequences of experiencing and expressing gratitude in writing for both psychological and physical well-being. Relative to participants in the control groups, people in the gratitude induction group experienced an increase in positive affect and optimism, reported more time spent in physical exercise, and better quality of sleep. Measures administered to participants' spouse/significant other indicated that the partner had also noticed the positive changes in the person's well-being. Finally, participants were asked about their helping interactions with others in the past week, and those in the gratitude induction condition reported more seeking of help from others, more positive reactions to receiving it, and more giving to others.

One account for these impressive effects of expressing gratitude on overall well-being is suggested by Lyubomirsky and Layous' positive activity model (2013) that regards the expression of gratitude as one positive activity among many other similar activities, such as acts of kindness or visualizing a bright future. The model suggests that the positive effects of these activities on individuals' affect and well-being increases when they occur more frequently and in a greater variety of situations (in the family, workplace, etc.). Regarding the explanation for the positive effects of gratitude on well-being, it is suggested that by expressing gratitude, people satisfy their needs for both autonomy and relatedness, i.e. *they* have decided to do something that will acknowledge that *others* care for them (Boehm et al. 2012). This explanation resonates with the previous findings that people feel gratitude when help is viewed as driven by the helper's genuine care (relatedness) and as emanating from their free will (autonomy).

An important behavioral consequence of gratitude is its effects on willingness for further helpfulness. In other words, will recipients of help who feel gratitude toward their benefactor be more willing to help others? How is such possible future helpfulness different from repaying a debt?

To examine the effects of gratitude on generosity participants had or had not been helped by a confederate, after which their feelings of gratitude toward the helper and willingness to help them were assessed (Bartlett and DeSteno 2006). To control for the possibility that rather than gratitude, general positive affect generated by having received help was responsible for the effect of prior helping on the recipient's future helpfulness, participants in a control condition were induced to a positive mood by watching an amusing video clip. The findings indicated that those who had been helped by the confederate were subsequently more willing to help the helper than those who had not. Importantly, the increased helpfulness of those who had been helped was mediated by feelings of gratitude, and not by general positive affect (Study 1). Further, feelings of gratitude toward one's benefactor, rather than recipients' compliance with the norm of reciprocity, drove helpfulness toward the former helper (Studies 2 and 3).

Feelings of gratitude orient people to cooperate with others, and away from an egoistic orientation to obtain available rewards. Based on this it was predicted that gratitude would be associated with a decrease in "economic impatience," i.e. preferring immediate smaller over delayed larger rewards. The authors write that cooperative relationships "require one to accept the immediate costs of providing support to another in return for the longer-term gains associated with a lasting relationship characterized by continuous exchange" (DeSteno et al. 2014, p. 1263). To examine this hypothesis, their participants had been induced to be in a grateful or a happy mood by recalling and writing about situations where they had felt grateful or happy. In a baseline control condition, they were asked to write about typical daily events. Economic impatience was subsequently assessed by asking participants to choose, on 27 separate multiple-choice dilemmas, between smaller cash amounts now and larger amounts later. Consistent with the hypothesis, participants evidenced less economic impatience when induced to feel grateful rather than happy (DeSteno et al. 2014). This finding is noteworthy because it shows that the effects of gratefulness transcend the ongoing interaction with one's benefactor and shape people's general social orientation in the direction of greater patience and lesser egoism, as reflected in their economic choices.

This link between gratitude and prosociality was examined in a meta-analysis of no less than 91 studies (Ma et al. 2017). The analysis focused on studies that explored the effects of benefit-triggered and trait gratitude on prosociality, defined as "behaviors, efforts or intentions designed to benefit or protect the well-being of another individual, group, organization or society" (p. 602). The findings established a significant link between gratitude and prosociality. Compared to those who did not experience gratitude in response to a benefit they had received, those who did were more helpful. Also, the higher an individual's score on a measure of dispositional tendency to feel and express gratitude after being helped by another person, or for good things in their lives, the more helpful they were toward others. Yet, benefit-triggered or situational gratitude had a stronger effect on subsequent generosity than did trait-gratitude.

Consequences for the Helper Another aspect of the positive consequences of gratitude is the effect of its expression on the helper's subsequent prosociality. This was examined in a series of laboratory and field experiments (Grant and Gino 2010). In the laboratory experiments, the expression of thanks by the recipient who had written a brief thank you note to the helper more than doubled the helper's willingness to give further assistance to the recipient (from 25 to 55% in Study 1, and from 32 to 66% in Study 2). Two possible psychological mechanisms link being thanked with prosociality. One is that being thanked satisfies people's need for competence, which underlies their greater helpfulness. The other is that being thanked increases the sense of mutual belongingness with the thankful individual. The findings indicate that the increased readiness to behave prosocially after having been thanked by the grateful recipient was mediated by the feelings that one was in communal relations of shared belongingness with the recipient, rather than by heightened self-efficacy (Grant and Gino 2010).

The positive consequences of expressions of thanks by a grateful recipient go beyond increasing further helpfulness. In a work environment, employees who had been thanked by their supervisor invested greater efforts (Grant and Gino 2010, Study 3). Also, the expectation that other team members would be thankful was enough to motivate team members who enjoyed high self-evaluations to realize their potential by investing efforts on a group task (Grant and Wrzesniewski 2010).

Finally, gratitude is more likely to be expressed after being helped reactively (i.e. receiving help after asking it) than proactively (i.e. receiving unsolicited help) (Lee et al. 2018a). This is because receiving unsolicited help leads the recipient to consider it unnecessary, less effective and threatening to self-esteem. Hearing the recipients say "thank you" leads the helpers to feel that they have greater impact on their coworkers, and to be more self-engaged in their work. These positive effects are due to that being thanked instills an experience of success, efficacy and meaningfulness in the workplace. These self-perceptions translate into greater engagement with one's coworkers and one's job.

Taken together with the earlier findings that gratitude is felt when the help is viewed as an expression of the helper's care and responsiveness, this underscores the role of gratitude and its expression in maintaining and solidifying existing close social bonds. Gratitude constitutes a positive relational cycle. It is associated with increased recipient well-being and a growing tendency to behave prosocially, while expressing it encourages and reinforces the helper's future prosociality and overall positive feelings.

CONSEQUENCES FOR QUALITY OF RELATIONSHIPS The similarity between the psychological antecedents of recipients' gratitude and the effects of its expression on their well-being suggests a positive gratitude-well-being cycle that begins with (i) the perception that helper acted autonomously and because he or she cared, resulting in feelings of gratitude that when expressed (ii) leads the recipient to increased feelings of personal autonomy and relatedness that (iii) leads to increased recipient's well-being, which in turn (iv) increases the grateful person's readiness to give, seek, and receive help. This positive cycle of gratitude is a reminder of Melanie Klein's (1950) assertion that gratitude is the basis of all human generosity.

This positive cycle of gratitude enhances the quality of relationships between helper and recipient. In fact, perceived investment of one's partner in the relationship was positively related to commitment to the relationship, measured nine months later, and this relationship was mediated by feelings of gratitude felt toward the partner who had invested in it (Joel et al. 2013). The positive role gratitude plays in close relationships is also demonstrated by the findings that performing positive behaviors toward one's partner elicits feelings of gratitude in the recipient that lead to reciprocal enactment of positive behaviors, which culminate in the strengthening of the intimate bond (Kubacka et al. 2011). These findings amplify the idea that feelings of gratitude and their expression create a positive relational cycle that constitutes the emotional glue that binds us together.

The positive effects of gratitude on the recipient, helper and their relationships is encapsulated in viewing gratitude-based helping relationships as increasing people's eudemonic well-being. The distinction between eudemonic and hedonic well-being is traced back to Aristotle (translated by Irwin 1985) and has been a central aspect in current discussions in humanistic and positive psychology of well-being (Ryan and Deci 2001). Broadly sketched, hedonic well-being refers to the person's happiness and eudemonic well-being goes beyond feelings of personal happiness. It is not an outcome of giving or receiving help but a "... process of fulfilling... one's virtuous potential and living as one was inherently intended to live." (Deci and Ryan 2008, p. 2). As the cycle of gratitude described above indicates the expression of gratitude by the recipient impacts positively on the helper and the quality of the relationships between helper and the recipient. This eudemonic perspective on gratitude is supported by the findings of research on the effects of gratitude on helpers in the workplace. Receiving gratitude led helpers to agree with statements saying that their work made a positive change in the life of their coworkers, and with statements indicating high work engagement (e.g. "today I was absorbed by the job"). These findings on the positive effects of gratitude and its expression demonstrate how feelings of gratitude that are expressed to the helper increases eudemonic well-being in the workplace (Lee et al. 2018b).

4.2.1.2 Dispositional Gratitude The research reviewed in the preceding sections centered on benefit-triggered/situational feeling of gratitude. This final section centers on dispositional gratitude that represents individuals' enduring tendency to be grateful for positive things that occurred in their life. These include positive events that are due to others' benevolence or to impersonal and general causes (i.e. relational and generalized gratitude, respectively). Definitions of dispositional gratitude reflect this duality. Generalized gratitude is underscored by a definition such as "life orientation toward noticing and appreciating the positive in the world" (Wood et al. 2010, p. 811), and relational gratitude in its definition as a "generalized tendency to recognize and respond with grateful emotion to [...] other people's benevolence" (McCullough et al. 2002, p. 112). Yet the measure of dispositional gratitude includes elements of the tendency to feel both "relational" and "generalized" gratitude. The measure is made up of six items, worded in the negative and positive direction, and assesses a person's habitual tendency to experience gratitude (i) intensely (e.g. "I feel grateful for what I received in life"); (ii) frequently ("a long time passes before I feel thankful to something or someone"); (iii) in a broad span of situations ("I sometimes feel gratitude for the smallest things"); and (iv) towards a relatively large number of people ("I am grateful to a wide variety of people") (i.e. Gratitude Questionnaire-6, abbreviated as GQ-6; McCullough et al., 2002). The total score of these four facets of gratitude represents the person's tendency for dispositional gratitude.

The conductance hypothesis views the accumulation of day-to-day experiences in which the person felt grateful in a wide range of situations as the antecedent of dispositional gratitude. The situational experiences of gratitude are said to be "conducted upward" to create a relatively pervasive tendency to feel grateful for good things in one's life and the benevolence of others (McCullough et al. 2004). Other antecedents are suggested by the relationships between people's GQ-6 scores, and their scores on the Big Five Personality Dimensions (John et al. 1991) on the one hand, and religiosity and spiritualistic tendencies on the other. High GQ-6 scorers score higher on the Agreeableness and Extraversion and lower on the Neuroticism scales of the Big 5 (McCullough et al. 2002; Wood et al. 2010). High scores on the dispositional scale are associated with people's religiosity, higher spirituality and lesser materialism (McCullough et al. 2002). Note here that these findings are consistent with the finding that people's dispositional generosity is positively associated with Agreeableness (Graziano and Habashi 2015) and intrinsic religiosity (Stavrova and Siegers 2014). Thus, these individuals are not only characteristically more helpful, but also more welcoming and appreciative of others' benevolent behavior toward them, by feeling and expressing their gratitude. These individuals seem to navigate the social world by depending on others when they are in need, appreciating others' help, and helping them when they need.

The consequences of scoring high on the dispositional gratitude scale resonate with the findings of the consequences of situational/benefit-triggered gratitude. High scorers on the GQ-6 report being happier, more optimistic, and having more positive feelings than low scorers, who in turn report having more negative emotions (e.g. depression, envy) (McCullough et al. 2002, 2004). Also, in accord with the previously discussed consequences of benefit-triggered gratitude, people who were dispositionally grateful perceived themselves and were perceived by others as being more helpful (McCullough et al. 2002). Similarly, dispositionally grateful people report having better relationships with others (Wood et al. 2010), and their peers report them as having better relations with them than do peers of less dispositionally grateful individuals (Emmons and McCullough 2003).

*

In summary, the study of the antecedents and consequences of gratitude has been on the increase in social psychology. The antecedents of gratitude reflect the instrumental and relational elements of self-support in receiving help. People experience gratitude when the help they have received is of greater than smaller value (i.e. instrumental-economic aspect of gratitude) and is viewed as a reflection of the helper's autonomous decision that is based on responsiveness and genuine care toward them (i.e. relational aspect of gratitude).

Although feeling indebted and feeling grateful result in reciprocity toward one's benefactor, indebtedness and gratitude represent two emotional opposites. While gratitude is a positive emotion that mediates the effects of positive interpersonal behaviors on interpersonal proximity, indebtedness is a negatively valanced emotion associated with social distance between oneself and one's benefactor. Gratitude, both benefit-triggered and dispositional, has positive consequences for the recipients and their relationships, i.e. increased well-being and prosociality, that increase with the growing frequency and variety of situations in which one feels grateful. When gratitude is expressed toward the helper, it sustains and encourages the helper's future helpfulness. In organizational settings, being thanked increases the helper's feeling of positive engagement with coworkers and their job.

Overall, the literature suggests a virtuous circle of gratitude that begins with receiving self-supportive help, which results in feeling gratitude, which increases recipients' overall well-being and has positive impact on their relationships, thereby increasing prosociality and communality. When expressed by thanking the helper, it has positive effects on the helper–recipient relationships, the helper's feelings and their own subsequent helpfulness. This positive cycle echoes Melanie Klein's view of gratitude as the basis of communality and solidarity in interpersonal relations and is encapsulated in viewing gratitude-based helping relations as increasing the participants' eudemonic well-being.

Rephrased in terms of the key emphases of this book, gratitude-dominated helping relations constitute a clear demonstration of the relations between helping others and shared belongingness.

4.2.2 The Negative Consequences of Receiving Help: The Self-Threat in Dependency

As emphasized throughout this book, being helped is a double-edged sword. While under certain conditions, it constitutes a supportive sign of shared belongingness, under others dependency may be negatively experienced by the recipient. The negative consequences of dependency on others' help emanate from three main psychological sources: (i) inconsistency with the internalized value of self-reliance; (ii) negative social comparison between one's lack of resources and the helper's resourcefulness (i.e. "comparison stress" in receiving help; Nadler and Fisher 1986), and (iii) feelings of indebtedness to one's benefactor that limit one's freedom of action, and the arousal of negative feelings of "reactance" (Brehm 1966).

For the sake of parsimony, the model of threat-to-self-esteem in receiving help binds the positive and negative aspects in receiving help together (Fisher et al. 1982). It views receiving help as a mixture of self-supportive and self-threatening elements for the recipient. Importantly, these elements are not mutually exclusive. They coexist in most helping interactions, with situational and personal variables (e.g. the helper's identity and the recipient's self-esteem, respectively), tilting the experience of being dependent on others' help in the self-supportive or self-threatening direction.

The following sections center on variables that amplify the self-threat in receiving help, thereby reducing readiness to seek and receive it. The reluctance to be dependent on others' help because of the self-threat associated with dependency has been observed in various contexts. In educational contexts, the implications of incompetence associated with seeking others' help led students to refrain from seeking help (e.g. Butler and Neuman 1995; Newman and Schwager 1992), and because of negative implications on their professional abilities teachers underutilized available and needed assistance (Gilman and Gabriel 2004). In organizational settings, workers avoided seeking their coworkers' assistance because of the negative implications of help-seeking for their professional prestige (e.g. Flynn 2003; Nadler et al. 2003). Finally, older people found the need to be dependent on others, due to frailty of body and mind, to be stressful and were therefore reluctant to seek or receive outside assistance (e.g. Baltes 1995).

The threat-to-self-esteem model suggests that characteristics of the help, the helper, and the recipient interact to determine whether receiving help would constitute a predominantly self-supportive or self-threatening experience for the recipient (Nadler and Fisher 1986). Taking a help characteristic as an example, for most people dependency that implies that one is not intelligent would be more self-threatening than help that implies that one is not very tall.

As can be seen in Figure 4.1, the model indicates that when receiving help is predominantly experienced as supportive, people would be willing to seek it and respond to with gratitude. If, however, receipt of help is experienced as primarily self-threatening, people may be unwilling to seek it and respond by negative affect and lower feelings of situational self-worth to receiving it. The effects of receiving self-threatening help on the recipient's behavior depend on the recipient's sense of control over the situation. If recipients perceive themselves as able to terminate the uneasy dependency by making efforts to

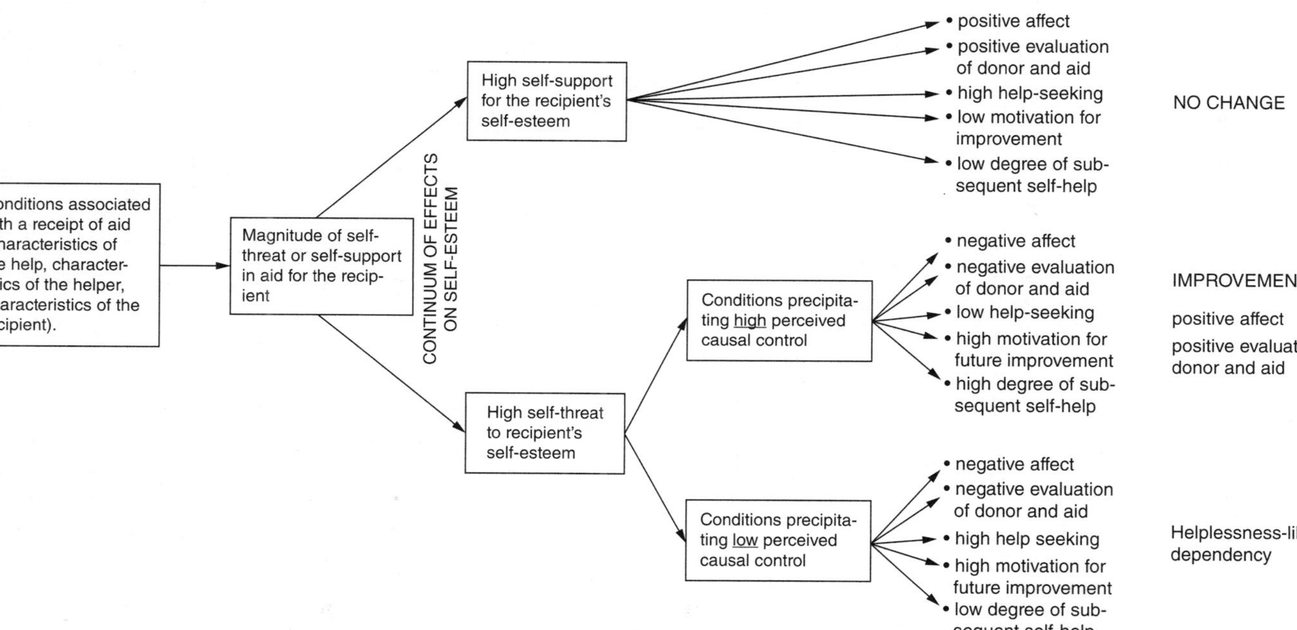

Figure 4.1 Schematic diagram of the threat × control model of reactions to help.

improve, self-threatening help would motivate them to invest efforts to regain future self-reliance. If, on the other hand, they do not view themselves as able to improve by investing efforts, receiving self-threatening help would result in long-term dependency on others (i.e. helpless passivity).

4.2.2.1 Who Is the Helper? Effects of Helper Identity on Receptivity to Help Are people readier to seek and receive help from someone close to them, or are they more comfortable depending on relative strangers? This question has dominated the research on effects of helper's characteristics on recipient reactions to help. Two parallel lines of research and theory have suggested opposite answers. The first suggests that the comparison stress experienced by a recipient who needs to depend on a resourceful helper renders the receipt of help from a socially close other a self-threatening experience. The second line, prevalent in the social support literature, indicates that people prefer to depend on socially close others in times of need (e.g. family members and close friends). Following a review of research, we propose a way of reconciling these two lines of research.

4.2.2.1.1 Comparison Stress: Similarity and Social Proximity Hurt How would a person know if their test score of 80 means they are good, mediocre, or poor performers? *Social comparison theory* tells us that we use similar others as a frame of reference for self-judgements (Festinger 1954). If my friends had obtained scores ranging between 65 and 70 on the same test, my score of 80 would lead me to conclude that I am relatively very good. If, however, their test scores ranged between 85 and 98, a test score of 80 would mean that I am a relative failure.

How is this process of social comparison relevant to the receiving of help being self-threatening or not? Dependency on others' help catalyzes social comparison. Helping interactions represent unequal social encounters where one has enough to give and the other is dependent on their good will. This underscores the present view of helping relations as having implications for relative status. Consistent with social comparison theory, this unfavorable comparison should be self-threatening when the helper is a similar other who serves as a frame of reference for recipients' self-judgments (Festinger 1954). Under these conditions, people who are likely to feel belittled by the receipt of help avoid seeking it, and react negatively to receiving it.

The hypothesis that people would feel threatened by dependency on similar others has been supported in an early study, where participants who had played a bogus stock market simulation believed themselves to have lost most of the game money they had been given and faced being excluded due to lack of resources. Participants in the help condition then received help in the form of additional resources in an envelope from another participant, supposedly sitting in an adjoining cubicle. This help was accompanied by a note saying, "it seems like you can use this." Participants in the no-help control condition were not "saved" that way. The partner, who helped or did not, had been presented as being attitudinally similar or dissimilar to the participants on a number of key attitudes (e.g. attitude on women's abortion rights). Following the help/no help manipulation, dependent measures were administered. Consistent with the comparison stress hypothesis, people who had received help from an attitudinally similar other experienced worse affect and reported lower feelings of self-worth. There were no such differences in the dissimilar other condition. These findings support the idea that dependency on others who represent a relevant frame of reference for oneself facilitates a process of negative comparison experienced by the recipient as negative and self-threatening (Fisher and Nadler 1974).

The adverse effects of comparison stress on the recipient are not limited to experimentally induced levels of similarity between helper and recipient and reflect a more general effect of social proximity. Another study in this research program compared the effects of receiving help from a friend or stranger on recipient affect and feelings of self-worth (Nadler et al. 1983). Half the participants were told that another participant in an adjoining cubicle was the friend they had come with to the experiment, and the other half that he was a stranger. Subsequently, all participants were to identify the culprit in a crime story (i.e. the experimental task). Half had been told that success in this task was related to intellectual skills (i.e. ego-central task), and the other half that it was related to luck. All participants then failed and received help from the other participant, enabling them to complete the task. The findings indicate that when participants believed that their performance was related to the ego-central quality of intelligence, receiving help from a friend resulted in negative feelings and low self-worth. This was not the case when the helper was a stranger. Further, participants who had been helped by their "friend" in what they believed was an ego-central task agreed more than did participants in the other experimental cells with the statement that the helper "helped me because he wanted to show me that he is better than me." This finding is of particular importance because it provides direct empirical support to the idea that receiving help from a socially close other is associated with comparison stress, resulting in negative recipient reactions.

The comparison stress associated with help from another who is psychologically relevant as a frame of reference for self-judgments has similar effects on people's willingness to seek needed help. Participants who had worked on a difficult anagram task could seek help from another participant described as attitudinally similar or dissimilar (Nadler 1987). Consistent with the previous results, when anagram-solving skills had been said to be related to one's IQ, significantly less help was sought from a similar than a dissimilar other. In other words, to avoid a psychologically relevant negative comparison associated with dependency on a similar helper who had "made it," people preferred failure on the task, thereby giving up on receiving a desired reward, rather than seeking help.

The role of comparison stress has also been demonstrated in research outside the social psychological laboratory. In a work environment, employees who had been helped by a peer evidenced lower ratings of competence and affect and greater discomfort, assessed by increased heart rate, than those who had not been similarly helped (Deelstra et al. 2003). The authors attribute these adverse consequences of receiving help to the self-threat associated with dependency on a coworker. Programs of "peer tutoring," where children are assisted in their schoolwork by their peers are another context where comparison stress is likely. Consistent with the previous findings, the higher the overall similarity between tutor and tutee in age, academic achievements, etc., the greater the discomfort reported by the latter (DePaulo et al. 1989). The role of comparison stress is further supported by the finding that such discomfort was more characteristic in reactions of fourth graders (about 10 years old) than second graders (about 8). Developmental research tells us that the older children are more sensitive to the self-implications of social comparison than the younger (Ruble and Frey 1987).

Research on receiving help in close relationships also points to the mixed blessing associated with receiving help from a socially close other (Gleason et al. 2008). In this study, participants filled out reports of daily helping interactions with their partner. The results show that consistent with findings in the social psychological laboratory, receiving support led recipients to experience a negative mood, especially in situations of high self-threat. At the same time, however, receiving help from one's partner led to better perceptions of them. These contradictory consequences of the negative effects that receiving help from a relationship partner has on one's feelings and perceived self-worth, and the positive effects it has on perceptions of the helper, echo similar findings in the social-psychological laboratory. Even when receiving help led recipients to experience negative feelings and low perceptions of self-worth, it had positive effects on their perceptions of the helper and future relations with them (Nadler 2015; Nadler and Fisher 1986). This is consistent with Gleason et al.'s (2008) statement that "support or aid can produce both increased psychological distress and sense of being cared for by the provider" (p. 286). This is a reminder that receiving help does not constitute an exclusively positive or negative experience, and may have contradictory effects on different dimensions.

4.2.2.1.2 Social Support vs. Comparison Stress: Connecting the Dots In contrast to the findings emanating from the comparison stress hypothesis that dependency on socially close others is relatively self-threatening and therefore often avoided, the social support literature indicates that in times of need people prefer to approach socially close others (e.g., close friends) for help (Collins and Feeney 2000). This preference was observed in a wide variety of contexts, including marital difficulties, problems at the workplace, and coping with stressful life situations (Wills 1983; Wills and DePaulo 1991).

Two broad explanations account for the inconsistency between the findings of experimental social psychology, i.e. people avoid dependency on others who are similar to them, and the social support literature, i.e. people prefer to approach close others in times of need. First, research that demonstrated the negative consequences of helpers' social proximity on receiving help studied situations of *instrumental* helping, where help was needed to facilitate task completion. In the social psychological laboratory, participants could not continue in a "stock market simulation" because of faulty investment decisions (Nadler et al. 1976) or stood to fail the anagram task they were working on (Nadler 1987). Similarly, field studies that documented comparison stress in receiving help investigated achievement-related situations in work settings (Bacharach et al. 2002; Nadler et al. 2003), where the task in which help had been needed reflected on the person's ability and therefore the comparison with the helper was psychologically relevant.

Conversely, the social support literature studied helping interactions that involved *emotional* rather than instrumental states of need. These included emotional difficulties due to loss of one's spouse (Stroebe et al. 2008) or to a serious illness (Bloom 1996). A key characteristic of the emotional context is that one's state of need is beyond control. One's skills or efforts have nothing to do with being depressed following the loss of a loved one. Under these circumstances, the aspects of shared belongingness associated with social proximity are salient and render dependency a positive experience.

Shared belongingness is related also to the second explanation for the inconsistency between the comparison stress and social support research programs. The social support literature focused on helping interactions with others with whom we have strong affective bonds, such as family members or close friends. These constitute communal sharing relational systems in which people are said to view themselves as undifferentiated from others who belong to the same social unit (Fiske 1991). Such relational systems are governed by communal norms that call on people to demonstrate concern for others in need and rely on their support when one needs help (Clark and Mills 2012); in such social systems, people do not necessarily compete over who is better, but relations are dominated by a "we" feeling of shared belongingness.

In the comparison stress research, on the other hand, the socially close helper is a person with whom one does not have an intimate social bond (e.g. a work colleague, fellow student). In such relationships, people's social behavior is governed by an "equality matching" relational model (Fiske 1991) and the giving and receiving of benefits are regulated by exchange norms (Clark and Mills 2012). Dependency on a similar other challenges the presumed equality between interactants and threatens to push the recipient downward in the social ladder, and is therefore associated with comparison stress.

Note that communal sharing social systems (e.g. family) and competition for a higher place on the hierarchy are not mutually exclusive. Communal-sharing systems may harbor intense competitive relations. The biblical stories of Esau and Jacob and Joseph and his brothers constitute a cultural reminder for the prevalence of intense rivalries within families. How is such fierce competition reconciled with the suggestion, above, that close-knit social systems are based on shared belongingness, and that therefore people are not threatened by dependency on others in the group? One possibility is that there is a figure-ground relationship between shared belongingness and competition in such relational systems that changes in different situations. When group members compete, the urge for a higher place on some hierarchy is the *figure* and the shared belongingness between interactants the *background*. When, however, one of the interaction partners needs assistance the figure-ground relationship flips over. Shared belongingness becomes salient, i.e. the figure, and competitive urges are subdued into the background.

*

In conclusion, receiving help is a mixed blessing. Research on gratitude demonstrated its self-supportive aspects, and research on threat to recipients' self-esteem its negative consequences for the recipient. The effects of helper's social proximity on recipient reactions is an important determinant of these consequences. When the need for help consists of an emotional difficulty due to causes beyond one's control, the element of shared belongingness associated with dependency on a socially close other dominate. When, however, the need for help is related to one's skills, dependency is a marker of one's relative inferiority, which is more psychologically relevant when the helper is socially close. Second, in close relations dominated by communal norms, the helper's social proximity is a marker of shared belongingness and dependency is unlikely to be self-threatening. From this perspective, receptivity to ego-central help from a close other may be an indication of intimacy in close relationships. In equality-based relational systems, individual achievement is important and dependency on an ego-central dimension is self-threatening, resulting in unwillingness to seek and receive help.

4.2.2.2 The How of Help: Characteristics of the Help Provided Ego-centrality. Research reviewed in the previous section indicates that people are not receptive to help from a socially close other, which induces comparison stress, but only when dependency reflects inferiority on an ego-central dimension such as intelligence. Note, however, that the same quality may be ego-central for one and non-central for another. For example, while manual dexterity is likely to be an ego-central quality for a professional violinist or a neurosurgeon, it is likely to be non-central for most other people. It should be emphasized that the ego-centrality of help is a *necessary*, but not *sufficient* condition for help to be self-threatening. The self-threat potential in dependency dampens one's willingness to seek and receive help only in the presence of other relevant variables, e.g. helper's similarity. In fact, when help reflects on an ego-central quality but the helper is a stranger people do not feel worse after having received it (Nadler and Fisher 1986), and are ready to seek it (Morris and Rosen 1973). This finding is relevant to the previous discussion on the effects of comparison stress on readiness to seek and receive help. Comparison stress is likely to arise when the helper serves as a frame of reference for self-judgments (e.g. a similar other, a colleague at the workplace) (Tesser 1988). When the task for which help is provided reflects on ego-central qualities it is a marker of the recipient's relative inferiority and elicits negative reactions to receiving help and unwillingness to seek it. When, however, the helper is a stranger, or another source of help that does not serve as a frame of reference for self-judgements (e.g. computerized source), dependency on help is not self-threatening even when it reflects on an ego-central quality.

Research on help-seeking among paraplegics and parents to mentally challenged children demonstrate the usefulness of the concept of ego centrality in understanding people's seeking and receiving help in persistent difficult life situations. One study examined the relationships between the different degrees of paraplegics' acceptance of their disability and their willingness to seek help in difficulties arising from their disability. The concept of acceptance of disability is conceptually related to ego centrality. It describes the degree to which people who have become disabled late in life continue to consider the lost/damaged ability as central to who they are (Linkowski 1971). People who continue to mourn their lost ability are said to have not accepted their disability. For example, a professional runner who has been confined to a wheelchair may view her lost running skills as a central aspect of who she is and continue to lament their loss for a long time. Alternatively, she may have moved "running" from the center of her self and replaced it with other activities that do not require the use of legs as central to their identity.

Consistent with research that people avoid dependency on ego-central qualities, it was hypothesized that people who had accepted their disability, i.e., view their lost/damaged ability as peripheral to their identity, would be more willing to seek others' help on daily tasks than those who have not, i.e., continue to view their lost/damaged identity as central to their identity. To examine this hypothesis, male paraplegics, confined to a wheelchair, had filled out the Acceptance of Disability scale (Linkowski 1971) and were later asked to imagine themselves in five daily situations in which they needed others' assistance (Nadler et al. 1979a). For example, on their way to a meeting they could not enter a building because of the stairs at the entrance. Respondents were asked to indicate the likelihood that (i) they would actively approach someone for help, (ii) wait until someone had noticed and offered them assistance, or (iii) give up on the meeting and leave. The findings indicated that the higher the "acceptance of disability" score, the more likely the person was willing to seek help.

Another study tested the same logic on parents of developmentally challenged children (Nadler et al. 1991). Parents had completed a modified version of the "acceptance of disability" scale that assessed the degree to which they regarded their child's condition as peripheral or central to their family's overall adequacy. Later they were asked to indicate their willingness to seek outside help to cope with difficulties arising from their child's condition. As before, the more parents viewed their family as adequate despite their child's condition, the greater was their willingness to seek outside help.

Taken together with the experimental findings reviewed above, people's need for independence is higher in ego-central than in non-central situations. Importantly, the meaning of ego centrality varies across people and situations. Also, receiving help on an instrumental task is linked to the degree to which it reflects on central qualities such as intelligence. In chronic difficulties such as physical disabilities, centrality is associated with acceptance of disability.

Autonomy- vs. *dependency-oriented help.* The distinction between dependency- and autonomy-oriented help is woven into the analysis of helping relations throughout the book. Because autonomy-oriented assistance provides recipients with skills or tools with which to solve the problem on their own, its receipt is less self-threatening than that of dependency-oriented help as it allows the recipient to retain a sense of self-reliance. Therefore, people are more likely to seek it, and respond positively to its receipt (Nadler 1998, 2002, 2015). In direct support for the relatively higher self-threat in dependency-oriented help, participants who had received autonomy-oriented assistance from a peer in solving a difficult task evidenced better feelings and higher perceptions of self-competence than those who had received dependency-oriented help (Alvarez and Van Leeuwen 2011). From the recipients' perspective, autonomy-oriented help is ideal because it satisfies their needs for both self-reliance and belongingness. On the other hand, dependency-oriented assistance may signify one's shared belongingness with the helper but be inconsistent with one's need for independence.

This does not mean that autonomy-oriented is uniformly preferable to dependency-oriented help. Sometimes, objective circumstances render dependency-oriented help the only viable course of action. If people are starving, teaching them to plant wheat is hardly appropriate, as what they need is an immediate and full solution in the shape of a loaf of bread. Dependency-oriented help is more appropriate also when recipients view themselves as unable to change the situation. For example, in the context of intergroup helping relations, members of low status groups who believe that their actions cannot change their disadvantaged position prefer dependency-oriented help. When, however, they expect their efforts to promote equality to succeed they prefer autonomy- to dependency-oriented assistance (Halabi et al. 2011).

Anonymity of help-seeking. While increasing the helper's prestige, visibility of helping relations also increases the self-threat associated with receiving help and decreases people's readiness to seek or receive it. This is because public receipt of help is tantamount to public admission of failure, and when related to ego-central qualities, it increases the self-threat associated with dependency and lowers people's receptivity to outside help (Nadler and Porat 1978). Consider for example the length to which providers of mental assistance go in order to secure the anonymity of people who approach them for help. One example are hotline programs that offer their callers the veil of anonymity when seeking help with a pressing personal difficulty (Raviv 1993). Protection of anonymity is of special importance when it comes to psychological difficulties that are generally viewed as reflecting on ego-central dimensions more than instrumental difficulties do.

One way people keep their anonymity as recipients is being helped inconspicuously. This occurs when the person in need is helped by observing or overhearing how another individual in a similar situation is being helped. To compare the effects of receiving conspicuous or inconspicuous help, participants had either received supportive advice on how to cope with an upcoming stressful experience directly from the experimenter, or overheard the same advice given to another individual (Bolger and Amarel 2007). The findings show that those who had received advice directly from the experimenter had a lower sense of efficacy than those who had received the same advice inconspicuously by overhearing it. Importantly, these perceptions mediated the effectiveness of the advice: the advice proved more effective for those who had received it inconspicuously.

Finally, social norms may affect the link between anonymity and readiness to seek and receive help on an ego-relevant dimension. It may be that the recent cultural trend that de-emphasizes privacy in social life makes it easier to expose one's weakness by seeking help in public. The new social media that enable and encourage people to "spill the beans" and reality shows that promote exhibitionism may make it more normative to share one's innermost thoughts and feelings with strangers. This may work to lower the threshold of privacy even when seeking help on ego-central problems.

Assumptive, requested, and negotiated help. The assumptive nature of the help is another characteristic that affects people's receptivity to it. Assumptive help is given without being solicited. Such help may be viewed by recipients as conveying the helper's assumption that they are unable to cope on their own (Schneider et al. 1996). When this conflicts with the recipients' perception that they can solve the problem, or at least be part of the solution, assumptive help is self-threatening. Further, compared to help requested by the recipient, assumptive help poses a threat to recipients' freedom of action, arousing adverse feelings of reactance (Brehm 1966). It obligates the recipient to the helper without the former having sought it. Perceived freedom of action may be restored and the negative feeling of reactance ameliorated by behaving toward the helper in a way that disregards the indebtedness toward them. Indeed, research indicates that when perceived freedom had been limited by being helped recipients reciprocated less than was expected of them (El-Alayili and Messe 2004). Finally, the finding that people feel more grateful after having received help they had requested compared to help they had not (i.e. "reactive" and "proactive" helping in their terminology) demonstrates the supportive nature of requested relative to assumptive help (Lee et al. 2018b).

The helper's giving in a "didactic" or "negotiated" style is a related characteristic that determines whether receiving of help would lead to reactance (Asser 1978). Similar to assumptive help, a didactic style of giving is one where the helper gives without engaging the recipient in a conversation on how they prefer to be helped. In negotiating giving, on the other hand, the helper negotiates with the recipient on how they prefer to be helped (how much, how long, etc.). Such a helping interaction involves the recipient as an equal and active social actor rather than a passive receptacle for the helper's generosity. It ameliorates the difficulty the recipient experiences while at the same time respecting their need for independence and self-control.

*

In summary, dependency on ego-central dimensions that limits the recipient's freedom of action is self-threatening, not likely to be sought, likely to be rejected when offered, and reacted to negatively when received. This non-receptivity is likely to be more salient when helping is conspicuous. Conversely, autonomy-oriented help is the outcome of negotiation between helper and recipient, representing an empowering and equality-based social interaction. This is a reminder that in many, if not most, helping interactions, being helped involves the recipient's perceived loss of control and freedom. Helpers' sensitivity to this aspect will help transform helping relations from hierarchical relations between haves and have-nots into social interactions that respect the recipient's needs for control and self-reliance. As implied by the threat-to-self-esteem model (Nadler and Fisher 1986), these are likely to be more constructive and effective interactions.

4.2.2.3 Effects of Recipient Characteristics on Receptivity to Help

4.2.2.3.1 Demographic Variables: Age and Gender *Age*. People's readiness to rely on others' help varies across the life span. We begin life as helpless newborns completely dependent on our caregivers. As we grow up, we learn to be increasingly self-reliant but, for the most part, remain dependent on adults' care. During adolescence, many conflicts emanate from the clash between adolescents' desire for independence and caregivers' reluctance to let go. Later in life, because of frail body and mind in old age, people lament their loss of independence with the growing dependency on others. From this perspective, the shifting weight associated with self-reliance during the life span is one way to view human development.

Research has supported the role of recipients' age in receptivity to help. First, the previous empirically based generalization that dependency on a similar other results in comparison stress that renders the receipt of help self-threatening is age-dependent. Children younger than eight generally do not engage in global judgments of self-worth that emanate from social comparison processes (Harter 1986). The pressures for autonomous performance in school, at ages seven to eight and beyond, change that, and children become sensitive to their performance relative to others and view themselves as more or less successful by way of comparison with their peers (Ruble et al. 1980). Therefore, dependency on similar others is usually self-threatening only in later childhood (Shell and Eisenberg 1992).

At the other end of the life span, loss of independence caused by mental and physical difficulties in old age is particularly self-threatening (Langer and Rodin 1976). Being dependent on others is a stark reminder of failing health. An interview study with men older than 65 revealed that their desire to maintain their independence reflects their wish to age successfully, as well as their masculine gender role identity (Smith et al. 2007). The latter finding that associates receptivity to help with the person's gender role draws attention to gender differences in receptivity to help.

Gender. In "Why Won't He Go to the Doctor?" Mansfield, Addis and Mahalik (2003) begin their paper by describing a greeting card that shows a caricature depicting Moses in the desert looking lost, with a caption that reads, "Why did Moses spend 40 years in the desert? Because he would not ask anyone for directions!" Similar descriptions of men preferring to be lost on the road rather than simply rolling down the window and asking for directions exist in countless accounts of gender differences in both popular culture and nonfictional literature, such as John Gray's 1992 book *Men are from Mars, Women are from Venus*. Do these accounts represent a fact or an unfounded social stereotype?

A consistent finding in the help-seeking literature is that women seek more help than do men (Wills and DePaulo 1991). This has been observed across a variety of problem situations, including depression, substance abuse, and negative life events (Addis and Mahalik 2003). Early studies based on large-scale surveys indicate that this gender difference cannot be explained by different levels of need (Kessler et al. 1981; Veroff 1981), and that it holds for seeking both professional and non-professional help (Padesky and Hammen 1981). Similarly, in the social psychological laboratory, male students who had been presented with a state of need common in campus life (i.e. failing to complete an assignment on time) were less likely to seek help to ameliorate the situation than were female students (Nadler et al. 1984).

One explanation for this consistent gender difference is that women are more likely to interpret a difficulty as a problem that requires outside assistance. Regarding women's greater propensity to seek outside help in emotional difficulties, Addis and Mahalik (2003) suggest that women are more likely to "recognize and label nonspecific feelings of distress as emotional problems" (p. 6). A broader explanation attributes this gender difference to differential implications of the feminine and masculine gender roles for independence. The masculine role emphasizes individual achievement and independence while the feminine gender role allows, and even encourages, reliance on more resourceful and knowledgeable others (Addis and Mahalik 2003). This explanation was empirically supported by the finding that adherence to the feminine and masculine gender roles, as assessed by the Psychological Androgyny scale (Bem 1974), predicted willingness to seek and receive help. Female respondents who adhered to the feminine role were more receptive to help, while males who adhered to the masculine role evidenced greater reluctance to depend on others' help than psychologically 'androgynous' women and men (i.e., describing themselves as having male and female gender role characteristics, resepectively) (Nadler et al. 1984).

This could have remained a non-evaluative simple matter of human differences were it not for the fact than in Western societies, at least, independence is more valued than dependence. Yet a closer examination of women's greater willingness to be depend on others' help suggests a more nuanced view than that which equates male self-reliance with strength. In fact, the readiness to seek and receive others' help has been conceptualized as representing women's higher level of active coping in that they use all available avenues to ameliorate a problem, while men's tendency to "barricade" themselves from the outside world in times of stress represents an ineffective coping strategy (Greenglass 1993). Viewed from this perspective, dependency on others' help does not represent weakness or maladjustment but an effective strategy of active social coping (Hobfoll et al. 1994; Nadler 2015).

Analyses of women's conduct as organizational leaders supports this view. While successful completion of the task is equally important for men and women managers, successful women managers do not shy away from admitting lack of knowledge and seeking help from their subordinates (Rosener 1990). A similar emphasis on the effective organizational leader as being able to empower others by helping them, and be empowered by them by seeking their help, is promoted by relational leadership theory (Uhl-Bien 2011). This theoretical perspective asserts that effective leaders are able to create positive relationships within the organization which includes giving support to, and seeking support from, others. From a broader perspective, men's reliance on themselves when in need, and women's initiation of interactions with others under similar circumstances is another demonstration of the view of helping relations as reflecting an interplay between needs for belongingness and independence. In fact, the need to protect one's place in the social hierarchy by displaying self-reliance is characteristic of men, while women seem to be able to balance between this need and their belongingness to others more effectively.

At this point, the reader may ask, which is the better coping strategy? As may be expected, the answer is neither and both. Consistent avoidance of help and consistent reliance on others are similarly ineffective. A more balanced view suggests that people need to (i) differentiate between situations they can cope with independently and those that will benefit from others' assistance, and (ii) be flexible enough to avoid seeking others' help in the former, and ready to rely on others in the latter.

This balanced view has been corroborated by research on help-seeking in an organizational setting (Nadler et al. 2003). Consistent with relational leadership theory, employees who had been characterized as being neither over- or under-utilizers of help were evaluated as better performers. Importantly, in this study, ratings of job performance were provided independently of the measurement of over- and under-utilization of help.

In a completely different context, research on resilient children (i.e. well-adjusted despite difficult life circumstances) lends support to the idea that effective coping is predicated on pursuing independence, combined with readiness to rely on others' help when the situation calls for it. Milgram and Palti (1993) compared personality traits of high- and low-achieving children in a disadvantaged community in Israel, and found that the successful (resilient) children differed from the less successful ones in what we labeled previously as "active social orientation." Although these children took personal initiative to cope with problems they were facing independently, their high sociability led them to be also more willing to rely on others' help. In a similar vein, resilient children in the inner city of Rochester, NY, exhibited both high levels of self-reliance *and* willingness to seek support (Parker et al. 1990).

4.2.2.4 Cultural Variables: Individualistic and Collectivistic Cultures

Just as cultural values affect people's willingness to give to others in need (pp. 45–51), they affect people's readiness to rely on others when they need help. Here too, the cultural emphasis on collectivistic or individualistic values (Hofstede and Bond 1984) is the major value orientation that affects receptivity to help. An early study compared evaluations by Dutch and American respondents of a target person who had been described as having sought help with daily problems (e.g. a stalled car) or not (Graf et al. 1979). The finding that help-seekers were evaluated less positively by American than by Dutch respondents was attributed to the greater emphasis in American society on the value of individual achievement. Similarly, participants living in an Israeli kibbutz (a close-knit collectivistic community) indicated that they would be more likely to seek others' help for daily problems than were participants from the big city where individualistic values dominate (Nadler 1986, Study 1). These findings are congruent with what one would expect regarding the link between collectivism–individualism and receptivity to help. As opposed to the previous studies based on paper-and-pencil measures of willingness to seek help in hypothetical situations, research that has examined actual help-seeking indicates that the link between individualism–collectivism and help-seeking is more complex. Participants raised in a kibbutz who had faced difficulties working on an anagram task sought *less* help than those raised in the individualistic environment of a Westernized big city (Nadler 1986, Study 2). This inconsistency with the paper-and-pencil study (Nadler 1986, Study 1) may be due to the fact that when asked about their evaluation of a hypothetical person who had sought help (Graf et al. 1979) or their response in a hypothetical need situation (Nadler 1986, Study 1), people reply by conforming to social norms. When, however, they are faced with the actual need to approach another person with a request for help, other psychological dynamics dominate.

Findings on differences in support-seeking between Asian- and European-Americans, i.e. representing more collectivistic and individualistic cultures, respectively, shed light on this unexpected finding that Kibbutz children had sought less help than city children. Two opposite predictions present themselves regarding the effects of collectivistic and individualistic values on willingness to seek and receive support from others. According to the *"collectivistic sharing"* prediction, collectivistic values will cause Asians to be readier than Westerners to seek others' support. The opposite prediction, which will be labeled the *"interdependent" prediction*, is based on the differences between the Western "independent self" and the Asian "interdependent self." It suggests that in Asian cultures (e.g. Japan) the "interdependent self" is primarily a relational entity. For the interdependent self, maintaining harmonious relations is more important than achieving personal goals while for the independent (Western) self, individual achievement is of paramount importance (Markus and Kitayama 1991). This suggests that bringing one's needs to the fore by seeking others' help requires others to cater to one's personal needs, which may harm social harmony and is therefore likely to be avoided by respondents from collectivistic cultures.

Empirical research corroborates the latter prediction. Asian American and European American students were asked to report the degree to which they had actually sought emotional support from others in their group. Consistent with the "interdependent self" hypothesis, Asian students reported that they relied less than did Western students on the emotional support of people in their group. These differences were observed in comparison between European Americans and Korean students and between European American and Asian American students (Taylor et al. 2004). Furthermore, and again in congruence with the interdependent-self prediction, this reluctance was especially salient with socially close others with whom harmonious relations are especially important (Kim et al. 2006). Further evidence supporting the logic of the interdependent-self hypothesis indicates that the lesser willingness of Asian Americans to seek emotional support was mediated by their concerns with disrupting the harmony of the group, and by fears of being criticized by those from whom they would have sought support (Kim et al. 2006; Taylor et al. 2004).

A related question is whether similar patterns would characterize *reactions to receiving help* in collectivistic and individualistic cultures. The logic of the collective sharing hypothesis suggests that Asians would respond more positively to receiving support than would Europeans. This is because being helped by others in the group expresses the mutual belongingness and mutual concern and caring that are more salient in collectivistic societies. Conversely, the logic of the interdependent-self hypothesis suggests that here too Asians would react more negatively than Europeans to receiving support from their network. Research indicates that the answer to this question is not straightforward, and that the effects of receiving support depend on whether it is implicit or explicit (Taylor et al. 2007), and on whether it had been solicited (Mojaverian and Kim 2013).

Implicit support reflects the sense of comfort one gains from being a member of a supportive network, without actually disclosing the problem by seeking the help of other members. *Explicit support* refers to the actual willingness to seek or receive emotional support from one's network. The findings about Asians' perceptions of support-seeking as disruptive of social harmony were obtained with regard to seeking explicit support: people were asked about times in which they had explicitly sought help from others in their group. Implicit support, on the other hand, is not disruptive to one's network and should therefore have more positive consequences for Asian American than European American participants (Taylor et al. 2007). To examine these hypotheses, Asian Americans and European Americans had been told to expect a stressful task and were later induced to experience implicit or explicit support from their network. In the implicit support condition, they were instructed to think about a group that was important to them and write down why this was so. In the explicit support condition, they were asked to write a letter to someone close to them and seek their advice on how to deal with the upcoming stressful task. The dependent variables included subjective and physiological measures of stress (i.e. cortisol levels) prior to experiencing the stressful task. As predicted, Asian Americans and European Americans evidenced less stress and more stress in the implicit support condition, respectively. This is consistent with findings by Uchida et al. (2008) that the link between *perceived availability of support* and well-being was stronger for participants from collectivistic compared to individualistic cultures.

Another relevant distinction is whether the assistance received has been solicited by recipients or given to them without having been solicited (i.e. requested vs. assumptive, and proactive vs. reactive help, respectively). Unsolicited support may indicate care and concern others in the group have for the person in need, and affirm interdependence and shared belongingness with them. This is likely to carry more significance in collectivistic societies. To examine this, Mojaverian and Kim (2013) exposed European Americans and Asian Americans to a stressful experimental situation consisting of having to solve difficult math problems for which they received assistance from a math student after they had actively sought it, or without having sought it. First, consistent with previous findings, Asian participants were less likely to seek help. Second, receiving unsolicited help led Asian participants to experience less task-related stress than receiving solicited help. For European Americans there was no difference in stress levels between the solicited and unsolicited help conditions. Importantly, the stress felt by Asians was mediated by an increase in "performance self-esteem" in the unsolicited help condition. These findings are of particular significance because they chart the path through which culture affects receptivity to help and its effects. When help represents shared belongingness, as is the case of Asians receiving unsolicited help, it increases recipients' "performance self-esteem," which bolsters their confidence in being able to tackle the upcoming task, thereby reducing stress, which is likely to result in better coping.

*

In summary, the research reviewed here highlights the effects of social values on receptivity to help. These depend on whether attitudes toward help seeking or actual help-seeking behavior are assessed. On the one hand, consistent with the idea that collectivism is associated with greater readiness for sharing, people in collectivist societies evidenced more positive attitudes toward help-seekers and help seeking than did those in individualistic societies. Yet, the research on the effects of collective values on actual seeking of support draws a different picture: people from the collectivistic societies avoided seeking support for personal problems more than did people from individualistic societies. The interdependent-self explanation is that people in collective societies are relatively more concerned with imposing their problems on others by *explicitly* seeking their support. Yet the receipt of unsolicited help is perceived by members of collectivistic societies as an affirmation of their shared belongingness with others in the group and therefore has more positive effects for the recipients. Finally, one's awareness of the availability of a supportive network – *implicit* support – does not impose on the network, and for members of collectivistic societies, it is linked to higher well-being and coping with stress.

4.2.2.5 The Recipient's Personality Characteristics In the preceding sections, we reviewed the links between people's demographic characteristics and their willingness to seek and receive help. This section addresses the role of personality variables in explaining differential receptivity to help. It focuses on three categories of personality dispositions: relational, self-related, and achievement-related. Relational dispositions describe a person's habitual patterns of social relationships with others (e.g. dependent personality and attachment). The main self-related disposition to be considered here is the self-esteem of the person in need and their need for achievement.

4.2.2.5.1 Relational Dispositions: The Dependent Personality and Attachment

THE DEPENDENT PERSONALITY The habitual tendency to turn to others for help as a primary reaction to experiencing difficulty has been described in research and theory on the dependent personality (Bornstein 2011). In psychoanalytic theory, the dependent personality is viewed as reflecting an "oral fixation." It was described by Erich Fromm as an habitual tendency of certain people to always search a magic helper, be grateful to those they depend on, and experience fear of losing them (Fromm 1947). This portrays the dependent personality in a non-flattering manner, as a maladjusted person who behaves in a needy manner, clings to others and when seeking their help, is likely to expect them to solve his or her predicament (i.e. prefer dependency-oriented help). The tendency of participants high on dependent personality to seek others' help as an immediate response to the experience of difficulty has been demonstrated in both laboratory (Shilkret and Masling 1981) and field studies (Sroufe et al. 1983).

Further research has indicated that dependency-related passivity is not an automatic response to every potential helper. The status of the potential helper affects the "dependent personality–help- seeking" link. In one study, participants rated high on dispositional dependence waited to see a professor twice as long as did low scorers (12 and 6 minutes, respectively). Yet when participants had been informed that the professor's ability to help diminished (i.e. he had been said to quit the university) the differences disappeared (Bornstein 2007). These and similar findings (cf. Bornstein 2011) dispel the view of dependent persons as uniformly passive and weak and portray them as strategic help-seekers who use help-seeking to strengthen their relationships with figures of authority and high status whose opinion, and potential helpfulness, is relatively more important than that of less influential helpers.

This more intricate view of the dependent personality is underscored by Pincus and Gurtman's (1995) distinction between "love dependency" and "submissive dependency." Love dependency expresses people's belongingness to each other. It is manifested in a person's readiness to rely on others, not as an immediate automatic response but after having considered whether one is able to overcome the predicament on his or her own. The description of love dependency echoes the previous description of women's', relative to men's higher readiness to seek help as *active social coping*. It reflects the person's motivation to optimally utilize available external resources. High scorers on love dependency are likely to seek autonomy- or dependency-oriented help based on their assessment of their own resources and ability to be part of the solution. Their help-seeking is likely to be associated with long-term self-reliance. Submissive dependency, on the other hand, originates in one's motivation to find the "magic helper" who will solve one's predicament. It is more likely to be manifested by the consistent seeking of dependency-oriented help, regardless of one's resources or abilities. Individuals characterized by submissive dependency are motivated to ingratiate themselves to others in positions of authority and high status.

In support of this analysis, people's scores on a submissive dependency scale were related to maladaptive patterns associated with anxious attachment and loneliness, while scores on love dependency were associated with patterns of secure attachment (Pincus and Wilson 2001). These findings bring into focus the links between receptivity to help and attachment to which we turn next.

Attachment and Receptivity to Help Attachment theory (Bowlby 1973) has been central to exploring the links between personality dispositions and social behavior (Mikulincer and Shaver 2007). The theory's basic premise is that interactions with significant others in early childhood create lifelong mental models about others' availability during stress. People's characteristic expectations that others will be available to them in times of stress is labeled *secure attachment* and is predictably expressed in readiness to turn to others for needed help (for more on secure and other types of attachment see previous discussion pp. 63–65). Research has supported this prediction. For example, in a field study, people's reaction to war-related stress (missile attacks on Israeli cities during the first Gulf War) was found to be affected by their attachment style (Mikulincer et al. 1993). Compared to avoidant and ambivalent individuals, secure individuals exhibited higher support-seeking to cope with the stress.

In a pioneering study, Simpson et al. (1992) provided a persuasive empirical demonstration of the effects of attachment styles on support seeking among romantically involved couples. Eighty-three heterosexual couples dating for an average of 17.9 months participated in this study. After their attachment styles and other relevant measures had been assessed, the women were informed that they would be exposed shortly to a stressful experimental procedure. To maximize the induction of this stress they were shown into a room with ominous-looking electrophysiological equipment and told to wait while the equipment was being prepared. They were then led to an adjoining room and seated next to their waiting male partner. The five-minute interaction between the woman and her partner was videotaped and analyzed to construct a measure of support-seeking and giving. The findings indicated that for securely attached women, the more anxiety they had felt the more active they were in seeking comfort and support from their partner. For women characterized as avoidants, however, the opposite pattern obtained: the higher their reported anxiety the lower their active seeking of support and comfort. This provides a clear experimental demonstration of how one's childhood-based expectations for the availability of others in times of stress translates into receptivity to others' help in adulthood.

This comparison focuses on the differences between securely and avoidantly attached individuals. It does not inform us about the receptivity to help of the anxiously attached. Attachment theory suggests that because the anxiously attached individuals crave closeness with others and at the same time fear their rejection, they will solicit help from others while exaggerating the need to forestall the possibility of being refused (Cassidy 2000; Lopez and Brennan 2000). In fact, others' help serves them as proof that they are liked (Vogel and Wei 2005). Empirical support was provided in that students' scores on the anxiety dimension of attachment were positively related to their intention to seek counseling for psychological and interpersonal concerns

(Cheng et al. 2015). The authors summarize their findings by writing that "because of a negative working model of self, anxiously attached persons tend to devalue their self-worth and overvalue others' opinions and approval" (p. 479).

A richer view of the link between attachment and receptivity to help is suggested by considering the distinction between dependency- and autonomy-oriented help, and between the "breadth" and "depth" of support-seeking. Because anxiously attached individuals crave others' liking and acceptance, they are likely to prefer dependency-oriented help, because it consists of more help and can be perceived as a relatively stronger indication of the helper's care and concern. The avoidantly attached individual is likely to reject all assistance. Yet, if circumstances are extreme and force him or her to depend on help, they are likely to prefer autonomy-oriented help that allows them to maintain a self-perception of relative independence and detachment from others. Compared to the anxiously and avoidantly attached, securely attached individuals' view of themselves is not predicated on receiving much help as a sign that others like them, nor on refusing all help because they fear being too close to others. Their receptiveness will be situationally determined. They will seek dependency-oriented help when the situation is extreme and they do not view themselves as able to help themselves, and autonomy-oriented assistance when perceiving themselves as able to be part of the solution. On the whole, the anxiously attached individual is likely to overutilize help, the avoidantly attached to underutilize it, and the securely attached to display a pattern of situationally adequate receptivity to others' assistance.

Avoidantly attached individuals generally display rigid self-reliance. Thus, for example, they are relatively less likely to seek professional psychological counseling, or support from non-professional others, in a variety of stressful situations (Dozier 1990). When they do seek help, they are likely to use indirect tactics of help seeking (e.g. using hints or stories about other people) (Collins and Feeney 2000). Yet, the distinction between "breadth" and "depth" of support suggests that this generalization may be incomplete. Breadth of support refers to the *number of others* one approaches, and depth refers to the *amount of support* one seeks from a given support provider. In a study based on a personal diary methodology in which participants noted the number of people they had approached for support and how much support they had requested in each encounter, the findings indicated that consistent with past research, avoidants sought less support than did securely and anxiously attached individuals (Armstrong and Kammrath 2015). However, this is due to having sought help from a smaller number of support providers; they sought as much support as secure and anxiously attached individuals in each support encounter. This suggests that relative to securely and anxiously attached individuals, avoidants must cross a higher threshold of perceived shared belongingness before seeking outside help. Once crossed, they do not shy away from seeking help. That threshold is lower for the securely attached. The receptiveness of the anxiously attached is more variable and depends on other variables. They may display overly self-reliant underutilization of help with some individuals or in certain situations, and overutilization with others in other situations.

The above indicates that the effects of attachment on receptivity to help are far from being represented by some simple tripartite patterns of help-seeking and receiving. The dependency or autonomy orientation of help and the breadth and depth of help-seeking moderate these patterns. Finally, conceptualizing these effects in terms of the need to cross a threshold of perceived shared belongingness demonstrates the theoretical and empirical richness of the relationship between a person's attachment style and their receptivity to help.

4.2.2.5.2 Self-related Characteristics

SELF-ESTEEM According to the threat-to-self-esteem model of receiving help, dependence on help may be a self-supportive or a self-threatening experience. This emphasis on the consequences of receiving help for the recipient's self-esteem suggests that people's chronic level of self-esteem will play a role in affecting their reactions to receiving help and willingness to seek it. In other words, high and low self-esteem individuals may be differently affected by being dependent on help and therefore display different levels of readiness to seek or receive it.

Two opposite predictions present themselves regarding the effects of self-esteem on receptivity to help: the *vulnerability* and the *consistency* predictions (Nadler 1986). The *vulnerability hypothesis* suggests that compared to high self-esteem, low self-esteem individuals have relatively few positive cognitions about themselves, which renders them more vulnerable to new negative information about themselves. Based on this logic, low self-esteem people in need will shun dependency on others as a way to solve their predicament when it reflects negatively on their self-worth, i.e. when the task on which help is needed is ego-relevant. Conversely, high self-esteem individuals in need who possess relatively many positive self-cognitions are less vulnerable and will therefore evidence greater readiness to rely on outside help even when it reflects negatively on their self-worth.

In contrast to the vulnerability hypothesis, the *consistency hypothesis* suggests that because dependency on ego-relevant dimensions is inconsistent with the positive self-evaluations of high self-esteem individuals they will shun dependency on others. On the other hand, dependency is relatively more consistent with the relatively more negative self-evaluations of low self-esteem individuals, who will therefore be more receptive to others' help. As the research below indicates, social psychological findings tend toward the consistency approach: when the experienced difficulty is ego-relevant, high self-esteem individuals will be less receptive to help than their low self-esteem counterparts.

In an early study that explored the effects of self-esteem on receptivity to help, participants could seek outside help to perform well on an unfamiliar task (i.e. determine the degree of neuroticism in a videotaped interaction; Tessler and Schwartz 1972). For half the participants, the task was said to be ego central (i.e. being good at determining neuroticism reflects one's intelligence), and for the other half it was said to be non-ego central (i.e. performance reflects luck). Consistent with the previous discussion of the effects of ego relevance on receptivity to help, an ego-centrality main effect indicated that participants were less willing to seek outside help when the task was presented as ego central. Yet, this finding was qualified by a significant task centrality × self-esteem interaction, indicating that when task performance was said to reflect non-ego central qualities, low and high self-esteem individuals sought similar amounts of help. Yet, when performance on the task was attributed to ego central qualities, high self-esteem individuals sought significantly less help. This finding is congruent with the consistency approach that when self-threat potential is high, self-esteem individuals are more sensitive than their low self-esteem counterparts to the self-threat associated with being helped.

In further support for the consistency hypothesis, high self-esteem individuals who had received help under conditions of self-threat (i.e. ego-central task and a similar helper) reported feeling worse than did participants in all other experimental conditions (Nadler et al. 1976). Also, high self-esteem participants who needed assistance to solve difficult anagrams were least likely to seek help in conditions of high-threat potential, i.e. a similar helper and ego-central task (Nadler 1987).

Similar findings were obtained when the self-threat potential in help was manipulated by inducing expectations that the help that one had sought could or could not be reciprocated. When a person in need expects that he or she would not be able to reciprocate, they risk remaining indebted to the helper. Under these conditions, high self-esteem individuals evidenced significantly lower readiness to seek help than did low self-esteem individuals (Nadler et al. 1985). Because self-esteem is a broad personal trait likely to be associated with other personality variables (e.g. achievement motivation; Abouserie 1995), it is important to note that similar support for the consistency hypothesis was obtained also when self-esteem had been experimentally manipulated (Nadler et al. 1979).

Finally, field observations have also supported the consistency prediction. Relative to women low in self-esteem, high self-esteem women sought less support from their network to cope with war-related stress (Hobfoll and London 1986), and high self-esteem domestic violence victims were less likely to seek counseling (Frieze 1979).

This research portrays the high self-esteem individual in need as reluctant to admit weakness or inability by seeking help. These individuals seem to prefer maintaining a posture of efficacy and self-reliance even when seeking help is the optimal way to cope. From this perspective, the readiness to rely on others' assistance has been aptly labeled the "utility of humility" by Weiss and Knight (1980), who found that low self-esteem individuals outperformed high self-esteem individuals on tasks that required substantial consultation among team members. Apparently, the higher readiness of the low-self-esteem individuals to seek advice from others and consult with them serves them well on tasks that emphasize group member interdependence.

These findings beg the question of the relationships between help seeking and effective coping. It seems that while high self-esteem individuals face the danger of rigid self-reliance leading them to underutilize available assistance, low self-esteem individuals may be over-dependent on others' help and seek it even if they can cope on their own. Both under- and overutilization are associated with poorer long-term coping (Nadler et al. 2003). However, consideration of the effects of people's self-esteem on their willingness to seek and receive help, and the consequences of receiving it on long-term coping, needs to consider the autonomy/dependency nature of the help in question, as discussed next.

The self-threat in receiving help is likely to be disarmed when help does not consist of a solution, but of tools with which recipients can be active in solving the problem (i.e. dependency- and autonomy-oriented help, respectively). Because with such help recipients can retain self-perceptions of independent coping, high self-esteem individuals are likely to be less rigidly self-reliant and be readier to seek and receive outside help. This reduces the danger of underutilization of help. For low self-esteem individuals, who view themselves as being habitually weak relative to others, receiving dependency-oriented help is not expected to be self-threatening. In fact, such assistance may be preferred (and present the danger of overutilization of others' help).

The habitual expectation that others would solve one's problems may result in a vicious cycle whereby people's low self-esteem leads them to be dependent on others, which further reinforces their negative self-evaluation. How can this vicious cycle be broken? One answer is the possibility that people who overutilize others' help as an immediate reaction to an experienced difficulty (e.g. dependent personality, low self-esteem) equate assistance with dependency-oriented help. Yet, if taught the distinction between dependency- and autonomy-oriented assistance, they may be less inclined to employ dependency-oriented help-seeking as a primary path of problem solution. In fact, (a) training low self-esteem individuals to make the distinction between autonomy- and dependency-oriented assistance, and (b) assess which is more appropriate, and (c) seek help accordingly, may result in more positive and enduring self-evaluations.

Need for Achievement Another personality variable closely related to people's willingness to seek and receive help is their dispositional need for achievement. On the one hand, the importance assigned by high achievers to successful task completion should lead them to be receptive to help that makes this outcome possible. On the other, successful performance that is due to others' help is incompatible with the individual achievement that the high achiever values. The next section focuses on the effects of recipient's need for achievement on their willingness to seek and receive help.

Achievement motivation and receptivity to help. Regarding the effects of achievement motivation on readiness to seek and receive help from others, two opposite predictions present themselves: avoidance of failure, and individual achievement. The avoidance of failure hypothesis suggests that because of their fear of failure, high achievers will use all available avenues to avoid failure. Thus, when experiencing difficulties, they will be readier to approach more knowledgeable and resourceful others for help than will low achievers for whom the consequences of failure are less overwhelming.

The individual achievement hypothesis suggests that because high achievers desire individual achievement that is based on demonstrating one's ability (Nichols 1984), they will be more concerned than low achievers to maintain their independence and tend to avoid seeking and receiving outside help to overcome their difficulties. At least two studies report a negative correlation between scores on a need for achievement scale and readiness to seek help on an experimental task and thus support the individual-achievement hypothesis (Nadler 1986; Tessler and Schwartz 1972). Also, outside the social psychological laboratory, elementary school children characterized as high achievers sought less help in the classroom than did children characterized as low achievers (Newman 1991). When, however, success was defined as a group achievement, high achievers sought *more* help to overcome a task-related difficulty than did low achievers (Nadler 1986). This finding further reinforces the interpretation that high achievers shy away from seeking help because they view it as undermining their *individual* achievements.

Conceptual developments on achievement motivation have gone beyond the distinction between high and low achievers to consider the reasons that motivate people to achieve. Achievement-goal theory proposes two achievement orientations: ego and mastery (Ames 1992; Harackiewicz et al. 2002). When achievement is dominated by ego orientation, people seek achievement as a means of avoiding negative appraisals about themselves and upholding positive self-esteem. When this orientation dominates, the high achiever continuously compares his or her achievements to others' (Nicholls 1984). When achievement is dominated by mastery orientation, on the other hand, the person is motivated to master the task at hand and acquire new skills and knowledge, and believes that skills are malleable by experience and work (Dweck 1986). Although each of these conceptual developments has had its own unique emphasis – for example, Dweck emphasizes beliefs about skill malleability while Nicholls centers on comparing achievements to others' – they share the distinction between achievement driven by the person's self-evaluative concerns and one motivated by the desire for learning and mastery.

Research in educational psychology has explored the significance of these two general achievement orientations for students' help-seeking. Mastery and ego achievement orientations imply two views of help that are conceptually related to autonomy- and dependency-oriented helping, respectively. The mastery-oriented high achiever views available help as an opportunity for personal development. Receiving tools and advice on how to solve the problem on one's own is consistent with the view of help as an autonomy-oriented opportunity for growth and development. The ego-oriented high achiever is likely to view any dependency on others' help as threatening positive self-evaluations. They are therefore likely to display rigid self-reliance and avoid help seeking even when this may cost them continued hardships. Consistent with this view, mastery-oriented students who had encountered a scholastic problem sought autonomy-oriented assistance, and ego-oriented students were unwilling to seek and receive help from their teachers (Butler and Neuman 1995; Ryan and Pintrich 1997).

Similar patterns were observed in the links between ego or mastery achievement orientations and teachers' receptivity to help. Mastery orientation was positively associated with teachers' willingness to seek outside help to cope with an educational problem, and this link was mediated by teachers' belief that outside assistance would promote their professional development. Teachers' ego orientation, on the other hand, was associated with relative unwillingness to seek or receive help and was mediated by their view of help seeking as signaling professional inadequacy (Butler 2007).

*

People's characteristic tendency to overutilize, underutilize, or adequately utilize help suggests a summary perspective on the effects of personality dispositions on receptivity to help. The submissive and passive dependency of the dependent personality on a more resourceful other represents overutilization, while the situationally determined reliance on others' help of the non-dependent individual represents adequate utilization. The important distinction between submissive and love dependency presented above reminds us that dependency on others may reflect shared belongingness and active social coping (i.e. high scores on love dependency). Research on adult attachment indicates that the willingness of the avoidant, anxious, and securely attached person to seek and receive others' help corresponds to under-, over-, and adequate utilization of help, respectively. Avoidants underutilize and the anxiously attached overutilize, while the securely attached individual's receptivity to help varies with the actual need and is therefore more adequate. Regarding the recipient's self-esteem, the high self-esteem individual may face the costs of underutilization (failure), while the low self-esteem individual faces the dangers associated with overutilization (long-term dependency). In a final subsection, we addressed the links between need for achievement and receptivity to help. As for achievement motivation, ego-oriented and mastery-oriented achievement are associated with under-and adequate utilization of help, respectively. Finally, as noted throughout these sections, the effects of personality variables on help seeking and receiving do not represent main effects but interact with relevant situational variables. For example, the effects of the dependent personality depend on the status of the available helper, and those of self-esteem on the ego relevance of the task, and the autonomy or dependency orientation of the available help.

5

Intergroup Helping Relations

The research in the preceding sections focused on interpersonal helping relationships. It sought to uncover variables and psychological processes that predict and explain individuals' willingness to help other individuals, and their willingness to seek and receive help. However, helping interactions occur also across group boundaries. Within society, people receive and give to others who are members of a different ethnic or cultural group, and between societies, nations may or may not come to the aid of others following a major catastrophe such as an earthquake. The receiving group may feel gratitude toward its benefactor or be suspicious about the true motivation underlying its generosity.

The study of such intergroup helping interactions is of great relevance because of developments outside and within social psychology. Outside our field, the globalized economy has led to greater cooperation across national and cultural borders and the recent refugee crisis has forced societies to address intergroup helping dilemmas. Conceptual developments within the social psychology of intergroup relations have also contributed to the growing interest in intergroup helping relations. Research on this subject has been a central area of interest for social psychologists since the inception of the field in the early twentieth century. This field of research and theory has undergone important conceptual and empirical development with the introduction of the social identity perspective on intergroup relations (i.e. social identity theory [SIT] and self-categorization theory, Turner and Reynolds 2001). This perspective is based on the idea that intergroup interactions occur also in the absence of physical groups. People carry the groups they belong to in their heads and when group affiliations are salient, what seems like an interpersonal interaction is actually an intergroup one. Thus for example, since intergroup conflict increases the salience of the members' collective identity (Ellemers et al. 2002), when an individual seeks help from another individual who is a member of the adversarial group (e.g. an Israeli seeking assistance from a Palestinian), this is psychologically an intergroup helping interaction. Other important implications of the social identity perspective for intergroup helping relations will be discussed later in this section, but regardless of the specific implication, all are based on the idea that when social identity is salient, giving and receiving from another individual can be experienced as an intergroup interaction.

This section begins by reviewing research on people's willingness to give to members of outgroups in need. It will consider research on discriminatory helping, where more help is given to the ingroup than to the outgroup; the motivations that govern helping ingroup and outgroup members; and ways in which discriminatory helping may be ameliorated. Next, attention will be drawn to helping relations in the context of structural inequality. Research conducted within the Intergroup Helping as Status Relations model (IHSR model) of intergroup helping (Nadler and Halabi 2006) will be reviewed. The final subsection will consider the practical implications of this body of research for promoting harmonious intergroup relations.

5.1 Giving Within the Group: Solidarity or Discrimination?

Intergroup relations have been commonly viewed in social psychology in tribal terms of "us" vs. "them" (Hawkins 1997). One expression of this view is that people are expected to help those with whom they share a collective identity before they turn to help others with whom they do not (i.e. ingroup and outgroup members, respectively). In support of this, Piliavin et al. (1981) indicate that a feeling of "we-ness" explains the ingroup favoritism in helpfulness. "We-ness" constitutes the affective component of shared collective identity. In a similar vein, Levine et al. (2005) showed that participants intervened more to help a person in need when the latter was perceived as being an ingroup rather than an outgroup member (i.e. being a fan of the same soccer team). Further support for the role of shared collective identity in helpfulness comes from interviews conducted with survivors of the 2005 terrorist attacks in the London subway. Findings indicate that the common threat experienced by survivors led to a feeling of shared group identity, which was translated into greater helpfulness than was evidenced in everyday life (Drury et al. 2009). Yet, these and other findings do not answer the following question: Do we help ingroup members *more*, or give *less* to outgroup members?

Does ingroup helpfulness represent discriminatory helping (giving less to strangers) or ingroup solidarity (giving more to ingroup members)? SIT (Tajfel and Turner 1979) suggests that the underlying motivation is to give less to others, while the ingroup favoring norm (Montoya and Pinter 2016) suggests that we give more to ingroup members because of our shared collective identity.

SIT views intergroup relations as competitive and centers on the discriminatory aspects in giving less to others. The classical research within this tradition, i.e. the minimal group paradigm, shows that members of experimental groups created ad hoc in the laboratory give less to an outgroup than to ingroup members (Tajfel 1970). This finding is of special significance because the ingroup and the outgroup have no relational history beyond the experimental laboratory in which they have been created. Therefore, the recurring finding of ingroup favoritism represents a "pure" intergroup phenomenon that is not tainted by past intergroup relations. The focus in this research is on the amount of resources given to an ingroup member *relative* to an outgroup member, rather than on the needs of ingroup members. Ingroup members are said to increase intergroup disparity in favor of the ingroup by discriminatory helping.

Conversely, the ingroup favoring norm conceived by Rabbie and Lodewijkx (1994) suggests that giving more to ingroup than outgroup members reflects the generic norm that people need to take care of their own before attending to the needs of strangers. The centrality of this norm in group life has been attributed to its evolutionary advantage. Groups that join efforts and resources to defend against external dangers and raise their young have an evolutionary advantage (Brewer 1999; Caporael and Brewer 1990). This view suggests that preferential helpfulness toward ingroup members in need is a positive and cooperative rather than competitive behavior. Such ingroup favoritism is not aimed at placing the outgroup lower than the ingroup but is a behavioral expression of the norm that group members "should take into account the interest of one's group before taking into account the interests of the other group" (Wildschut et al. 2002; p. 977). This approach to intergroup helpfulness has guided research that investigated the effects of individual variability in adherence to the ingroup favoring norm (e.g. Montoya and Pittinsky 2013), and the effects of the induction of beliefs regarding people's accountability for the well-being of other group members (Wildschut et al. 2002) on helping them.

At first glance, the differences between the SIT and ingroup favoring norm approaches may seem like hairsplitting. After all, both seek to explain the same basic phenomenon of giving more and more readily to one's own. Yet these two approaches suggest two different motivations that underlie the same phenomenon (see the following subsection). Further, they suggest different answers to the question of how to promote cooperation and giving across group boundaries. SIT suggests that this may be best achieved by convincing ingroup members that giving to strangers will not have adverse consequences of the ingroup's relative social position. Conversely, the ingroup favoring norm approach implies that the best way to promote helpfulness beyond the boundaries of the ingroup is by demonstrating to ingroup members that cooperation and helpfulness across group boundaries will benefit the ingroup (Montoya and Pinter 2016).

5.1.1 The Motivation for Ingroup and Outgroup Helping: Empathy and Attraction

The previous subsection discussed discriminatory helping. Here we address the intra-psychological processes that motivate helpfulness directed at an ingroup or outgroup member. Feelings of empathy are a central motivator of helpfulness (Batson 2011), but they impact differently on helping ingroup and outgroup members. Because perceived similarity and a feeling of psychological attachment are determinants of empathy (Batson et al. 2005), and people feel more similar and psychologically closer to ingroup than outgroup members, empathy is expected to be the emotional driver of helpfulness within the group. In support of this, dispositional empathy predicted volunteering to help AIDS patients by homosexual males, but failed to predict helpfulness by heterosexual females (Penner and Finkelstein 1998).

Conversely, members of outgroup in need of help are perceived as relatively dissimilar and psychologically distant from oneself, which is likely to diminish the role of empathy as the emotional driver of helping. Individual characteristics that render outgroup members personally attractive will de-emphasize their social categorization as outgroup members. When an outgroup member is personally appealing, the helper is likely to help them as individuals rather than as prototypical members of the outgroup. Therefore, personal attraction toward the other, rather than feelings of empathy, is expected to be associated with willingness to help them (Sturmer et al. 2005).

These hypotheses were supported by Sturmer et al. (2005), who found that empathy predicted intentions of homosexual male volunteers to help AIDS patients, while personal attraction predicted helping intentions of heterosexual male volunteers toward AIDS patients (Sturmer et al. 2005, Study 1). Although we do not mean to imply that homosexuality is equated with being afflicted with AIDS, the statistical reality of the disease renders AIDS patients as relatively more like "us" for homosexuals. In a second experiment, the ingroup or outgroup affiliation of the person needing help was experimentally manipulated, lending further support to the conclusion that empathy leads to helping ingroup but not outgroup members. This manipulation is designed to refute alternative explanations that may rise when intergroup categorizations are based on real group affiliation that has meanings based on history and ongoing events in the real world. Heterosexual or homosexual participants were told about another student suffering from hepatitis described as having homosexual or heterosexual preferences. Following the manipulation, measures of empathy and personal attraction toward the protagonist, and intentions to help them were taken. Consistent with the findings of the first study, empathy predicted helping intentions toward the ingroup member, and attraction predicted helping toward the outgroup member (Sturmer et al. 2005, Study 2).

These findings were replicated in a different context where German and Muslim participants indicated their willingness to help another newly arrived German or Muslim student, who had presented himself as Markus or Mohammed, respectively, in their first days on campus. Empathy predicted helping significantly more when the person in need had been described as culturally similar (Sturmer et al. 2006, Study 1). These findings were replicated in a second experiment that used ad hoc groups created in the laboratory. The finding that the strength of the empathy-helping relationships varied as a function of perceived intergroup similarity supports the psychological mechanisms responsible for these effects (Sturmer et al. 2006, Study 2).

Research that indicates that empathy drives helpfulness only toward ingroup members is inconsistent with the approach according to which the empathy-helping relationship is a general phenomenon that drives helpfulness toward all others in need, whether ingroup or outgroup members (Batson 2011). In an attempt to resolve this inconsistency, Lotz-Schmitt et al. (2017) suggested that empathy is a universal driver of helping toward ingroup members, and drives helping to outgroup members only after the disinhibiting psychological blocks associated with the "otherness" of the outgroup person in need have been removed. These blocks are most evident in relations with adversarial groups that are characterized by distrust, animosity and even dehumanization (e.g. Cehajic et al. 2009), but also in more benign intergroup relations. Social interactions with others who are viewed as "them" and not "us" evoke negative intergroup emotions (Pryor et al. 2004). Accordingly, learning that the other person, who is part of "them," is trustworthy and benevolent opens the path for empathy to be felt and drive helpfulness. In summary, when a similar other is in need, empathy is the primary and common driver of help-giving. With dissimilar others, empathy will arise only *after* the disinhibiting factors associated with the needy's "otherness" had been removed.

In an experiment supporting this explanation, German participants had read about a Canadian or Nigerian immigrant to Germany in need of help. Subsequently, they received information about the other's trustworthiness and benevolent character. This information was conveyed to participants in the form of ratings of the two immigrants supposedly made by a staff member of an absorption center. Participants' feelings of empathy and helping intentions toward the Canadian or Nigerian immigrant were subsequently measured. Consistent with the idea that empathy drives empathy toward ingroup members, empathy predicted helping intentions toward the Canadian regardless of information about their trustworthiness and benevolence. For Nigerian immigrants, the empathy-helping link was significant only when they had been presented as trustworthy and benevolent (Lotz-Schmitt et al. 2017). From this perspective, finding that personal attraction toward an outgroup member drives helpfulness (Sturmer et al. 2005) may mean that feelings of personal attraction toward an outgroup member, which de-emphasize their "otherness," represent another mechanism that lowers emotional blocks against feelings of empathy toward the person in need. Thus, empathy may explain helpfulness only toward outgroup members we trust and like.

The analysis suggested by Lotz-Schmitt et al. (2017) supports an evolutionary perspective on helping across group boundaries. The helper has to feel that his or her helpfulness will not be exploited. The interpersonal trust that exists in most social interactions with ingroup members allows the bystander to open up emotionally, empathize with the person in need and help them. With outgroup members such basic trust needs to be actively induced. This occurs when information indicates that the outgroup member is trustworthy or when one experiences personal attraction toward him or her, which allows the experience of empathy with his or her predicament, and drives subsequent helping. From this perspective, evolutionary fitness is served by blocking feelings of empathy when the other is a stranger, unlikeable, and therefore untrustworthy and potentially harmful.

5.2 Giving Across Group Boundaries

5.2.1 Strategic Helping

Although empathy is a prime motivator of assisting another person in need, helping is often driven by other, more egoistic motives. As the previous discussion of interpersonal helping indicated, giving to others may be reflect the helper's strategy for gaining prestige or protecting against threats to one's prestige. Help-giving across group boundaries may be similarly motivated by ingroup members' strategic concern of defending against threats to the ingroup's collective image, or the wish to gain prestige for one's group. Mauss (1954) described how in tribal societies, clan leaders give lavishly to their counterparts to gain status. Yet this apparent interpersonal interaction is in fact an intergroup interaction where one leader gives generously to other leaders in order to climb the rungs of the ladder of the *intergroup* hierarchy. Mauss writes that such lavish displays of generosity are to the "ultimate benefit of their own clan" (p. 4). This observation reiterates two generalizations about intergroup helping relations. First, when interactants' collective identities are salient, a seemingly interpersonal interaction may in fact be an intergroup helping interaction. Second, giving across group boundaries may be driven by the motivation to promote the ingroup's collective identity. Such help-giving that is motivated by the ingroup's strategic concerns, e.g. their collective identity, rather than by care for the outgroup is labeled "strategic intergroup helping" (van Leeuwen and Tauber 2009).

In an experimental demonstration of strategic helping, Scottish participants had suffered a threat to their group's collective identity that consisted of reading that the English considered them stingy. Subsequently, when given the opportunity, they contributed more to a Welsh than to a Scottish organization. Giving to an outgroup was chosen by the Scottish participants as a way to defend against the blow to their group's reputation because helping an outgroup is more diagnostic of benevolence than helping ingroup members (Hopkins et al. 2007).

A similar experiment was conducted with Dutch participants. In the threat-to-collective-identity condition, they had been told that the

Netherlands' integration into the European Union threatened Dutch unique identity. Subsequently, participants were asked whether the Netherlands should help Asian countries hard hit by flooding. Compared to the control condition, participants in the threat-to-collective-identity condition expressed greater support for the proposal that the Netherlands should help. This is another demonstration of how group members whose collective identity has been threatened seek to ameliorate the threat by putting their group on a pedestal of being a generous group. The identity-repair function of this helpfulness is demonstrated by the finding that greater willingness to assist people in the flooded areas was evident in skills central to Dutch collective identity (i.e. managing water sources) (van Leeuwen 2007).

Another demonstration of the utilitarian-strategic function of intergroup helping is the use of assistance as a way to communicate the ingroup's strategic wishes to the receiving outgroup. Thus, to communicate its desire to maintain national identity intact, the majority group in Indonesia behaved generously toward a separatist minority outgroup, thereby using the "carrot" of generosity to convince the outgroup to comply with its wishes (van Leeuwen and Mashuri 2013).

5.2.2 Discriminatory Helping: Giving Across Racial Boundaries

A specific case of cross-group help-giving that has received relatively much research attention centered on the willingness of European Americans to help African Americans. This is due partly at least to the fact that much of social psychological research and on helping in particular has been conducted in the US, where racial tensions in relations between whites and blacks exist. Because of these racial tensions, it was expected that whites would reveal their prejudicial and discriminatory tendencies toward blacks by being less likely to help a black compared to a white American in need (i.e. discriminatory helping).

Research on cross-racial help-giving conducted in the US in the 1970s supported this prediction (Benson et al. 1976; Gaertner and Bickman 1971). At this point, the reader may wonder whether the progress in racial/ethnic equality within the US and elsewhere has not made discriminatory helping a thing of the past. More recent research suggests a negative answer to this question. Racial prejudices toward victims of Hurricane Katrina in Louisiana and the earthquake in Haiti led to downplaying the severity of these natural catastrophes, increased blaming of the victims, and reduced willingness to help them (McManus and Saucier 2012). An extreme form of prejudice against other racial groups is the tendency to dehumanize them. In a study with Italian participants, dehumanization of earthquake victims in Japan, i.e. assigning them machine-like attributes, and Haiti, i.e. assigning them animal-like attributes, was associated with lesser readiness to help them (Vaes et al. 2012).

However, the generalization that prejudice would cause white people (for example) to give less help to a black than a white person in need is true only under certain conditions. In one study, white Americans intervened less often on behalf of a black victim than on behalf of a white victim in an emergency only when they were under the impression that other bystanders were present. When under the impression that only they and the victim were present, there was no difference in the likelihood of intervention (Gaertner and Dovidio 1977). One likely explanation for this effect of others' presence on helping across racial boundaries is that when others are thought to be present the costs of discriminating against the black victim by not intervening on their behalf are lower. Under these conditions, the would-be helper may tell him- or herself that others would, or already have intervened (cf. Darley and Latané 1968, pp. 36–38). These findings and interpretation suggest a modification of the generalized discriminatory helping hypothesis: people in an advantaged majority group would discriminate against a disadvantaged or stigmatized group member only when the costs of doing so by not helping them are relatively low.

Two literature reviews of cross-racial help-giving, 25 years apart, arrived at a similar conclusion. The first concluded that white Americans help black and white Americans equally in face-to-face interactions (Crosby et al. 1980). Under these conditions, the costs of refusing to help another person, regardless of his or her group affiliation, are particularly high. Similarly, a more recent review of the cross-racial helping literature concluded that discriminatory helping is likely to occur only when refusing help to the black person can be rationalized by the would-be helper. Being able to rationalize non-intervention renders non-helping less costly. One such rationalization is that helping is very risky; another is that "others will help" (Saucier et al. 2005). The rationalizations for refusing help to a black person by a white helper vary, but all lower the costs of not helping. They provide the prejudiced person with an acceptable reason to act out their prejudices. Moreover, prejudiced non-helpers may rationalize their failure to help a person from a stigmatized group retroactively: white participants that had refused help to a black person subsequently rationalized their inaction by claiming that it was not a real emergency (Kunstman and Plant 2008).

5.2.2.1 Discriminatory Helping as Aversive Racism In his treatise *White Racism: A Psychohistory*, Kovel (1970) distinguished between two forms of racism: aversive and dominative. *Dominative racism* is expressed in explicit violence and/or discrimination against stigmatized outgroups. *Aversive racism* expresses itself more subtly and passively by refusing contact and intimacy with members of prejudiced groups. When threatened with the prospect of close interaction with a black person, the aversive racist "walls himself off and turns away" (p. 23). A more recent social psychological account of aversive racism views the aversively racist person as being caught in the tension between two opposing psychological tendencies. On the one hand, the person's racist tendencies drive them to behave negatively and aggressively toward targets of racism. On the other, the social norm that one should treat others equally, regardless of their group affiliation, blocks the racist person's tendency to be openly negative toward others. Aversive racism is one way in which prejudiced persons solve this internal conflict. They behave in a discriminatory way toward stigmatized others as long as this is not seen as blatant violation of the norm against discrimination. For example, the aversively racist person may blame disadvantaged groups for their lowly social position and oppose policies of affirmative action that would better their situation. Although it reflects a prejudicial tendency toward the disadvantaged, this attitude may be rationalized as representing a legitimate social position regarding optimal economic policy (Dovidio and Gaertner 2004). Discriminatory helping constitutes another example of aversive racism. When not helping a black person in need may be rationalized (e.g. a risky situation), the costs of non-helping are low and the prejudiced white person discriminates while maintaining a positive moral image.

Although this section focused on discriminatory helping between European and African Americans, its implications extend to other contexts where members of socially advantaged groups encounter members of disadvantaged or stigmatized groups in need of help. In general, when rationalizations allow members of advantaged groups to perceive the refusal to help as not costly, prejudiced people would display aversive racism by not helping the stigmatized person in need. This may account for unwillingness to help a stigmatized group within society, as well as for the unwillingness of rich countries to help poorer countries (Fisher et al. 2008).

5.2.2.2 Overcoming Discriminatory Helping: Common Group Identity How can the tendency for discriminatory helping be overcome? One answer is suggested by the research on common identity in intergroup relations that is based on self-categorization theory's assertion that people's identity can be anchored in personal or collective self-categorization (e.g. "I am an intelligent and benevolent person" or "I am a citizen of …," respectively) and that the shift from one level of self-categorization to the other is situationally determined. An important premise of the theory is that people's sense of collective identity is malleable. In one condition, one may self-categorize in terms of one's country and in another in terms of the university he or she attends (e.g. international and inter-collegial sports competition, respectively) (Turner and Reynolds 2012). Based on this idea, the common identity model proposes that members of two separate groups can be induced to view themselves as united under an overarching common identity, while maintaining their separate collective identities. For example, students of psychology and economics may adopt the common identity of social sciences students, and African and White Americans the common American identity (Dovidio and Gaertner 2000).

The induction of common group identity has beneficial effects on attitudes toward the outgroup that shares the overarching common identity with the ingroup (Gaertner and Dovidio 2012), and reduces discriminatory helping tendencies. This was demonstrated in the formerly described study where Manchester United fans failed to help a fan of a rival team when separate group identities were salient. When, however, the collective identity of the ingroup and the rival group as "football lovers" had been made salient participants intervened equally to help ingroup and outgroup members in need (see previously described research by Levine et al., 2005, on pp. 35–36). Similar findings were reported by research showing that white students who had been induced to view fellow black students as team members working on the same task were more forthcoming in complying with their requests for assistance than when the black students were presented as individuals (Nier et al. 2001). Similar findings regarding the benevolent effects of common identity on cross-group helping were obtained with ad hoc groups created in the laboratory (Dovidio et al. 1997). Because the findings by Dovidio et al. (1997) are based on cross-group helping with groups that do not have a prior history, they bolster the internal validity of the link between common identity and reduced discriminatory helping.

Research on non-Jews who rescued Jews during the Holocaust, described in previous sections, echoes the same message. The study titled "The Altruistic Personality" compared a relatively large group of rescuers to a comparable group of non-rescuers on various psychological measures (Oliner and Oliner 1988). A key difference was the rescuers' higher scores on "extensitivity," that is the "propensity toward inclusiveness with respect to the diversity of individuals and groups to whom one will assume obligations" (Oliner and Oliner 1992, p. 370). Another example is the behavior by King Boris III and others in the Bulgarian leadership, who withstood Nazi pressures to expel Bulgarian Jews to the death camps. As Reicher et al. (2006) indicate, this decision was based on viewing Bulgarian Jews and non-Jews as sharing a common Bulgarian identity. Finally, the effects of dispositional tendency for extensitivity on readiness to help outgroups is evident in mundane daily helping interactions as well. People who had scored high on an especially constructed measure of extensitivity were equally ready to help family members and strangers, while low scorers exhibited greater readiness to help family members than strangers (Einolf 2010).

What are the antecedents of viewing one's ingroup and the outgroup as sharing a common identity? One answer, based on the literature reviewed previously, is situational emphasis on the ingroup's common identity with other groups. The research on rescuers of Jews during the Holocaust suggests a myriad of influences in one's family (e.g. parental emotional warmth and exhortation of moral values) (pp. 57–58).

Recently, Nai et al. (2018) reported that people who lived in a culturally diverse neighborhood were more helpful toward strangers than those living in a homogenous neighborhood and that this effect was mediated by adopting the overarching identity of "common humanity." In one study, participants who lived in an ethnically diverse neighborhood reported greater willingness to help strangers in the aftermath of the 2013 Boston Marathon bombing than those living in a homogenous neighborhood (Nai et al. 2018, Study 2). In another study, an ethnic and cultural diversity scores assigned to 128 nations was positively correlated with answers to the question, "In the past month, did you help a stranger?" (Study 3). To further explore the role of common identity as mediating the link between living in a socially diverse neighborhood and helping, the experience of living in a diverse or homogeneous neighborhood was experimentally induced (Study 5). European American participants were asked to imagine themselves living in an ethnically homogenous or diverse suburban neighborhood. Subsequently, they were asked to imagine that an explosion had occurred in their neighborhood and asked whether they would be ready to help a stranger who had fallen victim to this incident. Those who had imagined living in an ethnically diverse neighborhood evidenced greater readiness to help. More importantly, and of direct relevance to the present focus on common group identity, participants' identification with the broad category of "humanity" mediated this relationship.

*

To summarize, the section on intergroup helping opened with the question of whether the greater helpfulness within the group reflects within group solidarity, or a discrimination against the outgroup. Subsequently the section considered the motivations for helping ingroup and outgroup members. Overall, the arousal of empathy when an ingroup member is in need and the consequent helping express people's communion with others they consider part of "us." On the other hand, giving to an outgroup member may be a mechanism by which ingroup members gain prestige for their group, or defend against threats to collective identity. The psychological distance from "them" blocks empathy and lowers willingness to help across group boundaries. Giving to strangers is conditional upon reducing the psychological distance that separates groups. This occurs when the outgroup member is viewed as attractive, thereby de-emphasizing his or her "otherness," or when positive perceptions of the other had been actively induced. The automatic arousal of empathy with ingroup members in need and its conditional arousal with outgroup members increase evolutionary fitness. A subsequent subsection discussed discriminatory helping. The reluctance to help a member of a stigmatized group can be a form of aversive racism, which is more likely to occur when the costs of not helping are relatively low (i.e. can be easily rationalized). A final subsection addressed the question of how the tendency for discriminatory helping can be overcome by the adoption an overarching common identity which lowers the tendency to ignore the sufferings of people beyond ingroup boundaries.

5.3 Intergroup Helping Relations in Structurally Unequal Contexts

The research reviewed in previous sections indicates that while help-giving often reflects genuine concern and solidarity, at other times helping relations produce social inequality. This generalization serves as the basis for the threat-to-self-esteem model of interpersonal help seeking and receiving (p. 111). It is echoed in the research on giving and receiving across group boundaries, and demonstrated in historical and anthropological discussions of intergroup helping (Mauss, de Tocqueville, etc., pp. 15, 81, 145).

The previous sections have addressed interpersonal and intergroup relations without attention to the socio-structural context within which the groups interact. Yet intergroup relations are often hierarchical, taking place within societal contexts of structural inequality. The identity of the group ranking higher and lower in that hierarchy may vary across time and space, but the reality of structural inequality is characteristic of most if not all human societies. In certain periods and societal settings, gender may represent a key element of structural inequality, while at other times and places another social characteristic (e.g. religion, color of skin) may take precedence as the major social characteristic around which the social hierarchy is organized. The Intergroup Helping as Status Relations model (Nadler 2002; Nadler and Halabi 2006) accounts for the psychology of giving, seeking and receiving help in contexts of structural inequality. Integrating the social identity perspective on intergroup relations (Turner and Reynolds 2001) with recent research on helping relations, it proposes that groups create, maintain and challenge hierarchical relations by giving, seeking or receiving help to or from an outgroup.

5.3.1 The Intergroup Helping as Status Relations (IHSR) Model

The IHSR model proposes that the dynamics of helping relations between structurally unequal groups are shaped by characteristics of (i) the social structure, (ii) the help, and (iii) individual group members. We begin with a detailed description of the model, continue to research conducted within this framework, and conclude by discussing its implications.

5.3.1.1 The Social Structure: Security of Social Hierarchy The IHSR model rests on a distinction between intergroup helping relations in the context of secure or insecure status hierarchies. This distinction is borrowed from SIT's conceptualization of the ways in which members of disadvantaged groups cope with their lowly social position (Tajfel and Turner 1979). They may do so by promoting themselves as individuals (e.g. gaining education, joining a prestigious occupation), promoting the ingroup characteristics that others regard as unimportant (e.g. being warm people), or challenge the status quo and try to promote the status of the lowly positioned group (i.e. social action).

Whether or not coping with the group's disadvantaged position by challenging the unequal status quo occurs depends on the security of the existing status hierarchy. In a secure status hierarchy, the groups regard the unequal status quo as stable and legitimate. Because of this, the prospects of social change are viewed as relatively low and the unequal status quo remains unchallenged. Under these conditions, coping with the ingroup's low status through individual mobility or by promoting the ingroup's characteristics is more likely than openly challenging the unequal social structure. In an insecure status hierarchy, on the other hand, inequality is perceived as illegitimate and unstable, and therefore changeable. Under these conditions, members of low-status groups are more likely to actively challenge existing inequality and try to change it to a more equal social structure through violent or nonviolent political actions. To illustrate, consider gender relations. In previous centuries, gender relations represented a secure status hierarchy where men's superiority over women was seen as legitimate and stable. In present times, in the West at least, gender inequality represents an insecure status hierarchy that is viewed as illegitimate and therefore unstable because it is seen as having to change (Acker 2006).

How does the security of groups' status hierarchy affect intergroup helping relations? When status relations are secure, the advantaged group is expected to care for members of the disadvantaged group and help them as needed. The latter seek help from the advantaged group, and respond with gratitude to its receipt. In this social transaction, the high-status group cares for and protects the low-status group, which reciprocates by being receptive and grateful. The willing dependency of the disadvantaged on the advantaged solidifies and legitimizes social inequality. Thus, in secure status hierarchies, *helping relations represent a unidirectional top-down flow of assistance* – from the advantaged to the disadvantaged. To use the previous example, in previous centuries men were expected to care for and protect women, who through their receptivity and gratitude for such help legitimized the unequal hierarchy and their disadvantaged position in it.

When the status hierarchy is insecure, social change toward greater equality is viewed possible and dependency on the high-status group is inconsistent with low-status group members' quest for equality. Therefore, the latter are unlikely to seek help from the high-status group, and likely to reject their offers for help, even when this results in continued hardships. This is echoed in criticisms leveled against affirmative action programs that because beneficiaries are helped based on group affiliation their dependency institutionalizes their collective inferiority (Crosby and Clayton 2001). Conversely, because when the status hierarchy is viewed as insecure, the privileged position of the high-status group is threatened, it will attempt to defend against this threat by giving the low-status group assistance, even when not solicited. Importantly, these intergroup helping dynamics depend on whether help is autonomy- or dependency-oriented.

5.3.1.2 Characteristics of the Help: Autonomy- and Dependency-Oriented Help Dependency-oriented help underscores recipient's relative weakness and lowly position, while autonomy-oriented assistance implies that recipients are strong and resourceful enough to help themselves (Nadler and Halabi 2006). In a secure status hierarchy, assistance that is given "downward" from the privileged to the underprivileged is likely to be dependency oriented, to underscore the legitimate and stable inequality. Under these conditions, solving the low-status group's problem is the responsibility of the higher-status group. To paraphrase the previous conclusion, in secure hierarchies, *help will be dependency-oriented and flow unidirectionally top-down,* to be received gratefully (Nadler 2002).

When the status hierarchy is insecure and members of disadvantaged groups view their inequality as changeable, they will be willing to seek and receive only autonomy-oriented help. Such help implies that they are able to help themselves, and therefore more equal to their benefactor. The privileged group, whose social advantage is threatened when the status security is insecure, will seek to maintain its advantaged position by giving dependency-oriented help to the disadvantaged. These dynamics of intergroup helping relations may result in group misunderstandings that could exacerbate existing intergroup tensions (Nadler et al. 2009).

5.3.1.3 Personal Characteristics of Group Members Group members' personal characteristics are expected to moderate these patterns of intergroup helping relations. Because these relations emanate from group members' wish to promote or protect their collective identity, the latter's identification with the ingroup will moderate these patterns. For example, when status relations are insecure and the ingroup's lowly position is seen as changeable, those who are characteristically high ingroup identifiers will reject offers for dependency-oriented help from the advantaged group more strongly than low identifiers (Nadler, 2002; Nadler and Halabi 2006). Also, the focus on intergroup hierarchical relations suggests that dispositional characteristics related to people's concern with stratification in social life (e.g. authoritarianism,

Altemeyer 1998; system justification, Freeden 2010; social dominance orientation [SDO], Sidanius and Pratto 1999) will moderate these helping patterns. People who are characteristically more concerned with, and attentive to, hierarchical relations in social life will exhibit these tendencies more than those who are characteristically less concerned with them.

The model is presented in Figure 5.1.

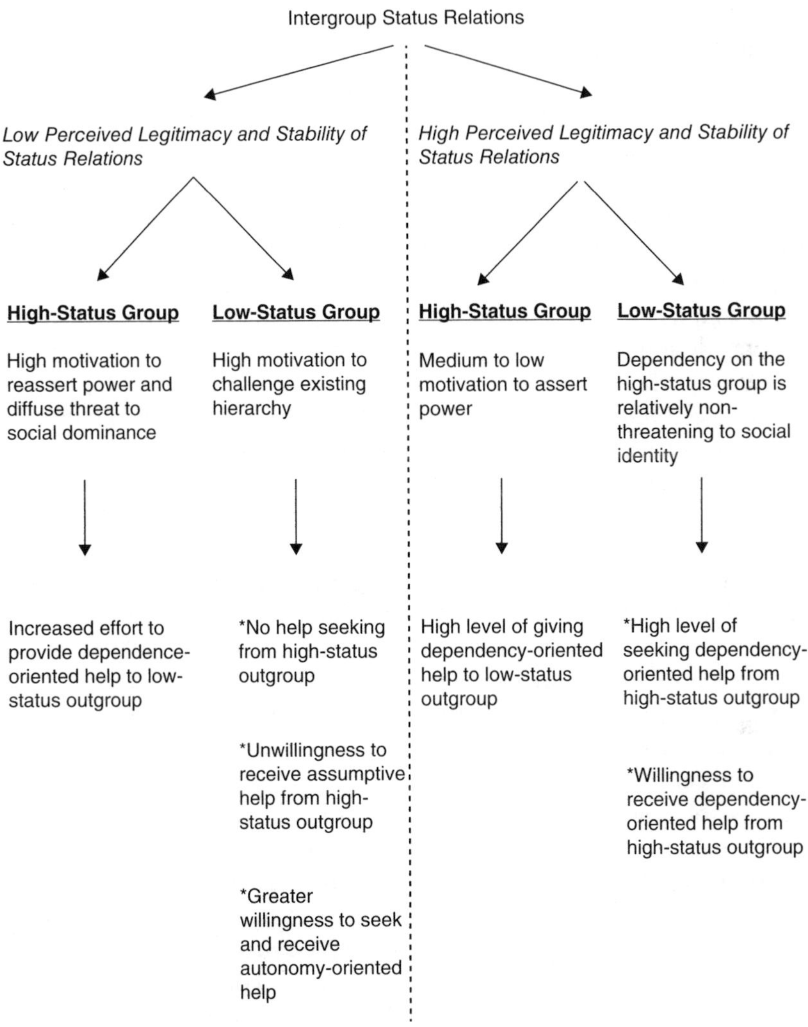

Figure 5.1 Intergroup helping relations as affected by perceived legitimacy and stability of status relations between groups.

5.3.2 *The Low-Status Group: Seeking and Receiving from the Advantaged Group*

We now turn to social psychological experimentation that examined the dynamics suggested by the IHSR and its extensions. We begin by research that centered on the low-status group's willingness to seek and receive help from the high-status group, and continue to research on help-giving by high- to low-status groups. Before we proceed, note that not all helpfulness across group boundaries is dominated by considerations of relative power, prestige, and status. Oftentimes the giving of assistance by the privileged to the less privileged group reflects genuine care and empathy. However, since the psychological processes associated with empathy-based giving are not unique to intergroup relations and have been the focus of much of this book, they are not discussed here.

The first group of experiments set out to examine the hypotheses of the IHSR model focused on the disadvantaged group. The first experiment in this research program used ad hoc groups in a 2 (stable vs. unstable status) × 2 (help vs. no help control conditions) experimental design (Nadler and Halabi 2006, Study 1). All participants were under the impression that they belonged to a lower-status group, having been told that their group was lower than the other on integrative and creative skills. The stability of this status difference was induced by telling half the participants that their integrative thinking score was based on a well-validated scale and was not likely to change (i.e. stable status condition), while the other half were told that their score was based on a new and relatively untried measure, and therefore their scores could change in future administrations (i.e. unstable status condition). Participants in the help condition received help from the higher-status outgroup to complete an experimental task they were working on, while those in the no-help control condition had not received such help. Thus, the experiment consisted of four equal experimental cells (i.e. unstable low status–help; unstable low status–no help; stable low status–help; and stable low status–no help).

Consistent with the hypothesis, participants in the unstable status condition who had received help from the higher status group on an experimental task evidenced more negative affect toward the helpful outgroup than participants in the no-help control condition. No such differences were observed in the stable status condition. These findings support the key assertion of the IHSR: under conditions of status insecurity, members of low-status groups respond negatively to help from high- status groups. Based on the rationale of the IHSR, this occurs because when status differences are unstable dependency on the higher-status group is inconsistent with the low-status group's motivation for group equality.

Following the empirical support for the model's key proposition using ad hoc groups, the research program moved to examine the model with real-world groups. In one experiment, Arab citizens of Israel, representing a disadvantaged minority group in Israeli society, received help from an Israeli Jew i.e., the majority group in Israeli society. Participants had been induced to believe that the socioeconomic gap between these two groups remained the same or was increasingly narrowing over the last decade (stable and unstable hierarchy, respectively). Arabs helped by Jews responded significantly more negatively to receiving help in the unstable than in the stable status condition (Nadler and Halabi 2006, Study 2).

Consistent with the presumed role of personal dispositions in this context, the negative reactions of members of the disadvantaged group to help from the advantaged outgroup under conditions of status insecurity were more characteristic of high than low identifiers with the ingroup (Nadler and Halabi 2006, Study 3).

The following experiment in this research program examined the IHSR model's three building blocks simultaneously. The dependent variable was participants' willingness to seek help from the high-status group. Participants were students in an Israeli high school and their identification with their school had been manipulated by having half of them write a short essay on why they liked their school, and the other half on local environmental concerns. They were then instructed to work on a demanding task and told that they could seek autonomy- or dependency-oriented help (hint or full answer, respectively) online from a student in another school. The other high school was located in a different city and was identified as one of the most prestigious in the country. The security of status relations between the two high schools was manipulated by telling half the participants that the gap in academic achievements between their school and the prestigious other school was steadily narrowing, or remained the same over the last ten years (unstable or stable status hierarchy, respectively). The findings provided full support for the predictions of the IHSR model. A significant three-way interaction (stability of status hierarchy × ingroup identification × autonomy/dependency-oriented help) indicated that *when help was autonomy-oriented, participants sought a similar amount of help in all conditions.* When, however, help was *dependency-oriented, high identifiers in the unstable hierarchy cell sought significantly less help than in all other cells.* (Nadler and Halabi 2006, Study 4).

Other research on reluctance by disadvantaged groups to rely on the support of advantaged groups supported the logic of the model. In one study, African Americans who had been helped by a European American evidenced lower self-esteem than those who had not received such help (Schneider et al. 1996). Because this study did not include a control condition, these findings were somewhat ambiguous. This ambiguity was resolved by another experiment that compared reactions to receiving help from the higher-status outgroup to reactions to receiving the same amount of help from an ingroup helper. In this experiment, Arab citizens of Israel had more negative self-views after receiving help from an Israeli Jew compared to an Arab (Halabi et al. 2011). Although neither Schneider et al. (1996) nor Halabi et al. (2011) manipulated or measured perceived security of the relevant status hierarchy, at the time when these studies were conducted (i.e. late twentieth and early twenty-first centuries) neither African Americans nor Israeli Arabs were likely to have regarded their under-privileged status as stable. A more direct demonstration of the role of perceived security is the finding that the more Israeli Arabs saw their disadvantaged position as illegitimate and unstable the lower was their receptivity to help from an Israeli Jew (Halabi et al. 2012).

Regarding the moderating effects of the kind of help, in these experiments, participants had received "assumptive help" that had not been solicited ("proactive help"; see Lee et al. 2018b, p. 121). Assumptive and dependency-oriented help convey a similar message about recipients' weakness and inability to help themselves. Being helped that way by the advantaged outgroup is a humiliating experience for low-status recipients who seek to upgrade the status of their group. The finding that Romanian students in Britain, who had perceived their ingroup's lower status as unstable and changeable, sought only autonomy-oriented help from native British students supports the roles of the structural variable of the perceived stability of the status hierarchy and of kind of help in determining the low-status group's receptivity to help from the high-status one (Onu et al. 2015).

Finally, consistent with the IHSR model, personal characteristics of members of low-status groups affect receptivity to help from high-status groups. Israeli Arabs who scored high on system justification – a dispositional tendency to legitimize the unequal hierarchy (Jost and Kay 2005) – sought dependency-oriented help from Israeli Jews, whereas low scorers sought only autonomy-oriented help (Chernyak-Hai et al. 2014). In the next section, we turn to the opposite direction of intergroup helping relations in a structurally unequal context by considering processes that underlie helping by the advantaged to the disadvantaged.

5.3.3 *The High-Status Group: Giving to the Disadvantaged*

Besides empathy-based assistance, helping extended by the advantaged to the disadvantaged group has been attributed to two psychological mechanisms: guilt-based and defensive helping. Guilt-based helping occurs when the advantaged group views itself as responsible, partially or fully, for the predicaments of the disadvantaged outgroup and tries to make amends (Leach 2002). These guilt feelings do not necessarily represent personal guilt; rather, these are feelings of collective guilt that group members feel, or may be induced to feel, for events that may have occurred even before they were born. This guilt by association is derived from one's membership in a particular group (Branscombe and Miron 2004).

An empirical demonstration of the effects of collective guilt by association on outgroup helping is the finding that European Americans who felt guilty about their group's advantaged position over African Americans (white guilt) expressed greater support for affirmative action (Iyer et al. 2003). Similarly, white South Africans who felt guilty over the wrongdoings of the apartheid regime supported expenditure of funds for social programs that would benefit black South Africans (Klandermans et al. 2008).

The effects of collective guilt on generosity toward the victimized outgroup are moderated by group members' in-group identification. Dutch students who were low identifiers with their national group expressed guilt over wrongdoings committed by the Netherlands in Asia during the colonial era, and supported expenditures by the present day Dutch government for disadvantaged societies in that region. High identifiers, on the other hand, defended against feelings of collective guilt by rejecting the ingroup's responsibility for past wrongdoings, and were less supportive of giving to societies who had formerly suffered from Dutch colonialism (Doosje et al. 1998).

Collective pride rather than collective guilt drives the readiness of high identifiers, who refuse to admit their group's wrongdoings, to help a victimized outgroup. Dutch students, who were high identifiers and had been induced to feel proud of Dutch people who saved Jews during the Second World War were readier to assist present day victims of Nazism. Consistent with the previous findings of Doosje et al. (1998), the willingness of low identifiers to help present-day victims of Nazism was associated with induced collective guilt (i.e. being reminded of the collaboration of Dutch people with the Nazis) (Van Leeuwen et al. 2013).

The research on the effects of collective social emotions, i.e. collective guilt and pride, on helping the disadvantaged assessed readiness for top-down and relatively passive helping (e.g. supporting programs that will benefit the less privileged). A more active and equality-based helping consists of readiness to join the disadvantaged in social action to promote equality. This is likely when members of the advantaged group view the disadvantaged position of the low-status group as violating moral standards they believe in, which causes them to experience moral outrage (Thomas et al. 2009). This is supported by the finding that feelings of moral outrage increased the readiness of members of the advantaged group to join the disadvantaged group in political action to promote equality (Van de Vyver and Abrams 2015). Such joint social action is more likely to yield enduring social change that would benefit the disadvantaged, rather than a temporary amelioration of their predicament. Joint social action is a truly altruistic act by members of the advantaged group, because it is costly to them in that it undermines their own privileged position. In the next section, I address research on defensive helping, which represents the opposite motivation.

5.3.3.1 Defensive Helping: Helping to Protect Ingroup's Status SIT holds that committed group members respond defensively to threats to their group identity – to their group's distinctiveness, its reputation and moral image, and its relative status in an existing structural hierarchy (Ellemers et al. 2002). A common defensive response to such threats is devaluation of the outgroup that poses the threat (Branscombe and Wann 1994). Helping an outgroup can be one vehicle of devaluation. The finding that highly committed Dutch participants whose group's distinctiveness had been threatened (i.e. by joining the EU, the Netherlands lost its unique identity), displayed generosity toward an outgroup in need (victims of flooding) demonstrates how outgroup helping may be used to defuse threats to the ingroup's distinct identity (Van Leeuwen 2007). Similarly, that Scottish participants who had learned that others viewed their group as stingy behaved generously toward an outgroup demonstrates how helping an outgroup can be used to remedy a threat to the ingroup's reputation (Hopkins et al. 2007).

The advantaged ingroup's status is threatened when the outgroup moves upward in the hierarchical ladder, thereby undermining its relative superior position The advantaged group can defend against this threat by maintaining the status quo and its privileged position in it. This can be done by explicit and direct means, such as not allowing the disadvantaged outgroup to obtain tools that will facilitate their upward movement. For example, the high-status group may deny educational opportunities to the low-status group. When moral, legal or other limitations render such explicit efforts difficult, the advantaged group can defend against threats to its position via more implicit means, such as attempting to assert the disadvantaged group's dependency on its help; in a word, defensive helping.

Unlike help that aims to reestablish the ingroup's reputation that is directed towards a group that is unrelated to the threat to the ingroup's prestige/reputation (e.g., Scots labeled as stingy by the English displayed generosity towards the Welsh, Hopkins et al., 2007), defensive help is targeted at the source of the threat to the privileged ingroup's status. Defensive helping is characterized by (i) its target, i.e. the threatening low-status group; (ii) its lack of responsiveness to others' actual needs; and (iii) its dependency-oriented nature. The research program presented below demonstrates these features of defensive helping and, more importantly, the conditions under which it is more likely.

The first experiment used ad hoc groups and demonstrated that participants induced to identify with their ingroup gave more help to an outgroup that posed a threat to the ingroup's status (was said to do better on an important task) than did low identifiers (Nadler et al. 2009, Study 1). The fact that this finding characterized the behavior of high identifiers supports the interpretation that this outgroup helping was driven by the helpers' motivation to protect themselves against threats to collective identity. Further, the artificial nature of these ad hoc groups contributes to the internal validity of the concept of defensive helping.

A second experiment employed real life groups and demonstrated that such help is directed at the source of the threat and is nonresponsive to recipient's actual need for help (Nadler et al. 2009, Study 2). Participants in this experiment, high school students, had received information about the scholastic achievements of their own and two similar local schools. One of these other schools was said to outperform the participants' school, and the other was described as having similar achievements. This created a threatening and non-threatening outgroup, respectively. In a control condition, neither school was a source of threat. Subsequently, participants could help a student who had been presented as being from either the threatening or the non-threatening school. Consistent with the defensive helping hypothesis, participants who identified highly with their school gave significantly more help to a student from a school that had been said to outperform their own. In support of the idea that defensive helping is nonresponsive to the other's need for help, the student from the threatening outgroup was given as much help on difficult as on easy questions, while the student from the non-threatening school received significantly more help on difficult questions.

In the third experiment, defensive helping was examined in the context of structural inequality, where social mobility of the low-status outgroup threatened the structurally advantaged position of the high-status group (Nadler et al. 2009, Study 3). Consistent with the importance assigned to it by the IHSR model, the perceived stability of the status difference between the two groups was manipulated. Further, this experiment examined the role of self-categorization processes by comparing defensive helping when the groups' separate or common identity were salient. Thus, the experiment consisted of a 2 (stable vs. unstable hierarchy) × 3 (separate identities vs. common identity vs. control) between-participants design. Finally, participants could provide the outgroup member who needed help with either dependency- or autonomy-oriented assistance.

Participants were Israeli high school students who had been told they would interact with a student from another school of lower scholastic status in the same region. In the stable hierarchy condition, participants had been told that the scholastic gap between their high-status school and the other school has remained unchanged over the last five years. In the unstable hierarchy condition, they had been told that the scholastic gap between the two schools was steadily narrowing over the same period. Subsequently, to manipulate participants' self-categorization of separate or common school identities, participants were asked to read a short text. In the separate identity condition, participants read about the uniqueness of their school compared to other schools in the region, while in the common identity condition they read about the uniqueness of all schools in the region, compared to schools in other regions of the country. Following these manipulations, participants were asked to help the outgroup member on a difficult analogies task. A major feature of this study was that they could give the outgroup member either the answer to the question or a hint (i.e. dependency- and autonomy-oriented help, respectively).

The findings replicate and extend the understandings proposed by previous research. When the separate identities of the two groups were salient, the participants from the advantaged group responded defensively to the upward movement of the disadvantaged in the unstable, but not stable, hierarchy condition. They experienced it as threatening their advantaged position and provided the disadvantaged group with significantly more dependency-oriented help, thereby seeking to maintain the hierarchical gap.

These findings are consistent with findings of an earlier research, that longtime Canadians who perceived immigrants as a threat to their economic status recommended giving them dependency- rather than autonomy-oriented help (i.e. financial grants vs. professional training) (Jackson and Esses 2000). In the common identity-unstable hierarchy condition, members of the advantaged group gave the disadvantaged group members who had been said to move toward equality much autonomy-oriented help. Thus, under conditions of common identity the information that the disadvantaged group was moving upward was taken as an indication of its positive potential to achieve equality that needed to be supported with empowering help. Under these conditions, the motivation to protect the ingroup's high status was replaced by a motivation to support the low-status group's quest for social equality.

Another demonstration of how perceived common identity disarms status concerns in helping relations between structurally unequal groups comes from research on the willingness of the advantaged to seek help from the disadvantaged. In one experiment, psychology students could seek autonomy- or dependency-oriented help from students of social work (i.e. high and low professional status groups, respectively) under conditions of unstable or stable status hierarchy (Halabi et al. 2014). Consistent with the logic of the IHSR model, the psychology students evidenced relative unwillingness to seek dependency-oriented help from the lower-status group of social work students. When, however, the common identity of the group members as mental health professionals had been made salient, the psychology students indicated relatively high willingness to seek dependency-oriented help from the social work students. Beyond the conceptual significance of these findings for a fuller understanding of intergroup helping relations, they are of much applied importance, as they point the way to minimizing status concerns in intergroup helping interactions and turning them into empowering interactions. From a broader perspective, this research focuses on intergroup helping as either a vehicle for maintaining an unequal status quo or a means to promote greater equality.

Finally, reactions to threats to group status vary across individual group members. In addition to ingroup identification, people's SDO (Sidanius and Pratto 1999) affects their reactions to such threats. High SDO Individuals endorse attitudes and policies that reinforce social hierarchies, while those who score low endorse attitudes and policies that promote equality. Given the nature of defensive helping as a vehicle to maintain unequal hierarchy, high

SDO individuals are expected to employ defensive helping tactics more than would low SDO individuals. Supporting this, when Jews' advantaged position in Israeli society was threatened, high SDO Israeli Jews endorsed giving dependency-oriented help to Israeli Arab students (i.e. the disadvantaged group and source of threat) (Halabi et al. 2008). Thus, defensive helping that seeks to fend off a threat to the existing hierarchy and to one's advantaged position in it is more likely to be employed as a tactic by those who are characteristically disposed to support inequality in interpersonal and intergroup relations.

5.3.3.2 Perceptions of Help Seeking by High- and Low-Status Group Members This section focuses on the effects of the help seeker's status affiliation on the helper's perceptions and the kind of help that is given to them. Imagine a high school teacher asked by two students for help on a school assignment. One request comes from a student of a high socioeconomic status whose parents are well to do professionals and whose address places them in an expensive part of the city. The second request comes from a student of a low SES background whose parents are manual laborers living in a poorer neighborhood in the same city. All other things being equal, will the teacher provide the same kind of help to both students, and if not, what will be the future consequences of the different patterns of help-giving?

Seeking others' help can be perceived by the helper and others as a sign of either weakness or strength. On the one hand, self-reliance and perseverance in the face of difficulties is a marker of strength and motivation, while turning to others under the same circumstances implies weakness and inability to cope. This theme has been amplified in much of the foregoing discussion on seeking and receiving help in both interpersonal and intergroup context. Yet, compared to those who do not seek others' help even when the alternative is failure, those who do may be viewed as coping effectively by employing all available means to overcome their predicament. In fact, in the previous discussion of gender differences in help seeking, the greater willingness of women than men to rely on outside help was conceptualized as *effective* social coping. Importantly, these two opposite meanings assigned to the same act are likely to result in giving different kinds of help in the same situation. When help seeking implies weakness it is likely to result in the provision of dependency-oriented help, but when viewed as an indication of active social coping, it is likely to result in autonomy-oriented assistance.

What determines these alternative interpretations of help seeking? One answer is the help seeker's social status. Broadly defined, social status is any characteristic on which groups are hierarchically ordered as higher or lower and which reflects people's performance expectations (Berger et al. 1985). Thus, regardless of the specific content (gender, skin color, etc.), high status individuals are expected to be more able and perform better than low status individuals. Applied to the present context of help seeking, a help request by a low-status individual is expected to be attributed to his or her chronic lack of ability and to be responded to with dependency-oriented help. The same request by a high-status person is likely to be attributed to a transient difficulty that can be ameliorated by giving the help seeker autonomy-oriented help.

Recent research supported this analysis. In one experiment, participants were exposed to a high- or low-status person who had or had not sought their help in solving a difficult problem. Status was manipulated by information about the problem solver's SES. Consistent with the suggestion that the meaning of seeking help is determined by the status of the help seeker, high-status individuals who had sought help were perceived as more able and less likely to need help in the future than their counterparts who had not sought help. Conversely, low-status individuals who had sought help were perceived as less able and more likely to need help in the future than low-status individuals who had not sought help. These different perceptual patterns affected the kind of help given. The help sought by low-status participants was attributed to their lack of ability and they were given dependency-oriented help (the solution), while high-status help seekers were given autonomy-oriented assistance (a hint) (Nadler and Chernyak-Hai 2014, Study 2).

These findings were corroborated in a study where Italian teachers interacted with six- to eight-year-olds to solve a problem (D'Errico et al. 2011). The latter were either recent immigrants from Romania or native Italian children. The teacher–child interactions were videotaped and analyzed. Consistent with Nadler and Chernyak-Hai (2014), more dependency-oriented help was given to immigrants. Moreover, these low-status children behaved less autonomously than did their Italian counterparts (e.g. did not provide alternatives to the teacher's suggestions), and this lesser autonomy was mediated by the teacher's previous dependency-oriented helping. Leone and her colleagues labeled such helping interactions as "overhelping" – helping driven by the helper's needs or stereotypes rather than the recipient's actual needs (Leone 2009; Leone et al. 2008). These findings represent the vicious cycle of dependency-oriented helping in educational settings. The needy's low status promotes dependency-oriented help, which shapes their future behavior in the passive and dependent direction, thereby further reinforcing their disadvantaged social position.

The findings reported above convey a gloomy message to those seeking social equality. The social dynamic where the status of the needy person determines the kind of help he or she receives reproduces the unequal status by pushing the disadvantaged to the lowly status to which they "belong." Under these circumstances, dependency-oriented assistance helps the disadvantaged stay where they are, and may even push them further down the social ladder.

The last experiment reviewed in this section dispels some of the gloom associated with "overhelping" and "helping them stay where they are." In this experiment, participants rated high- and low-status individuals who had been said to have sought dependency- or autonomy-oriented help ("solve it for me" vs. "show me how to solve it," respectively) (Nadler and Chernyak-Hai 2014, Study 4). The findings send a cautious message of hope: in general, people who had sought autonomy-oriented help were more favorably perceived and better evaluated than those who had sought dependency-oriented help. This was especially so for low-status individuals. When they had asked the helper to "show me and I'll do it" they were perceived as particularly efficacious, motivated, and able to cope.

5.4 Closing Comments: Intergroup Helping

The section on intergroup helping relations began by addressing people's tendency to give more to others in need that belong to their ingroup rather than to an outgroup. This phenomenon was viewed as stemming from one's desire to give more to one's own and less to the "other" – the ingroup favoritism norm and discriminatory helping, respectively. Following a discussion of the implications of either of these two perspectives on intergroup helping, we turned to empathy and interpersonal attraction – the antecedents of helping ingroup and outgroup members, respectively – and to the strategic concern that may underlie giving to an outgroup: ameliorating threats to collective identity. The lesser willingness to give to stigmatized racial or ethnic groups was conceptualized as reflecting "aversive racism." Research indicates that people are likely to reveal their prejudices by declining to help members of such groups when the social costs of doing so are low.

A final subsection considered how inducing common identity between the ingroup and outgroup facilitates outgroup helping.

The second section was devoted to intergroup helping relations in a structurally unequal context. Research conducted within the IHSR model supported the idea that intergroup helping relations between structurally unequal groups may be a social mechanism for the disadvantaged group to either reinforce or challenge existing inequality by receiving or declining the advantaged group's help, respectively. Looking at the other side of the divide between advantaged and disadvantaged groups, high-status groups may use "generosity" or give help in a way that reproduces inequality. Relying on social identity theory, these processes are affected by characteristics of the existing social structure (security of status relations) and those of group members' social identity (ingroup commitment). Further, consistent with theorizing on helping relations, this research has underscored the different meanings and implications of dependency- and autonomy-oriented help in this context.

The consideration of helping relations between structurally unequal groups suggests a close link between intergroup helping and social change. One question concerns the conditions under which the high-status group will oppose change by using "soft" and "indirect" means such as maintaining the outgroup's dependency on its help, and the conditions under which it will use more "direct" and "harsh" means to maintain the unequal status quo (discrimination). The answer may depend on the normative context. If discrimination and other direct means are frowned upon, the high-status group may resort to subtler means to maintain its superiority. Giving the low-status group dependency-oriented help is one such tactic. This is more likely to occur at the first stages of social change, when inequality is no longer viewed as legitimate, yet the social structure has not yet changed. The reluctance of the disadvantaged to depend on the advantaged group's help, particularly when it is dependency-oriented, may be an early harbinger of such change. These social dynamics represent a fertile ground for intergroup misunderstandings that might exacerbate intergroup tensions. In fact, intergroup animosity may increase when the advantaged group's generosity is spurned by the low-status group (Nadler et al. 2009). The links between helping and social change need to be explored and better understood by future research and theory.

As I close this section, note that the distinction between intergroup and interpersonal helping relations should not be viewed as an impermeable wall. First, as emphasized by social identity and self-categorization theories, individuals carry the groups they belong to in their heads. When two people's social identities are salient what is objectively a helping interaction between two persons is subjectively an intergroup interaction. Second, many of the processes used to describe intergroup helping relations are also applicable to the analysis of interpersonal helping. For example, status differences between two individuals (e.g. employer and employee) may also be stable or unstable, thereby affecting helping relations in a similar way to that described by the IHSR model in the intergroup context. In fact, although the specific relevant variable may vary between the two levels of analysis (e.g. self-esteem and ingroup commitment in interpersonal and intergroup interactions, respectively), the processes that affect helping in structurally unequal contexts are the same. The discussion of interpersonal and intergroup helping corresponds to the beginning and concluding sections of the entire book. It opens the door to the next, and final, section that will summarize main themes, and raise dilemmas and avenues of future research about giving, seeking and receiving help.

6

Concluding Comments

The view of giving and receiving help as reflecting, and impacting, on solidarity and hierarchy in interpersonal and intergroup relations has been a dominant theme throughout the book. We conclude by revisiting these two aspects in helping relations and continue to the present emphasis on the need to go beyond the help/no help distinction in this research context. Finally, we underline the importance of these conceptual distinctions for the transformation of helping interactions into equality-based social relations.

6.1 Solidarity and Hierarchy in Helping Relations

Helping relations have been conceptualized as the stage on which two basic human needs play out: the need for belongingness and the need for independence. The need for belongingness is manifested in the webs of solidarity that bind interpersonal and intragroup relationships together, and is expressed in giving and the willing receiving from others with whom we share a feeling of belongingness. Under certain circumstances, in some sociocultural contexts and for some people, this shared belongingness is narrow and restricted to family and close friends, while in others, and for other people, it is extended to include all humanity, or even all living creatures. The point is that once shared belongingness exists, people are likely to help others in need and be receptive to their help.

Social Psychology of Helping Relations: Solidarity and Hierarchy, First Edition. Arie Nadler.

From this perspective, the first part of the book's focus on the help-giving question centers on social psychological research aiming to identify variables and processes that determine the boundaries of shared belongingness, thereby affecting willingness to help and be helped. This aspect of helping relations, which resonates with concepts such as "generosity" and "caring," centers on the *social* in human relationships, while the need for independence, which emanates from people's desire for individual competence and relative excellence, centers on the *individual* aspect in social behavior. It reflects people's motivation to excel in what they do, thereby expressing their individuality.

This desire for individual achievement is inconsistent with reliance on others' help, and being on the receiving end of help is associated with a lower position on the social hierarchy. This hierarchy may be temporary or permanent and represent a structural aspect of interpersonal and intergroup relations. Yet, regardless of the hierarchy's relative permanence, giving is associated with prestige and higher status while receiving is associated with relative incompetence and lower status. The second part of the book that focuses on recipient reactions and intergroup helping relations centers on this hierarchical aspect in helping.

6.2 Beyond the Help/No Help Dichotomy

As noted previously, the present book goes beyond the dichotomy between helping and not helping to consider the different kinds of help that are given, sought or received. The key distinction considered here – between autonomy- and dependency-oriented help – implies that that the needy person is not a passive receptacle of the helper's generosity. Rather, when help is autonomy-oriented, the recipient is viewed as an active and competent actor who experiences a transient difficulty that can be remedied by relying on others' instructions or advice on how to cope by oneself. Autonomy-oriented help allows the recipient to rely on others *and* maintain a sense of independence. Since it consists of providing tools or teaching skills, it increases the prospects for the recipient's future self-reliance, compared to dependency-oriented help that simply solves the problem. The latter implies that the person in need is relatively incompetent and chronically dependent and is unlikely to promote future self-reliance. Rather, it represents an additional link in a chain of long-term dependency.

The distinction between autonomy- and dependency-oriented help has important conceptual and applied implications demonstrated throughout the book. First, it once more raises the question with which the book opens: What is help? Is it an act that reduces the needy's current predicament, or one that increases his or her prospects for future self-reliance? Helping solve the recipient's predicament represents dependency-oriented help and is beneficial for the helpers: it improves their affect and has positive effects on their self-esteem and overall well-being. Dependency-oriented help is also beneficial for recipients: it ameliorates their difficulties and increases their overall well-being – albeit only in the present and immediate future. Yet if help means perpetuating or increasing the likelihood that the recipient would need help in the future, it is doubtful whether dependency-oriented help benefits the recipient. Becoming used to relying on others' benevolence to cope with difficulties is unlikely to increase the prospects of future self-reliance.

Another implication concerns the empathy-helping link. Most, if not all, past research on that link has focused on the binary choice of helping vs. not helping as the main dependent measure. Thus, voluminous research indicates that when people are dispositionally empathic toward others, or are situationally induced to be so, empathy results in greater readiness to harness resources and energies to remedy the needy's immediate predicament (Batson 2011). Yet, if the goal of helping is to reduce the likelihood that recipients would depend on help in the future (i.e. increase their self-reliance) rather than ameliorate their current difficulties, the effects of empathy on helping would be to give *less* rather than more help. In fact, the empathic person would give the needy partial help that would increase their prospects of future self-reliance rather than solve their current difficulties.

Another, and related, important distinction is between the "negotiating" and "didactic" models of helping relations. The negotiating model presupposes the needy as active and able individuals, while the didactic model views them as passive and relatively incompetent. In the negotiating model, help is negotiated rather than given top-down. The person in need is expected to articulate his or her wishes and the kind of help that he or she prefers, and the helper is expected to be willing to tailor the help accordingly. In didactic helping relations, on the other hand, the helper knows best. He or she provides help without negotiating with the recipient, so that their help is considered assumptive. It is given by the helper without having been asked for it, and is therefore likely to be self-threatening for the recipient and limit their perceived freedom.

From a broad perspective, *dependency-oriented*, *didactic*, and *assumptive* help seek to solve the presenting problem and are therefore oriented toward the present or the immediate future. The persons in need who seek or accepts such help is motivated to ease their present predicament. *Autonomy-oriented*, *negotiated*, and *non-assumptive* help are all future oriented. The recipients' long-term self-reliance rather than their immediate relief is at focus.

Admittedly, sometimes what the needy person must receive is dependency-oriented, assumptive help that is provided didactically. For example, the starving person needs a loaf of bread rather than learning how to grow wheat. Yet such extreme scenarios are rare. The person in need who prefers autonomy-oriented assistance that is negotiated with the helper is motivated to reduce the probability that they would become or remain dependent on others in the future. Importantly, these future-oriented helping interactions regard assisting others as a social interaction between equals rather than an interaction between a resourceful, omniscient helper and a helpless recipient. In terms of Alan Fiske's relational models, this suggests reshaping helping interactions from being hierarchical relational systems to being relationships based on equality-matching or communal-sharing relational assumptions.

6.3 From Helping to Equality-Based Interactions

What determines whether a negotiated future-oriented or a didactic present-oriented model of helping is adopted? One such determinant is the needy's social status. The book shows that when people in need are affiliated with a lower social class or a stigmatized group, the helper tends to adopt a didactic model of helping. These individuals are more likely to receive dependency-oriented help than their more advantaged counterparts, and their seeking of help is taken as evidence of their inability, whereas the same help seeking by the more advantaged is taken as evidence of their motivation to employ all possible avenues to avoid failure. These and other similar phenomena reviewed in the book render helping relations as contributing to potential vicious cycle of inequality. Because giving help as a subtle tactic to maintain inequality are clad with the bright robes of benevolence, they are more dangerous than direct and explicit means of maintaining inequality (e.g. discrimination).

An important task for social psychological research in this area is to identify the processes and variables that will turn helping between the haves and have nots into cooperation between differentially resourceful but *equal* individuals. Some of the ways of doing so are addressed in this book. For example, cognitively redrawing group boundaries to include helper and recipient within the same overarching social identity transforms helping from being dependency-oriented to being autonomy-oriented, thereby turning helping into an empowering event that decreases the prospects of future dependency. Also, research suggests that inducing members of low-status or stigmatized groups to seek autonomy-oriented help leads helpers to adopt a negotiating model of helping relations toward them, thereby breaking the aforementioned vicious cycle. These examples, and other findings and concepts reviewed in this book, amplify the link between helping relations and social change and highlight the applied importance of the findings and concepts reviewed.

We began this book by noting that research on helping has been driven from its inception by two goals: gaining basic knowledge on social behavior, and contributing to a more caring society. The present emphasis on helping as reflecting human solidarity and hierarchical relations adds to the goal of creating a more caring society that of creating an equal society. The cultural revolution of the 1960s, when the field began to take shape, encouraged to application of knowledge gained by social psychological research to generate social change. Today, the need to create a caring society is as pressing as ever. The world continues to witness extreme and publicly advertised acts of brutality and violence. Beheadings of reporters, children suffocating from poisonous gas, and barbarous terrorist attacks against innocent civilians. These, together with a refugee crisis of historical proportions, raise anxieties that give rise to ideologies that justify inequality, discrimination, and alienation toward the other. Dependency-oriented, didactic and assumptive models of helping relations may inadvertently, or intentionally, reinforce these negative social tendencies. Therefore, social psychological research on interpersonal and intergroup helping needs to go beyond the question of generosity to contribute to equality- and solidarity-based helping relations between differentially resourceful individuals and groups.

References

Abele, A.E., Cuddy, A.J.C., Judd, C.M., and Yzerbyt, V.Y. (2008). Fundamental dimensions of social judgment. *European Journal of Social Psychology* 38 (7): 1063–1065. https://doi.org/10.1002/ejsp.574.

Abouserie, R. (1995). Self-esteem and achievement motivation as determinants of students' approaches to studying. *Studies in Higher Education* 20 (1): 19–26. https://doi.org/10.1080/03075079512331381770.

Acker, J. (2006). Inequality regimes: gender, class, and race in organizations. *Gender & Society* 20 (4): 441–464. https://doi.org/10.1177/0891243206289499.

Addis, M.E. and Mahalik, J.R. (2003). Men, masculinity, and the contexts of help seeking. *American Psychologist* 58 (1): 5–14. https://doi.org/10.1037/0003-066X.58.1.5.

Ahmed, A.M. (2009). Are religious people more prosocial? A Quasi-experimental study with *Madrasah* Pupils in a rural community in India. *Journal for the Scientific Study of Religion* 48 (2): 368–374. https://doi.org/10.1111/j.1468-5906.2009.01452.x.

Ahmed, A.M. and Salas, O. (2011). Implicit influences of Christian religious representations on dictator and prisoner's dilemma game decisions. *The Journal of Socio-Economics* 40 (3): 242–246. https://doi.org/10.1016/j.socec.2010.12.013.

Aknin, L.B., Dunn, E.N., Whillans, A.V. et al. (2013). Making a difference matters: impact unlocks the emotional benefits of prosocial spending. *Journal of Economic Behavior and Organization* 88: 90–95. http://dx.doi.org/10.1016/j.jebo.2013.01.008.

Aknin, L.B., Sandstorm, G.M., Dunn, E.W., and Norton, M.I. (2011). It's the recipient that counts: spending money on strong social ties leads to

Social Psychology of Helping Relations: Solidarity and Hierarchy, First Edition. Arie Nadler.

greater happiness than spending on weak social ties. *PLoS One* 6: e17018. http://dx.doi.org/10.1371/journal.pone.0017018.

Algoe, S.B. (2012). Find, remind, and bind: the functions of gratitude in everyday relationships: gratitude in relationships. *Social and Personality Psychology Compass* 6 (6): 455–469. https://doi.org/10.1111/j.1751-9004.2012.00439.x.

Algoe, S.B. and Haidt, J. (2009). Witnessing excellence in action: the "other-praising" emotions of elevation, gratitude, and admiration. *The Journal of Positive Psychology* 4 (2): 105–127. https://doi.org/10.1080/17439760802650519.

Algoe, S.B., Haidt, J., and Gable, S.L. (2008). Beyond reciprocity: Gratitude and relationships in everyday life. *Emotion* 8 (3): 425–429. https://doi.org/10.1037/1528-3542.8.3.425.

Altemeyer, B. (1998). The other "Authoritarian Personality". *Advances in Experimental Social Psychology* 30: 47–92. https://doi.org/10.1016/S0065-2601(08)60382-2.

Alvarez, K. and van Leeuwen, E. (2011). To teach or to tell? Consequences of receiving help from experts and peers. *European Journal of Social Psychology* 41 (3): 397–402. https://doi.org/10.1002/ejsp.789.

Ames, C. (1992). Classrooms: goals, structures, and student motivation. *Journal of Educational Psychology* 84: 261–271. http://dx.doi.org/10.1037/0022-0663.84.3.261.

Anderson, C. and Galinsky, A.D. (2006). Power, optimism, and risk-taking. *European Journal of Social Psychology* 36 (4): 511–536. https://doi.org/10.1002/ejsp.324.

Anik, L., Aknin, L.B., Norton, M.I. et al. (2013). Prosocial spending increases job satisfaction and organizational commitment. *PLoS ONE* 8 (9): e75509.

Annas, J. (1977). Plato and Aristotle on friendship and altruism. *Mind* 86 (344): 532–554.

Applebaum, L.D. (2001). The influence of perceived deservingness on policy decisions regarding aid to the poor. *Political Psychology* 22 (3): 419–442. https://doi.org/10.1111/0162-895X.00248.

Archer, J. and Lloyd, B. (2002). *Sex and gender*, 2e. New York, NY: Cambridge University Press.

Aristotle and Irwin, T. (1985). *Nicomachean Ethics*. Indianapolis, Ind: Hackett Publishing Company.

Armstrong, B.F. and Kammrath, L.K. (2015). Depth and breadth tactics in support seeking. *Social Psychological and Personality Science* 6 (1): 39–46. https://doi.org/10.1177/1948550614546049.

Aronfreed, J. (1968). Aversive control of socialization. *Nebraska Symposium on Motivation* 16: 271–320.

Asser, E.S. (1978). Social class and help-seeking behavior. *American Journal of Community Psychology* 6 (5): 465–475. https://doi.org/10.1007/BF00941422.

Axelrod, R. and Hamilton, W.D. (1981). The evolution of cooperation. *Science* 211: 1390–1396.

Bacharach, S.B., Bamberger, P.A., and Sonnenstuhl, W.J. (2002). Driven to drink: managerial control, work-related risk factors, and employee problem drinking. *Academy of Management Journal* 45 (4): 637–658. https://doi.org/10.5465/3069302.

Bakan, D. (1966). *The Duality of Human Existence: An Essay on Psychology and Religion*. Oxford, England: Rand Mcnally.

Balliet, D., Li, N.P., and Joireman, J. (2011). Relating trait self-control and forgiveness within prosocials and proselfs: compensatory versus synergistic models. *Journal of Personality and Social Psychology* 101 (5): 1090–1105. https://doi.org/10.1037/a0024967.

Baltes, M.M. (1995). Dependency in old age: gains and losses. *Current Directions in Psychological Science* 4 (1): 14–19. https://doi.org/10.1111/1467-8721.ep10770949.

Bandura, A. (2000). Exercise of human agency through collective efficacy. *Current Directions in Psychological Science* 9 (3): 75–78. https://doi.org/10.1111/1467-8721.00064.

Bandura, A., Caprara, G.V., Barbaranelli, C. et al. (2003). Role of affective self-regulatory efficacy in diverse spheres of psychosocial functioning. *Child Development* 74 (3): 769–782. https://doi.org/10.1111/1467-8624.00567.

Baron, R.A. and Byrne, D. (1987). *Social Psychology: Understanding Human Interaction*, 5e. Needham Heights, MA, US: Allyn & Bacon.

Baron, R.A. and Byrne, D. (1987). *Social Psychology: Understanding human interaction*, 5e. Needham heights, Mass: Allyn & Bacon.

Baron, R.A., Byrne, D., and Branscombe, N.R. (2006). Upper saddle river. In: *Social Psychology*, 11e. New Jersey: Pearson Education.

Baron, R.A., Byrne, D.E., and Branscombe, N.R. (2007). *Mastering Social Psychology*. Boston; London: Pearson/Allyn and Bacon.

Baron, J. and Ritov, I. (2009). Chapter 4 protected values and omission bias as deontological judgments. *Psychology of Learning and Motivation* 50: 133–167. https://doi.org/10.1016/S0079-7421(08)00404-0.

Baron-Cohen, S. (2003). *The Essential Difference: The Truth About the Male and Female Brain*. New York, NY, US: Basic Books.

Bar-Tal, D., Nadler, A., and Blechman, N. (1980). The relationship between Israeli children's helping behavior and their perception of parents' socialization practices. *The Journal of Social Psychology* 111 (2): 159–167.

Bartlett, M.Y. and DeSteno, D. (2006). Gratitude and prosocial behavior: helping when it costs you. *Psychological Science* 17 (4): 319–325. https://doi.org/10.1111/j.1467-9280.2006.01705.x.

Bartz, J.A., Zaki, J., Bolger, N., and Ochsner, K.N. (2011). Social effects of oxytocin in humans: Context and person matter. *Trends in Cognitive Science* 15: 301–309.

Batson, C. (2015). The egoism-altruism debate: a psychological perspective. In: *Caring Economics: Conversations on Altruism and Compassion, between Scientists, Economists, and the Dalai Lama* (eds. T. Singer and M. Ricard), 15–25. New York: Picador.

Batson, C.D. (1998). Altruism and prosocial behavior. In: *The Handbook of Social Psychology*, 4e (eds. D.T. Gilbert, S.T. Fiske and G. Lindzey), 282–315. Boston, New York: McGraw-Hill; Distributed exclusively by Oxford University Press.

Batson, C.D., Duncan, B.D., Ackerman, P. et al. (1981). Is empathic emotion a source of altruistic motivation? *Journal of Personality and Social Psychology* 40: 290–302. http://dx.doi.org/10.1037/0022-3514.40.2.290.

Batson, C.D., Turk, C., Shaw, L.L., and Klein, T.R. (1995). Information function of empathic emotion: Learning that we value the other's welfare. *Journal of Personality and Social Psychology* 68: 300–313.

Batson, C.D., Lishner, D.A., Cook, J., and Sawyer, S. (2005). Similarity and nurturance: two possible sources of empathy for strangers. *Basic and Applied Social Psychology* 27 (1): 15–25. https://doi.org/10.1207/s15324834basp2701_2.

Batson, D.C. (2011). *Altruism in humans*. New York, NY: Oxford University Press.

Baumeister, R.F. and Leary, M.R. (1995). The need to belong: desire for interpersonal attachments as a fundamental human motivation. *Psychological Bulletin* 117 (3): 497–529. https://doi.org/10.1037/0033-2909.117.3.497.

Bem, S.L. (1974). The measurement of psychological androgyny. *Journal of Consulting and Clinical Psychology* 42 (2): 155–162. https://doi.org/10.1037/h0036215.

Ben-Ner, A., McCall, B.P., Stephane, M., and Wang, H. (2009). Identity and in-group/out-group differentiation in work and giving behaviors: experimental evidence. *Journal of Economic Behavior & Organization* 72 (1): 153–170. https://doi.org/10.1016/j.jebo.2009.05.007.

Benson, P.L., Karabenick, S.A., and Lerner, R.M. (1976). Pretty pleases: the effects of physical attractiveness, race, and sex on receiving help. *Journal of Experimental Social Psychology* 12 (5): 409–415. https://doi.org/10.1016/0022-1031(76)90073-1.

Bentham, J. (1948). *A Fragment on Government and an Introduction to the Principles of Morals and Legislation*. Blackwell.

Berger, J., Wagner, D.G., and Zelditch, M. (1985). Theoretical and metatheoretical themes in expectation states theory. *Perspectives on Sociological Theory* 2: 148–168.

Berkowitz, L. and Daniels, L.R. (1963). Responsibility and dependency. *The Journal of Abnormal and Social Psychology* 66 (5): 429–436. https://doi.org/10.1037/h0049250.

Berkowitz, L. and Daniels, L.R. (1964). Affecting the salience of the social responsibility norm: effects of past help on the response to dependency relationships. *The Journal of Abnormal and Social Psychology* 68 (3): 275–281. https://doi.org/10.1037/h0040164.

Berkowitz, L. and Friedman, P. (1967). Some social class differences in helping behavior. *Journal of Personality and Social Psychology* 5: 217–225.

Bierhoff, H.-W. (2002). *Prosocial Behaviour*. Hove: Psychology Press.

Blader, S.L. and Chen, Y.-R. (2012). Differentiating the effects of status and power: a justice perspective. *Journal of Personality and Social Psychology* 102 (5): 994–1014. https://doi.org/10.1037/a0026651.

Blau, P.M. (1963). *The Dynamics of Bureaucracy: Study of Interpersonal Relations in Two Government Agencies*, Rev. ed. Chicago: University of Chicago Press.

Bloom, J.R. (1996). Social support of the cancer patient and the role of the family. In: *Cancer and the Family* (eds. L. Baider, C.L. Cooper and A.K. De-Nour), 53–70. Oxford, UK: Wiley.

Boehm, C. (1999). The natural selection of altruistic traits. *Human Nature* 10 (3): 205–252. https://doi.org/10.1007/s12110-999-1003-z.

Boehm, C. (2012). Costs and benefits in hunter-gatherer punishment. *Behavioral and Brain Sciences* 35 (01): 19–20. https://doi.org/10.1017/S0140525X11001403.

Boehm, J., Lyubomirsky, S., & Sheldon, K. (2012). The role of need satisfying emotions in a positive activity intervention. *Unpublished Raw Data*.

Bolger, N. and Amarel, D. (2007). Effects of social support visibility on adjustment to stress: experimental evidence. *Journal of Personality and Social Psychology*92(3):458–475.https://doi.org/10.1037/0022-3514.92.3.458.

Boone, J.L. (1998). The evolution of magnanimity: when is it better to give than to receive? *Human Nature* 9 (1): 1–21. https://doi.org/10.1007/s12110-998-1009-y.

Bornstein, D. (2007). *How to Change the World: Social Entrepreneurs and the Power of New Ideas* (Updated Edition). New York: Oxford University Press, USA.

Bornstein, R.F. (2011). An interactionist perspective on interpersonal dependency. *Current Directions in Psychological Science* 20 (2): 124–128. https://doi.org/10.1177/0963721411403121.

Bourdieu, P. (1989). Social space and symbolic power. *Sociological Theory* 7 (1): 14. https://doi.org/10.2307/202060.

Bowersox, M.S. (1981). Women in corrections: competence, competition, and the social responsibility norm. *Criminal Justice and Behavior* 8 (4): 491–499. https://doi.org/10.1177/009385488100800407.

Bowlby, J. (1973). *Attachment and Loss: Separation: Anxiety and Anger (Vol. 2)*. New York: Basic Books.

Branscombe, N.R. and Miron, A.M. (2004). Interpreting the ingroup's negative actions toward another group. In: *The Social Life of Emotions* (eds. L.Z. Tiedens and C.W. Leach), 314–335. Cambridge: Cambridge University Press.

Branscombe, N.R. and Wann, D.L. (1994). Collective self-esteem consequences of outgroup derogation when a valued social identity is on trial. *European Journal of Social Psychology* 24 (6): 641–657. https://doi.org/10.1002/ejsp.2420240603.

Brehm, J.W. (1989). Psychological reactance: theory and applications. *NA - Advances in Consumer Research* 16: 72–75.

Brehm, J.W. (1966). *A Theory of Psychological Reactance*. New York: Academic Press.

Brewer, M.B. (1999). The psychology of prejudice: ingroup love and outgroup hate? *Journal of Social Issues* 55 (3): 429–444. https://doi.org/10.1111/0022-4537.00126.

Brickman, P., Rabinowitz, V.C., Karuza, J. et al. (1982). Models of helping and coping. *American Psychologist* 37 (4): 368–384.

Brown, J.L., Dow, D.D., Brown, E.R., and Brown, S.D. (1978). Effects of helpers on feeding of nestlings in the grey-crowned Babbler (Pomatostomus temporalis). *Behavioral Ecology and Sociobiology* 4 (1): 43–59. https://doi.org/10.1007/BF00302560.

Brown, S.L., Brown, R.M., House, J.S., and Smith, D.M. (2008). Coping with spousal loss: Potential buffering effects of self-reported helping behavior. *Personality and Social Psychology Bulletin* 34: 849–861.

Bryan, J.H. and Test, M.A. (1967). Models and helping: naturalistic studies in aiding behavior. *Journal of Personality and Social Psychology* 6 (4, Pt.1): 400–407. https://doi.org/10.1037/h0024826.

Buckley, K.E. and Anderson, C.A. (2006). A theoretical model of the effects and consequences of playing video games. In: *Playing video games: Motives, responses and consequences* (eds. P. Vordere and B. Jennings), 363–378. Mahwah, NJ: Erlbaum.

Burnstein, E., Crandall, C., and Kitayama, S. (1994). Some neo-Darwinian decision rules for altruism: Weighing cues for inclusive fitness as a function of the biological importance of the decision. *Journal of Personality and Social Psychology* 67 (5): 773–789. https://doi.org/10.1037/0022-3514.67.5.773.

Butler, R. (2007). Teachers' achievement goal orientations and associations with teachers' help seeking: Examination of a novel approach to teacher motivation. *Journal of Educational Psychology* 99 (2): 241–252. https://doi.org/10.1037/0022-0663.99.2.241.

Butler, R. and Neuman, O. (1995). Effects of task and ego achievement goals on help-seeking behaviors and attitudes. *Journal of Educational Psychology* 87 (2): 261–271. https://doi.org/10.1037/0022-0663.87.2.261.

Byrne, D.E. (1971). *The Attraction Paradigm*. New York: Acad. Press.

Canter, D., Breaux, J., and Sime, J. (1980). Domestic, multiple occupancy, and hospital fires. In: *Fires and Human Behaviour* (ed. D. Canter), 117–136. New York: Wiley.

Caporael, L. and Brewer, M. (1990). We ARE Darwinians, and this is what the fuss is all about. *Motivation and Emotion* 14 (4): 287–293. https://doi.org/10.1007/BF00996186.

Carlisle, T.R. and Zahavi, A. (1986). Helping at the nest, allofeeding and social status in immature arabian babblers. *Behavioral Ecology and Sociobiology* 18 (5): 339–351. https://doi.org/10.1007/BF00299665.

Carlo, G., Okun, M.A., Knight, G.P., and de Guzman, M.R.T. (2005). The interplay of traits and motives on volunteering: agreeableness, extraversion and prosocial value motivation. *Personality and Individual Differences* 38 (6): 1293–1305. https://doi.org/10.1016/j.paid.2004.08.012.

Carpenter, T.P. and Marshall, M.A. (2009). An examination of religious priming and intrinsic religious motivation in the moral hypocrisy paradigm. *Journal for the Scientific Study of Religion* 48 (2): 386–393. https://doi.org/10.1111/j.1468-5906.2009.01454.x.

Cassidy, J. (2000). Adult romantic attachments: a developmental perspective on individual differences. *Review of General Psychology* 4 (2): 111–131. https://doi.org/10.1037//1089-2680.4.2.111.

Čehajić, S., Brown, R., and González, R. (2009). What do I care? Perceived ingroup responsibility and dehumanization as predictors of empathy felt for the victim group. *Group Processes & Intergroup Relations* 12 (6): 715–729. https://doi.org/10.1177/1368430209347727.

Chalmers, D.M. (2013). *And the Crooked Places made Straight: The Struggle for Social Change in the 1960s* (Second edition updated). Baltimore: The Johns Hopkins University Press.

Cheng, H.-L., McDermott, R.C., and Lopez, F.G. (2015). Mental health, self-stigma, and help-seeking intentions among emerging adults: an attachment perspective. *The Counseling Psychologist* 43 (3): 463–487. https://doi.org/10.1177/0011000014568203.

Chernyak-Hai, L., Halabi, S., and Nadler, A. (2014). "Justified dependency": effects of perceived stability of social hierarchy and level of system justification on help-seeking behavior of low-status group members. *Group Processes & Intergroup Relations* 17 (4): 420–435. https://doi.org/10.1177/1368430213507320.

Chuah, S.-H., Hoffmann, R., Jones, M., and Williams, G. (2009). An economic anatomy of culture: attitudes and behaviour in inter- and intranational ultimatum game experiments. *Journal of Economic Psychology* 30 (5): 732–744. https://doi.org/10.1016/j.joep.2009.06.004.

Cialdini, R.B., Darby, B.L., and Vincent, J.E. (1973). Transgression and altruism: a case for hedonism. *Journal of Experimental Social Psychology* 9 (6): 502–516. https://doi.org/10.1016/0022-1031(73)90031-0.

Cialdini, R.B. and Trost, M.R. (1998). Social influence: social norms, conformity, and compliance. In: *The Handbook of Social Psychology*, 4e (eds. D.T. Gilbert, S.T. Fiske and G. Lindzey), 151–192. Boston, New York: McGraw-Hill; Distributed exclusively by Oxford University Press.

Clark, M.S. and Mills, J. (1993). The difference between communal and exchange relationships: what it is and is not. *Personality and Social Psychology Bulletin* 19 (6): 684–691. https://doi.org/10.1177/0146167293196003.

Clark, M.S. and Mills, J.R. (2012). Chapter 38: A theory of communal (and exchange) relationships. In: *Handbook of Theories of Social Psychology*, vol. 2 (eds. P.A.M.V. Lange, A.W. Kruglanski and E.T. Higgins). Los Angeles: SAGE. Retrieved from http://libproxy.wustl.edu/login?url=https://search.credoreference.com/content/title/sageuksocpsyii.

Collins, N.L. and Feeney, B.C. (2000). A safe haven: an attachment theory perspective on support seeking and caregiving in intimate relationships. *Journal of Personality and Social Psychology* 78 (6): 1053–1073. https://doi.org/10.1037/0022-3514.78.6.1053.

Cosmides, L. and Tooby, J. (1995). Cognitive adaptaions for social exchange. In: *The Adapted Mind: Evolutionary Psychology and the Generation of Culture* (ed. J.H. Barkow), 163–224. New York: Oxford University Press.

Costa, P.T. and McCrae, R.R. (2009). The five-factor model and the NEO Inventories. In: *Oxford Handbook of Personality Assessment* (ed. J.N. Butcher), 299–322. New York, NY: Oxford University Press.

Côté, S., Piff, P.K., and Willer, R. (2013). For whom do the ends justify the means? Social class and utilitarian moral judgment. *Journal of Personality and Social Psychology* 104 (3): 490–503. https://doi.org/10.1037/a0030931.

Cronin, H. (1991). *The Ant and the Peacock: Altruism and Sexual Selection from Darwin to Today* (Reprinted). Cambridge: Cambridge University Press.

Crosby, F., Bromley, S., and Saxe, L. (1980). Recent unobtrusive studies of black and white discrimination and prejudice: a literature review. *Psychological Bulletin* 87 (3): 546–563. https://doi.org/10.1037/0033-2909.87.3.546.

Crosby, F.J. and Clayton, S. (2001). Affirmative action: psychological contributions to policy. *Analyses of Social Issues and Public Policy* 1 (1): 71–87. https://doi.org/10.1111/1530-2415.00004.

Cross, S.E. and Madson, L. (1997). Models of the self: self-construals and gender. *Psychological Bulletin* 122 (1): 5–37. https://doi.org/10.1037/0033-2909.122.1.5.

Damrosch, L. (2007). *Jean-Jacques Rousseau: Restless Genius* (First Mariner Books edition). Boston, New York: Houghton Mifflin Company.

Darby, B.W. and Schlenker, B.R. (1989). Children's reactions to transgressions: effects of the actor's apology, reputation and remorse. *British Journal of Social Psychology* 28 (4): 353–364. https://doi.org/10.1111/j.2044-8309.1989.tb00879.x.

Darley, J.M. and Batson, C.D. (1973). "From Jerusalem to Jericho": a study of situational and dispositional variables in helping behavior. *Journal of Personality and Social Psychology* 27 (1): 100–108. https://doi.org/10.1037/h0034449.

Darley, J.M. and Latane, B. (1968). Bystander intervention in emergencies: diffusion of responsibility. *Journal of Personality and Social Psychology* 8 (4, Pt.1): 377–383. https://doi.org/10.1037/h0025589.

Darwin, C. (1871). *The descent of man and selection in relation to sex.* London, England: Murray.

Darwin, C. (1982). *The Origin of Species by Means of Natural Selection, or, the Preservation of Favoured Races in the Struggle for Life.* Harmondsworth: Penguin.

Davis, M.H. (1994). *Empathy: A social psychological approach.* Boulder, CO: Westview Press.

Davis, M.H., Mitchell, K.V., Hall, J.A. et al. (1999). Empathy, expectations, and situational preferences: personality influences on the decision to participate in volunteer helping behaviors. *Journal of Personality* 67 (3): 469–503. https://doi.org/10.1111/1467-6494.00062.

Dawkins, R. (1976/2006). *The Selfish Gene: With a New Introduction by the Author.* UK: Oxford University Press.

de Guzman, M.R.T., Carlo, G., and Pope Edwards, C. (2008). Prosocial behaviors in context: examining the role of children's social companions.

International Journal of Behavioral Development 32 (6): 522–530. https://doi.org/10.1177/0165025408095557.

Derrida, J. (1992). *Given time: I. Counterfeit money*. Chicago: Chicago University Press.

De Steno, D., Li, Y., Dickens, L., and Lerner, J.S. (2014). Gratitude: A tool for reducing economic impatience. *Psychological Science* 25: 1262–1267.

De Tocqueville, A. (1956). *Democracy in America: Specially Edited and Abridged for the Modern Reader*. New American Library.

de Waal, F. (2006). The animal roots of human morality. *New Scientist* 192 (2573): 60–61. https://doi.org/10.1016/S0262-4079(06)60737-9.

de Waal, F.B.M., Macedo, S., and Ober, J. (2009). *Primates and Philosophers: How Morality Evolved*. Princeton, N.J.; Woodstock: Princeton University Press.

Deci, E.L. and Ryan, R.M. (2008). Hedonia, eudaimonia, and well-being: an introduction. *Journal of Happiness Studies* 9 (1): 1–11. https://doi.org/10.1007/s10902-006-9018-1.

Deelstra, J.T., Peeters, M.C.W., Schaufeli, W.B. et al. (2003). Receiving instrumental support at work: when help is not welcome. *Journal of Applied Psychology* 88 (2): 324–331. https://doi.org/10.1037/0021-9010.88.2.324.

Demoulin, S., Nadler, A., Halabi, S., and Harpaz-Gorodeisky, G. (eds.) (2009). Intergoup helping as status-organizing processes: implications for intergroup misunderstandings. In: *Intergroup Misunderstandings: Impact of Divergent social Realities*. New York: Psychology Press.

Denham, S.A. and Grout, I. (1992). Mothers' emotional expressiveness and coping: relations with preschoolers emotional competence. *Genetic, Social, and General Psychology Monographs* 118 (1): 73–101. Accessed from PsycInfo.

DePaulo, B.M., Dull, W.R., Greenberg, J.M., and Swaim, G.W. (1989). Are shy people reluctant to ask for help? *Journal of Personality and Social Psychology* 56 (5): 834–844. https://doi.org/10.1037/0022-3514.56.5.834.

D'Errico, F., Leone, G., and Mastrovito, T. (2011). When teachers' intervention makes an immigrant child more dependent. In: *Cultural Diversity in the Classroom* (eds. J.A. Spinthourakis, J. Lalor and W. Berg), 129–143. Wiesbaden: VS Verlag für Sozialwissenschaften https://doi.org/10.1007/978-3-531-93494-5_8.

Derrida, J. and Derrida, J. (2004). *Counterfeit Memory* (6th pr). Chicago: University of Chicago Press.

Diekman, A.B., Brown, E.R., Johnston, A.M., and Clark, E.K. (2010). Seeking congruity between goals and roles: a new look at why women opt out of science, technology, engineering, and mathematics careers. *Psychological Science* 21 (8): 1051–1057. https://doi.org/10.1177/0956797610377342.

Diekman, A.B. and Clark, E.K. (2015). Beyond the damsel in distress: gender differences and similarities in enacting prosocial behavior. In: *The Oxford Handbook of Prosocial Behavior* (eds. D.A. Schroeder and W.G. Graziano), 376–391. Oxford, New York: Oxford University Press.

Doosje, B., Branscombe, N.R., Spears, R., and Manstead, A.S.R. (1998). Guilty by association: when one's group has a negative history. *Journal of*

Personality and Social Psychology 75 (4): 872–886. https://doi.org/10.1037/0022-3514.75.4.872.

Doutrelant, C. and Covas, R. (2007). Helping has signalling characteristics in a cooperatively breeding bird. *Animal Behaviour* 74 (4): 739–747. https://doi.org/10.1016/j.anbehav.2006.11.033.

Dovidio, J.F., Allen, J.L., and Schroeder, D.A. (1990). Specificity of empathy-induced helping: evidence for altruistic motivation. *Journal of Personality and Social Psychology* 59 (2): 249–260. https://doi.org/10.1037/0022-3514.59.2.249.

Dovidio, J.F. and Gaertner, S.L. (2004). Aversive racism. *Advances in Experimental Social Psychology* 36: 1–52. https://doi.org/10.1016/S0065-2601(04)36001-6.

Dovidio, J.F., Gaertner, S.L., Hodson, G. et al. (2006a). Recategorization and crossed categorization: The implications of group salience and representations for reducing bias. In: *Multiple Social Categorization: Processes, Models and Applications*, 65–89. New York, NY, US: Psychology Press.

Dovidio, J.F., Gaertner, S.L., Validzic, A. et al. (1997). Extending the benefits of recategorization: evaluations, self-disclosure, and helping. *Journal of Experimental Social Psychology* 33 (4): 401–420. https://doi.org/10.1006/jesp.1997.1327.

Dovidio, J.F., Piliavin, J.A., Schroeder, D.A., and Penner, L. (2006b). *The Social Psychology of Prosocial Behavior.* Mahwah, N.J: Lawrence Erlbaum Publishers.

Dozier, M. (1990). Attachment organization and treatment use for adults with serious psychopathological disorders. *Development and Psychopathology* 2 (01): 47. https://doi.org/10.1017/S0954579400000584.

Drury, J., Cocking, C., and Reicher, S. (2009). Everyone for themselves? A comparative study of crowd solidarity among emergency survivors. *British Journal of Social Psychology* 48 (3): 487–506. https://doi.org/10.1348/014466608X357893.

Dunn, E.W., Aknin, L.B., and Norton, M.I. (2008). Spending money on others promotes happiness. *Science* 319 (5870): 1687–1688. https://doi.org/10.1126/science.1150952.

Dunn, E.W., Aknin, L.B., and Norton, M.I. (2014). Prosocial spending and happiness: using money to benefit others pays off. *Current Directions in Psychological Science* 23 (1): 41–47. https://doi.org/10.1177/0963721413512503.

Dunn, E. and Norton, M.I. (2013). *Happy Money: The Science of Smarter Spending* (1st Simon & Schuster hardcover ed.). New York: Simon & Schuster.

Dweck, C.S. (1986). Motivational processes affecting learning. *American Psychologist* 41 (10): 1040–1048. https://doi.org/10.1037/0003-066X.41.10.1040.

Eagly, A.H. (2009). The his and hers of prosocial behavior: an examination of the social psychology of gender. *American Psychologist* 64: 644–658.

Eagly, A.H. and Crowley, M. (1986). Gender and helping behavior: a meta-analytic review of the social psychological literature. *Psychological Bulletin* 100 (3): 283–308. https://doi.org/10.1037/0033-2909.100.3.283.

Eagly, A.H. and Karau, S.J. (2002). Role congruity theory of prejudice toward female leaders. *Psychological Review* 109 (3): 573–598. https://doi.org/10.1037/0033-295X.109.3.573.

Eagly, A.H., Wood, W., and Diekman, A.B. (2000). Social role theory of sex differences and similarities: a current appraisal. In: *The Developmental Social Psychology of Gender*, 123–174. Mahwah, NJ, US: Lawrence Erlbaum Associates Publishers.

Eccles, J.S. (1994). Understanding women's educational and occupational choices: *applying the Eccles et al. model of achievement-related choices. Psychology of Women Quarterly* 18 (4): 585–609. https://doi.org/10.1111/j.1471-6402.1994.tb01049.x.

Einolf, C.J. (2010). Does extensivity form part of the altruistic personality? An empirical test of Oliner and Oliner's theory. *Social Science Research* 39 (1): 142–151. https://doi.org/10.1016/j.ssresearch.2009.02.003.

Eisenberg, N. (2014). *Altruistic Emotion, Cognition, and Behavior (PLE: Emotion)*, 1e. Psychology Press.

Eisenberg, N., Fabes, R.A., Carlo, G. et al. (1992). The relations of maternal practices and characteristics to children's vicarious emotional responsiveness. *Child Development* 63 (3): 583–602. https://doi.org/10.1111/j.1467-8624.1992.tb01648.x.

Eisenberg, N. and Miller, P.A. (1987). The relation of empathy to prosocial and related behaviors. *Psychological Bulletin* 101 (1): 91–119. https://doi.org/10.1037/0033-2909.101.1.91.

El-Alayli, A. and Messé, L.A. (2004). Reactions toward an unexpected and counternormative favor-giver: Does it matter if we think we can reciprocate? *Journal of Experimental Social Psychology* 40: 633–641.

Ellemers, N., Spears, R., and Doosje, B. (2002). Self and social identity. *Annual Review of Psychology* 53 (1): 161–186. https://doi.org/10.1146/annurev.psych.53.100901.135228.

Emmons, R.A. and McCullough, M.E. (2003). Counting blessings versus burdens: an experimental investigation of gratitude and subjective well-being in daily life. *Journal of Personality and Social Psychology* 84 (2): 377–389. https://doi.org/10.1037/0022-3514.84.2.377.

Eysenck, H.J. (1970). *Crime and Personality* (3rd Revised ed.). London: Paladin.

Feather, N.T. and McKee, I.R. (2009). Differentiating emotions in relation to deserved or undeserved outcomes: a retrospective study of real-life events. *Cognition & Emotion* 23 (5): 955–977. https://doi.org/10.1080/02699930802243378.

Fehr, E. and Fischbacher, U. (2003). The nature of human altruism. *Nature* 425: 785.

Fehr, E. and Rockenbach, B. (2004). Human altruism: economic, neural, and evolutionary perspectives. *Current Opinion in Neurobiology* 14 (6): 784–790. https://doi.org/10.1016/j.conb.2004.10.007.

Festinger, L. (1954). A theory of social comparison processes. *Human Relations* 7 (2): 117–140. https://doi.org/10.1177/001872675400700202.

Feygina, I. and Henry, P.J. (2015). Culture and prosocial behavior. In: *The Oxford Handbook of Prosocial Behavior* (eds. D.A. Schroeder and W.G. Graziano), 188–208. Oxford; New York: Oxford University Press.

Fischer, P., Krueger, J.I., Greitemeyer, T. et al. (2011). The bystander-effect: a meta-analytic review on bystander intervention in dangerous and non-dangerous emergencies. *Psychological Bulletin* 137 (4): 517–537. https://doi.org/10.1037/a0023304.

Fisher, J.D., Nadler, A., Hart, E., and Whitcher, S.J. (1981). Helping the needy helps the self. *Bulletin of the Psychonomic Society* 17 (4): 190–192. https://doi.org/10.3758/BF03333708.

Fisher, J.D., Nadler, A., Little, J.S., and Saguy, T. (2008). Help as a vehicle to reconciliation, with particular reference to help for extreme health needs. In: *The Social Psychology of Intergroup Reconciliation* (eds. A. Nadler, T.E. Malloy and J.D. Fisher), 447–468. Oxford, New York: Oxford University Press.

Fisher, J.D., Nadler, A., and Whitcher-Alagna, S. (1982). Recipient reactions to aid. *Psychological Bulletin* 91 (1): 27–54. https://doi.org/10.1037/0033-2909.91.1.27.

Fisher, J.D. and Nadler, A. (1974). The effect of similarity between donor and recipient on recipient's reactions to aid1. *Journal of Applied Social Psychology* 4 (3): 230–243. https://doi.org/10.1111/j.1559-1816.1974.tb02643.x.

Fiske, A.P. (1991). *Structures of Social Life: The Four Elementary Forms of Human Relations: Communal Sharing, Authority Ranking, Equality Matching, Market Pricing*. New York; Toronto; New York: Free Press; Collier Macmillan Canada; Maxwell Macmillan International.

Flynn, F.J. (2003). How much should I give and how often? The effects of generosity and frequency of favor exchange on social status and productivity. *Academy of Management Journal* 46 (5): 539–553. https://doi.org/10.5465/30040648.

Flynn, F.J., Reagans, R.E., Amanatullah, E.T., and Ames, D.R. (2006). Helping one's way to the top: self-monitors achieve status by helping others and knowing who helps whom. *Journal of Personality and Social Psychology* 91 (6): 1123–1137. https://doi.org/10.1037/0022-3514.91.6.1123.

Frankel, V.E. (1984). *Man's search for meaning*. New York: Washington Square Press.

Frankl, V.E. (2006). *Man's Search for Meaning*. Boston: Beacon Press.

Freeden, M. (2010). Social and psychological bases of ideology and system justification – edited by John T. Jost, Aaron C. Kay, and Hulda Thorrisdottir: Book Reviews. *Political Psychology* 31 (3): 479–482. https://doi.org/10.1111/j.1467-9221.2010.00769.x.

Freud, S. (1930). *Civilization and its discontents*. Oxford, UK: Hogarth.

Frieze, I.H. (1979). Perceptions of battered wives. In: *New Approaches to Social Problems: applications of attribution theory* (eds. I.H. Frieze, D. Bar-Tal and J.S. Carroll), 79–108. San Francisco, CA: Jossey-Bass.

Fromm, E. (1947). *Man for Himself: An Inquiry Into Psychology of Ethica.* Holt, Rinehart and Winston.

Gaertner, S. and Bickman, L. (1971). Effects of race on the elicitation of helping behavior: the wrong number technique. *Journal of Personality and Social Psychology* 20 (2): 218–222. https://doi.org/10.1037/h0031681.

Gaertner, S.L. and Dovidio, J.F. (1977). The subtlety of White racism, arousal, and helping behavior. *Journal of Personality and Social Psychology* 35 (10): 691–707. https://doi.org/10.1037/0022-3514.35.10.691.

Gaertner, S.L. and Dovidio, J.F. (2009). A common ingroup identity: a categorization-based approach for reducing intergroup bias. In: *Handbook of Prejudice, Stereotyping, and Discrimination* (ed. T.D. Nelson), 489–505. New York, NY, US: Psychology Press.

Gaertner, S.L. and Dovidio, J.F. (2012). The common ingroup identity model. In: *Handbook of Theories of Social Psychology*, vol. 2 (eds. P.A.M. Van Lange, A.W. Kruglanski and E.T. Higgins), 439–457. Thousand Oaks, CA: Sage.

Gaertner, S.L., Dovidio, J.F., Anastasio, P.A. et al. (1993). The common ingroup identity model: recategorization and the reduction of intergroup bias. *European Review of Social Psychology* 4 (1): 1–26. https://doi.org/10.1080/14792779343000004.

Gangestad, S.W. and Snyder, M. (2000). Self-monitoring: appraisal and reappraisal. *Psychological Bulletin* 126 (4): 530–555. https://doi.org/10.1037/0033-2909.126.4.530.

Garcia, S.M., Weaver, K., Moskowitz, G.B., and Darley, J.M. (2002). Crowded minds: the implicit bystander effect. *Journal of Personality and Social Psychology* 83 (4): 843–853. https://doi.org/10.1037/0022-3514.83.4.843.

Geller, D. and Bamberger, P.A. (2012). The impact of help seeking on individual task performance: the moderating effect of help seekers' logics of action. *Journal of Applied Psychology* 97 (2): 487–497. https://doi.org/10.1037/a0026014.

Gentile, D.A., Anderson, C.A., Yukawa, S. et al. (2009). The effects of prosocial video games on prosocial behaviors: international evidence from correlational, longitudinal, and experimental studies. *Personality and Social Psychology Bulletin* 35 (6): 752–763. https://doi.org/10.1177/0146167209333045.

Gergen, K., & Gergen, M. (1974). Understanding foreign assistance through public opinion. *Yearbook of World Affairs, 27.*

Gergen, K.J., Gergen, M.M., and Meter, K. (1972). Individual orientations to prosocial behavior. *Journal of Social Issues* 28 (3): 105–130. https://doi.org/10.1111/j.1540-4560.1972.tb00035.x.

Gergen, K.J., Morse, S.J., and Kristeller, J.L. (1973). The manner of giving: cross-national continuities in reactions to aid. *Psychologia: An International Journal of Psychology in the Orient* 16 (3): 121–131.

Ghiselin, M.T. (1974). *The Economy of Nature and the Evolution of Sex.* Berkeley: University of California Press.

Gillath, O., Shaver, P.R., Mikulincer, M. et al. (2005). Attachment, caregiving, and volunteering: placing volunteerism in an attachment-theoretical framework. *Personal Relationships* 12 (4): 425–446. https://doi.org/10.1111/j.1475-6811.2005.00124.x.

Gilman, R. and Gabriel, S. (2004). Perceptions of school psychological services by education professionals: results from a multi-state survey pilot study. *School Psychology Review* 33 (2): 271–286.

Gintis, H., Bowles, S., Boyd, R., and Fehr, E. (2003). Explaining altruistic behavior in humans. *Evolution and Human Behavior* 24 (3): 153–172. https://doi.org/10.1016/S1090-5138(02)00157-5.

Gintis, H., Smith, E.A., and Bowles, S. (2001). Costly signaling and cooperation. *Journal of Theoretical Biology* 213 (1): 103–119. https://doi.org/10.1006/jtbi.2001.2406.

Gleason, M.E.J., Iida, M., Shrout, P.E., and Bolger, N. (2008). Receiving support as a mixed blessing: evidence for dual effects of support on psychological outcomes. *Journal of Personality and Social Psychology* 94 (5): 824–838. https://doi.org/10.1037/0022-3514.94.5.824.

Glick, P. and Fiske, S.T. (1996). The ambivalent sexism inventory: differentiating hostile and benevolent sexism. *Journal of Personality and Social Psychology* 70 (3): 491–512. https://doi.org/10.1037/0022-3514.70.3.491.

Glick, P. and Fiske, S.T. (2001). An ambivalent alliance: hostile and benevolent sexism as complementary justifications for gender inequality. *American Psychologist* 56 (2): 109–118. https://doi.org/10.1037/0003-066X.56.2.109.

Goffman, E. (1961). *Asylums*. Garden City, NY: Anchor books.

Gordon, A.L. (1893). *Poems by Adam Lindsay Gordon* (ed. M.A.H. Clarke).

Gouldner, A.W. (1960). The norm of reciprocity: a preliminary statement. *American Sociological Review* 25 (2): 161. https://doi.org/10.2307/2092623.

Goux, J.J. (2002). *Seneca against Derrida: Gift and alterity* (eds. E. Wyschogrod, J.-J. Goux and E. Boyton) *The Enigma of Gift and Sacrifice*. NY: Fordham University Press.

Graf, R.G., Freer, S., and Plaizier, P.C. (1979). Interpersonal perception as a function of help-seeking: a United States-Netherlands contrast. *Journal of Cross-Cultural Psychology* 10 (1): 101–110. https://doi.org/10.1177/0022022179101007.

Grant, A.M. and Gino, F. (2010). A little thanks goes a long way: explaining why gratitude expressions motivate prosocial behavior. *Journal of Personality and Social Psychology* 98 (6): 946–955. https://doi.org/10.1037/a0017935.

Grant, A.M. and Wrzesniewski, A. (2010). I won't let you down… or will I? Core self-evaluations, other-orientation, anticipated guilt and gratitude, and job performance. *Journal of Applied Psychology* 95 (1): 108–121. https://doi.org/10.1037/a0017974.

Grant, R.W. and Tarcov, N. (eds.) (1996). *Some Thoughts Concerning Education and The Conduct of the Understanding*. Hackett Publishing.

Gray, J. (1992). *Men are from Mars, women are from Venus: a practical guide for improving communication and getting what you want in your relationships*, 1e. New York, NY: HarperCollins.

Graziano, W.G. and Tobin, R.M. (2002). Agreeableness: dimension of personality or social desirability artifact? *Journal of Personality* 70 (5): 695–728. https://doi.org/10.1111/1467-6494.05021.

Graziano, W.G. and Habashi, M.M. (2015). Chapter 12: searching for the pro-social personality. In: *The Oxford Handbook of Prosocial Behavior* (eds. D.A. Schroeder and W.G. Graziano), 231–255. Oxford, New York: Oxford University Press.

Graziano, W.G., Habashi, M.M., Sheese, B.E., and Tobin, R.M. (2007). Agreeableness, empathy, and helping: a person × situation perspective. *Journal of Personality and Social Psychology* 93 (4): 583–599. https://doi.org/10.1037/0022-3514.93.4.583.

Greenberg, J. (1980). Attentional focus and locus of performance causality as determinants of equity behavior. *Journal of Personality and Social Psychology* 38 (4): 579–585. https://doi.org/10.1037/0022-3514.38.4.579.

Greenglass, E.R. (1993). Social support and coping of employed women. In: *Women, work, and Coping: A Multidisciplinary Approach to Workplace Stress* (eds. B.C. Long and S.E. Kahn), 154–169. Montreal; Buffalo: McGill-Queen's University Press.

Greitemeyer, T. (2009a). Effects of songs with prosocial lyrics on prosocial behavior: further evidence and a mediating mechanism. *Personality and Social Psychology Bulletin* 35 (11): 1500–1511. https://doi.org/10.1177/0146167209341648.

Greitemeyer, T. (2009b). Effects of songs with prosocial lyrics on prosocial thoughts, affect, and behavior. *Journal of Experimental Social Psychology* 45 (1): 186–190. https://doi.org/10.1016/j.jesp.2008.08.003.

Greve, F. (2009, May 23). America's poor are its most generous. *The Seattle Times. Retrieved from* http://seatletimes.nwsource.com

Griffin, M.T. (2013). *Seneca on society: A guide to De Beneficiis.* Oxford, UK: Oxford University Press.

Griskevicius, V., Tybur, J.M., Sundie, J.M. et al. (2007). Blatant benevolence and conspicuous consumption: When romantic motives elicit strategic costly signals. *Journal of Personality and Social Psychology* 93: 85–102.

Gurven, M., Zanolini, A., and Schniter, E. (2008). Culture sometimes matters: intra-cultural variation in pro-social behavior among Tsimane Amerindians. *Journal of Economic Behavior & Organization* 67 (3–4): 587–607. https://doi.org/10.1016/j.jebo.2007.09.005.

Haidt, J. (2003). Elevation and the positive psychology of morality. In: *Flourishing: Positive Psychology and the Life Well-Lived* (eds. C.L.M. Keyes and J. Haidt), 275–289. Washington DC, US: American Psychological Association.

Halabi, S., Dovidio, J.F., and Nadler, A. (2008). When and how high status groups offer help: Effects of social dominance orientation and status threat. *Political Psychology* 29: 841–858.

Halabi, S., Dovidio, J.F., and Nadler, A. (2012). Responses to intergroup helping: effects of perceived stability and legitimacy of intergroup relations on Israeli Arabs' reactions to assistance by Israeli Jews. *International Journal of Intercultural Relations* 36 (2): 295–301. https://doi.org/10.1016/j.ijintrel.2011.12.002.

Halabi, S., Dovidio, J.F., and Nadler, A. (2014). Seeking help from the low status: Effects of status stability, type of help and social categorization. *Journal of Experimental Social Psychology*. 53: 139–144.

Halabi, S., Nadler, A., and Dovidio, J.F. (2011). Reactions to receiving assumptive help: the moderating effects of group membership and perceived need for help1: RECEIVING HELP. *Journal of Applied Social Psychology* 41 (12): 2793–2815. https://doi.org/10.1111/j.1559-1816.2011.00859.x.

Hall, D.L., Matz, D.C., and Wood, W. (2010). Why don't we practice what we teach? A meta analytic review of religious racism. *Personality and Social Psychology Review* 14: 126–139. http://dx.doi.org/10.1177/1088868310364151.

Hamilton, W.D. (1964). The genetical evolution of social behaviour. II. *Journal of Theoretical Biology* 7 (1): 17–52. https://doi.org/10.1016/0022-5193(64)90039-6.

Harackiewicz, J.M., Barron, K.E., Pintrich, P.R. et al. (2002). Revision of achievement goal theory: necessary and illuminating. *Journal of Educational Psychology* 94(3): 638–645. https://doi.org/10.1037/0022-0663.94.3.638.

Hardy, C. and Van Vugt, M. (2006). Nice guys finish first: The competitive altruism hypothesis. *Personality and Social Psychology Bulletin* 32: 1402–1413.

Harris, D.B. (1957). A scale for measuring attitudes of social responsibility in children. *The Journal of Abnormal and Social Psychology* 55 (3): 322–326. https://doi.org/10.1037/h0048925.

Harter, S. (1986). Cognitive-developmental processes in the integration of concepts about emotions and the self. *Social Cognition* 4 (2): 119–151. https://doi.org/10.1521/soco.1986.4.2.119.

Hartshorne, H. and May, M.A. (1928). *Studies in the Nature of Character, I Studies in Deciet.* New York: MacMillan Co.

Hartshorne, H., May, M.A., and Maller, J.B. (1929). *Studies in the Nature of Character, II Studies in Service and Self-Control.* New York: MacMillan Co.

Hartshorne, H., May, M.A., and Shuttleworth, F.K. (1930). *Studies in the Nature of Character, Vol. 3: Studies in the Organization of Character.* New York: MacMillan Co.

Haslam, N. and Fiske, A.P. (1999). Relational models theory: a confirmatory factor analysis. *Personal Relationships* 6 (2): 241–250. https://doi.org/10.1111/j.1475-6811.1999.tb00190.x.

Hawkins, M. (1997). *Social Darwinism in European and American Thought, 1860–1945: Nature as Model and Nature as Threat.* Cambridge; New York: Cambridge University Press.

Hay, D.F. and Cook, K.V. (2007). The transformation of prosocial behavior from infancy to childhood. In: *Socioemotional Development in the Toddler Years* (eds. C.E. Brwonell and C.B. Kopp), 101–131. New York, NY: Guilford press.

Hay, D.F. and Cook, K.V. (2010). The transformation of prosocial behavior from infancy to childhood. In: *Socioemotional Development in the Toddler Years: Transitions and Transformations* (eds. C. Brownell and C. Kopp), 100–131. New York: Guilford Publications.

Hazan, C. and Shaver, P. (1987). Romantic love conceptualized as an attachment process. *Journal of Personality and Social Psychology* 52 (3): 511–524. https://doi.org/10.1037/0022-3514.52.3.511.

Hearold, S. (1986). WITHDRAWN: a synthesis of 1043 effects of television on social behavior. In: *Public Communication and Behavior* (ed. G. Comstock), 65–133. Elsevier.

Heider, F. (1958). *The Psychology of Interpersonal Relations.* Hoboken: Wiley.

Henrich, J., Boyd, R., Bowles, S. et al. (2005). "Economic man" in cross-cultural perspective: behavioral experiments in 15 small-scale societies. *Behavioral and Brain Sciences* 28 (06) https://doi.org/10.1017/S0140525X05000142.

Hobbes, T., Malcolm, N., and Hobbes, T. (2014). *Thomas Hobbes Leviathan: Editorial Introduction.* Oxford: Clarendon Press.

Hobfoll, S.E., Dunahoo, C.L., Ben-Porath, Y., and Monnier, J. (1994). Gender and coping: the dual-axis model of coping. *American Journal of Community Psychology* 22 (1): 49–82. https://doi.org/10.1007/BF02506817.

Hobfoll, S.E. and London, P. (1986). The relationship of self-concept and social support to emotional distress among women during war. *Journal of Social and Clinical Psychology* 4 (2): 189–203. https://doi.org/10.1521/jscp.1986.4.2.189.

Hodgkinson, V.A. and Weitzman, M.S. (1994). *Giving and Volunteering in the United States: Findings from a National Survey, 1994 Edition.* Washington, DC: Independent Sector.

Hoffman, M.L. (2000). *Empathy and Moral Development: Implications for Caring and Justice.* Cambridge, England: Cambridge University Press.

Hofstede, G. (1991). Empirical models of cultural differences. In: *Contemporary Issues in Cross-Cultural Psychology*, 4–20. Lisse, Netherlands: Swets & Zeitlinger Publishers.

Hofstede, G. and Bond, M.H. (1984). Hofstede's culture dimensions: an independent validation using Rokeach's Value survey. *Journal of Cross-Cultural Psychology* 15 (4): 417–433. https://doi.org/10.1177/0022002184015004003.

Hopkins, N., Reicher, S., Harrison, K. et al. (2007). Helping to improve the group stereotype: on the strategic dimension of prosocial behavior. *Personality and Social Psychology Bulletin* 33 (6): 776–788. https://doi.org/10.1177/0146167207301023.

House, J., Landis, K., and Umberson, D. (1988). Social relationships and health. *Science* 241 (4865): 540–545. https://doi.org/10.1126/science.3399889.

Huxley, T.H. (1894). *Darwiniana.* New York, NY: Appleton.

Iyer, A., Leach, C.W., and Crosby, F.J. (2003). white guilt and racial compensation: the benefits and limits of self-focus. *Personality and Social Psychology Bulletin* 29 (1): 117–129. https://doi.org/10.1177/0146167202238377.

Jackman, M.R. (1994). *The velvet glove: paternalism and conflict in gender, class, and race relations*. Berkeley: University of California Press.

Jackson, L.M. and Esses, V.M. (2000). Effects of perceived economic competition on people's willingness to help empower immigrants. *Group Processes & Intergroup Relations* 3 (4): 419–435. https://doi.org/10.1177/1368430200003004006.

Janoff-Bulman, R., Sheikh, S., and Baldacci, K.G. (2008). Mapping moral motives: Approach, avoidance, and political orientation. *Journal of Experimental Social Psychology* 44 (4): 1091–1099. https://doi.org/10.1016/j.jesp.2007.11.003.

Jetten, J., Spears, R., and Manstead, A.S.R. (1997). Strength of identification and intergroup differentiation: the influence of group norms. *European Journal of Social Psychology* 27 (5): 603–609. https://doi.org/10.1002/(SICI)1099-0992(199709/10)27:5<603::AID-EJSP816>3.0.CO;2-B.

Joel, S., Gordon, A.M., Impett, E.A. et al. (2013). The things you do for me: perceptions of a romantic partner's investments promote gratitude and commitment. *Personality and Social Psychology Bulletin* 39 (10): 1333–1345. https://doi.org/10.1177/0146167213497801.

John, O.P., Donahue, E.M., and Kentle, R.L. (1991). *The Big Five Inventory–Versions 4a and 54*, 54. Berkeley, CA: University of California, Berkeley, Institute of Personality and Social Research.

Johnson, M.K., Rowatt, W.C., and LaBouff, J. (2010). Priming Christian religious concepts increases racial prejudice. *Social Psychological and Personality Science* 1 (2): 119–126. https://doi.org/10.1177/1948550609357246.

Joireman, J.A., Needham, T.L., and Cummings, A.-L. (2002). Relationships between dimensions of attachment and empathy. *North American Journal of Psychology* 4 (1): 63–80.

Jost, J.T. and Hunyady, O. (2005). Antecedents and consequences of system-justifying ideologies. *Current Directions in Psychological Science* 14 (5): 260–265. https://doi.org/10.1111/j.0963-7214.2005.00377.x.

Jost, J.T. and Kay, A.C. (2005). Exposure to benevolent sexism and complementary gender stereotypes: consequences for specific and diffuse forms of system justification. *Journal of Personality and Social Psychology* 88 (3): 498–509. https://doi.org/10.1037/0022-3514.88.3.498.

Kant, I. (1930). *Lectures on Ethics* (trans. L. Infield). London, UK: Methuen.

Karabenick, S.A. and Berger, J.-L. (2013). Help seeking as self-regulated learning strategy. In: *Applications of Self-Regulated Learning Across Diverse Disciplines: A Tribute to Barry J. Zimmerman* (eds. B.J. Zimmerman, H. Bembenutty and D.H. Schunk), 237–261. Charlotte, North Carolina: Information Age Publishing.

Keltner, D. (2009). *Born to Be Good: The Science of a Meaningful Life*, 1e. New York: W.W. Norton & Co.

Keltner, D., Kogan, A., Piff, P.K., and Saturn, S.R. (2014). The Sociocultural Appraisals, Values, and Emotions (SAVE) framework of prosociality: core processes from gene to meme. *Annual Review of Psychology* 65 (1): 425–460. https://doi.org/10.1146/annurev-psych-010213-115054.

Kemmelmeier, M., Jambor, E.E., and Letner, J. (2006). Individualism and good works: cultural variation in giving and volunteering across the United States. *Journal of Cross-Cultural Psychology* 37 (3): 327–344. https://doi.org/10.1177/0022022106286927.

Kessler, R.C., Brown, R.L., and Broman, C.L. (1981). Sex differences in psychiatric help-seeking: evidence from four large-scale surveys. *Journal of Health and Social Behavior* 22 (1): 49. https://doi.org/10.2307/2136367.

Kim, H.S., Sherman, D.K., Ko, D., and Taylor, S.E. (2006). Pursuit of comfort and pursuit of harmony: culture, relationships, and social support seeking. *Personality and Social Psychology Bulletin* 32 (12): 1595–1607. https://doi.org/10.1177/0146167206291991.

King, E.B., George, J.M., and Hebl, M.R. (2005). Linking personality to helping behaviors at work: an interactional perspective. *Journal of Personality* 73 (3): 585–608. https://doi.org/10.1111/j.1467-6494.2005.00322.x.

Klandermans, B., Werner, M., and van Doorn, M. (2008). Redeeming apartheid's legacy: collective guilt, political ideology, and compensation. *Political Psychology* 29 (3): 331–349. https://doi.org/10.1111/j.1467-9221.2008.00633.x.

Klein, M. (1950). On the criteria for the termination of a psycho-analysis. *The International Journal of Psychoanalysis* 31: 78–80.

Klein, M. (1984). *Love, Guilt and Reparation and Other Works 1921–1945.* New York: Free Press.

Knafo-Noam, A., Uzefovsky, F., Israel, S. et al. (2015). The prosocial personality and its facets: genetic and environmental architecture of mother-reported behavior of 7-year-old twins. *Frontiers in Psychology* 6 https://doi.org/10.3389/fpsyg.2015.00112.

Kogan, A., Oveis, C., Carr, E.W. et al. (2014). Vagal activity is quadratically related to prosocial traits, prosocial emotions, and observer perceptions of prosociality. *Journal of Personality and Social Psychology* 107 (6): 1051–1063. https://doi.org/10.1037/a0037509.

Kogut, T. and Ritov, I. (2005). The singularity effect of identified victims in separate and joint evaluations. *Organizational Behavior and Human Decision Processes* 97 (2): 106–116. https://doi.org/10.1016/j.obhdp.2005.02.003.

Kogut, T., Slovic, P., and Västfjäll, D. (2015). Scope insensitivity in helping decisions: is it a matter of culture and values? *Journal of Experimental Psychology: General* 144 (6): 1042–1052. https://doi.org/10.1037/a0039708.

Korchmaros, J.D. and Kenny, D.A. (2001). Emotional closeness as a mediator of the effect of genetic relatedness on altruism. *Psychological Science* 12: 262–265.

Korchmaros, J.D. and Kenny, D.A. (2006). An evolutionary and close-relationship model of helping. *Journal of Social and Personal Relationships* 23 (1): 21–43. https://doi.org/10.1177/0265407506060176.

Kovel, J. (1970). *White Racism: A Psychohistory.* New York, NY, US: Pantheon Books.

Karabenick, S.A. and Gonida, E.N. (2018). Academic help seeking as a self-regulated learning strategy: Current issues, future directions. In: *Handbook of Self-Regulation of Learning and Performance*, 2e (eds. D.H. Schunk and J.A. Greene), 421–433. New York, NY: Routledge/Taylor & Francis group.

Kraus, M.W. and Keltner, D. (2009). Signs of socioeconomic status: a thin-slicing approach. *Psychological Science* 20 (1): 99–106. https://doi.org/10.1111/j.1467-9280.2008.02251.x.

Krause, N. and Shaw, B.A. (2000). Giving social support to others, socioeconomic status, and changes in self-esteem in later life. *The Journals of Gerontology: Series B: Psychological Sciences and Social Sciences* 55: s323–s2333. http://dx.doi.org/10.1093/geronb/55.6.S323.

Kropotkin, P. (1902). *Mutual Aid: A Factor in Evolution.* New York, NY: Doubleday.

Kropotkin, P. (2012). *Mutual Aid: a Factor of Evolution.* Dover Publications.

Kruger, D. (2003). Evolution and altruism combining psychological mediators with naturally selected tendencies. *Evolution and Human Behavior* 24 (2): 118–125. https://doi.org/10.1016/S1090-5138(02)00156-3.

Kubacka, K.E., Finkenauer, C., Rusbult, C.E., and Keijsers, L. (2011). Maintaining close relationships: gratitude as a motivator and a detector of maintenance behavior. *Personality and Social Psychology Bulletin* 37 (10): 1362–1375. https://doi.org/10.1177/0146167211412196.

Kunstman, J.W. and Plant, E.A. (2008). Racing to help: racial bias in high emergency helping situations. *Journal of Personality and Social Psychology* 95 (6): 1499–1510. https://doi.org/10.1037/a0012822.

Lamy, L., Fischer-Lokou, J., and Guéguen, N. (2009). Induced reminiscence of love and chivalrous helping. *Current Psychology* 28 (3): 202–209. https://doi.org/10.1007/s12144-009-9059-9.

Langer, E.J. and Rodin, J. (1976). The effects of choice and enhanced personal responsibility for the aged: a field experiment in an institutional setting. *Journal of Personality and Social Psychology* 34 (2): 191–198. https://doi.org/10.1037/0022-3514.34.2.191.

Latané, B. and Darley, J.M. (1970). *The Unresponsive Bystander: Why Doesn't He Help? Century Psychology Series.* New York: Appleton-Century Crofts.

Leach, C.W. (2002). II. The social psychology of racism reconsidered. *Feminism & Psychology* 12 (4): 439–444. https://doi.org/10.1177/0959353502012004005.

Lee, H.W., Bradburn, J., Johnson, R.E. et al. (2018a). The benefits of receiving gratitude for helpers: a daily investigation of proactive and reactive helping at work. *Journal of Applied Psychology* https://doi.org/10.1037/apl0000346.

Lee, H.W., Johnson, R.E., Lin, S.J., and Chang, C. (2018b). The benefits of receiving gratitude for helpers: A daily investigation of proactive or reactive helping at work. *Journal of Applied Psychology* 104: 117–213.

Leone, G. (2009). *Le ambivalenze dell'aiuto* [The ambivalence of helping]. Rome: *Carocci.*

Leone, G., D'Errico, F., Carmencita, S., and Marzano, M. (2008). Empatia e costi psicologi dell'aiuto [empathy and the psychological costs of help]. In: *La mente del cuore: le emozioni nel lavoro, nella scuola, nella vita* (ed. I. Poggi). Armando: Roma.

Lepper, M.R., Greene, D., and Nisbett, R.E. (1973). Undermining children's intrinsic interest with extrinsic reward: a test of the "overjustification" hypothesis. *Journal of Personality and Social Psychology* 28 (1): 129–137. https://doi.org/10.1037/h0035519.

Levine, M. and Manning, R. (2013). Social identity, group processes, and helping in emergencies. *European Review of Social Psychology* 24 (1): 225–251. https://doi.org/10.1080/10463283.2014.892318.

Levine, M., Prosser, A., Evans, D., and Reicher, S. (2005). Identity and emergency intervention: how social group membership and inclusiveness of group boundaries shape helping behavior. *Personality and Social Psychology Bulletin* 31 (4): 443–453. https://doi.org/10.1177/0146167204271651.

Levine, R.V., Martinez, T.S., Brase, G., and Sorenson, K. (1994). Helping in 36 U.S. cities. *Journal of Personality and Social Psychology* 67 (1): 69–82. https://doi.org/10.1037/0022-3514.67.1.69.

Levine, R.V., Norenzayan, A., and Philbrick, K. (2001). Cross-cultural differences in helping strangers. *Journal of Cross-Cultural Psychology* 32 (5): 543–560. https://doi.org/10.1177/0022022101032005002.

Lewin, K. (1951). *Field Theory in Social Science: Selected Theoretical Papers* (ed. D. Cartwright). Oxford, England: Harpers.

Linkowski, D.C. (1971). A scale to measure acceptance of disability. *Rehabilitation Counseling Bulletin* 14 (4): 236–244.

London, P. (1970). The rescuers: motivational hypothesis about Christians who saved Jews from Nazis. In: *Altruism and Helping Behavior: Social Psychological Studies of Some Antecedents and Consequences* (eds. J. Macaulay and L. Berkowitz), 241–250. New York: Academic Press.

Lopez, F.G. and Brennan, K.A. (2000). Dynamic processes underlying adult attachment organization: toward an attachment theoretical perspective on the healthy and effective self. *Journal of Counseling Psychology* 47 (3): 283–300. https://doi.org/10.1037/0022-0167.47.3.283.

Lotz-Schmitt, K., Siem, B., and Stürmer, S. (2017). Empathy as a motivator of dyadic helping across group boundaries: the dis-inhibiting effect of the recipient's perceived benevolence. *Group Processes & Intergroup Relations* 20 (2): 233–259. https://doi.org/10.1177/1368430215612218.

Lund, D.A., Dimond, M.F., Caserta, M.S. et al. (1985). Identifying elderly with coping difficulties after two years of bereavement. *Omega: Journal of Death and Dying* 16 (3): 213–224.

Lyon, S.M. (2004). "Indirect" symbolic violence and rivalry between equals in rural Punjab, Pakistan. *Durham Anthropology Journal* 12 (1): 37–50.

Lyubomirsky, S. and Layous, K. (2013). How do simple positive activities increase well-being? *Current Directions in Psychological Science* 22 (1): 57–62. https://doi.org/10.1177/0963721412469809.

Ma, L.K., Tunney, R.J., and Ferguson, E. (2017). Does gratitude enhance prosociality?: a meta-analytic review. *Psychological Bulletin* 143 (6): 601–635. https://doi.org/10.1037/bul0000103.

Macaulay, J. (1970). A shill for charity. In: *Altruism and Helping Behavior: Social Psychological Studies of Some Antecedents and Consequences* (eds. J. Macaulay and L. Berkowitz). Academic Press.

MacKenzie, M.J., Vohs, K.D., and Baumeister, R.F. (2014). You didn't have to do that: belief in free will promotes gratitude. *Personality and Social Psychology Bulletin* 40 (11): 1423–1434. https://doi.org/10.1177/0146167214549322.

Maimonides, M. (1998). *The Mishneh Torah.* New York: Rambam/ Maimonides and Monzaim Publishers.

Malcolm, N. (2014). *Clarendon Edition of the Works of Thomas Hobbes.* Oxford, UK: Oxford University Press.

Maner, J.K., Luce, C.L., Neuberg, S.L. et al. (2002). The effects of perspective taking on motivations for helping: still no evidence for altruism. *Personality and Social Psychology Bulletin* 28 (11): 1601–1610. https://doi.org/10.1177/014616702237586.

Manning, R., Levine, M., and Collins, A. (2007). The Kitty Genovese murder and the social psychology of helping: The parable of the 38 witnesses. *American Psychologist* 62: 555–562.

Mares, M.-L. and Woodard, E. (2005). Positive effects of television on children's social interactions: a meta-analysis. *Media Psychology* 7 (3): 301–322. https://doi.org/10.1207/S1532785XMEP0703_4.

Markus, H.R. and Kitayama, S. (1991). Culture and the self: implications for cognition, emotion, and motivation. *Psychological Review* 98 (2): 224–253. https://doi.org/10.1037/0033-295X.98.2.224.

Martin, G.B. and Clark, R.D. (1982). Distress crying in neonates: species and peer specificity. *Developmental Psychology* 18 (1): 3–9. https://doi.org/10.1037/0012-1649.18.1.3.

Maslow, A.H. (1954). *Personality and Motivation*, vol. 1, 987. Harlow, England: *Longman*.

Maslow, A.H. (1982). *Toward a Psychology of Being*, 2e. New York: Van Nostrand Reinhold.

Mathews, K.E. and Canon, L.K. (1975). Environmental noise level as a determinant of helping behavior. *Journal of Personality and Social Psychology* 32 (4): 571–577. https://doi.org/10.1037/0022-3514.32.4.571.

Mauss, M. (1954). *The Gift: Forms and Functions of Exchange in Archaic Societies.* Glencoe, IL: Free Press. (Original work published 1907).

Mauss, M., Douglas, M., & Halls, W. D. (2002). *The gift: the form and reason for exchange in archaic societies.* Retrieved from http://site.ebrary.com/id/10053848

McLelland, D.C. (1967). *The Achieving Society.* New York, N.Y.: Free press.

McCrae, R.R. and Costa, P.T. (1987). Validation of the five-factor model of personality across instruments and observers. *Journal of Personality and Social Psychology* 52 (1): 81–90. https://doi.org/10.1037/0022-3514.52.1.81.

McCullough, M.E., Emmons, R.A., and Tsang, J.-A. (2002). The grateful disposition: a conceptual and empirical topography. *Journal of Personality and Social Psychology* 82 (1): 112–127. https://doi.org/10.1037/0022-3514.82.1.112.

McCullough, M.E., Kimeldorf, M.B., and Cohen, A.D. (2008). An adaptation for altruism: the social causes, social effects, and social evolution of gratitude. *Current Directions in Psychological Science* 17 (4): 281–285. https://doi.org/10.1111/j.1467-8721.2008.00590.x.

McCullough, M.E., Tsang, J.-A., and Emmons, R.A. (2004). Gratitude in intermediate affective terrain: links of grateful moods to individual differences and daily emotional experience. *Journal of Personality and Social Psychology*86(2):295–309.https://doi.org/10.1037/0022-3514.86.2.295.

McGinley, M., Lipperman-Kreda, S., Byrnes, H.F., and Carlo, G. (2010). Parental, social and dispositional pathways to Israeli adolescents' volunteering. *Journal of Applied Developmental Psychology* 31 (5): 386–394. https://doi.org/10.1016/j.appdev.2010.06.001.

McManus, J.L. and Saucier, D.A. (2012). Helping natural disaster victims depends on characteristics and perceptions of victims. A response to "who helps natural disaster victims?": helping natural disaster victims. *Analyses of Social Issues and Public Policy* 12 (1): 272–275. https://doi.org/10.1111/j.1530-2415.2012.01287.x.

Meier, B.P., Moeller, S.K., Riemer-Peltz, M., and Robinson, M.D. (2012). Sweet taste preferences and experiences predict prosocial inferences, personalities, and behaviors. *Journal of Personality and Social Psychology* 102 (1): 163–174. https://doi.org/10.1037/a0025253.

Meierhenrich, J. (2008). Varieties of reconciliation: varieties of reconciliation. *Law & Social Inquiry* 33 (1): 195–231. https://doi.org/10.1111/j.1747-4469.2008.00098.x.

Midlarsky, E. and Bryan, J.H. (1972). Affect expressions and children's imitative altruism. *Journal of Experimental Research in Personality* 6 (2–3): 195–203.

Midlarsky, E., Fagin Jones, S., and Corley, R.P. (2005). Personality correlates of heroic rescue during the Holocaust. *Journal of Personality* 73 (4): 907–934. https://doi.org/10.1111/j.1467-6494.2005.00333.x.

Mikulincer, M., Florian, V., and Weller, A. (1993). Attachment styles, coping strategies, and posttraumatic psychological distress: the impact of the Gulf War in Israel. *Journal of Personality and Social Psychology* 64 (5): 817–826. https://doi.org/10.1037/0022-3514.64.5.817.

Mikulincer, M. and Shaver, P.R. (2007). *Attachment in Adulthood: Strcuture, Dyanmics and Change.* New York, NY: Guilford Press.

Mikulincer, M. and Shaver, P.R. (eds.) (2010). *Prosocial Motives, Emotions, and Behavior: The Better Angels of our Nature.* Washington: American Psychological Association.

Mikulincer, M. and Shaver, P.R. (2015). An attachment perspective on prosocial attitudes and behavior. In: *The Oxford Handbook of Prosocial behavior* (eds. D.A. Schroeder and W.G. Graziano). Oxford; New York: Oxford University Press.

Mikulincer, M., Shaver, P.R., Gillath, O., and Nitzberg, R.A. (2005). Attachment, caregiving, and altruism: boosting attachment security increases compassion and helping. *Journal of Personality and Social Psychology* 89 (5): 817–839. https://doi.org/10.1037/0022-3514.89.5.817.

Milgram, N.A. and Palti, G. (1993). Psychosocial characteristics of resilient children. *Journal of Research in Personality* 27 (3): 207–221. https://doi.org/10.1006/jrpe.1993.1015.

Milgram, S. (1970). The experience of living in cities. *Science* 167 (3924): 1461–1468.

Miller, D.R. and Swanson, G.E. (1958). *The Changing American Parent: A Study in the Detroit Area.* Oxford, England: Wiley.

Miller, J.G., Bland, C., Källberg-Shroff, M. et al. (2014). Culture and the role of exchange vs. communal norms in friendship. *Journal of Experimental Social Psychology* 53: 79–93. https://doi.org/10.1016/j.jesp.2014.02.006.

Miller, M.J., Woehr, D.J., and Hudspeth, N. (2002). The meaning and measurement of work ethic: construction and initial validation of a multidimensional inventory. *Journal of Vocational Behavior* 60 (3): 451–489. https://doi.org/10.1006/jvbe.2001.1838.

Mischel, W. (1968). *Personality and Assessment.* Hoboken, NJ, US: Wiley.

Mischel, W. (1969). Continuity and change in personality. *American Psychologist* 24 (11): 1012–1018. https://doi.org/10.1037/h0028886.

Mojaverian, T. and Kim, H.S. (2013). Interpreting a helping hand: cultural variation in the effectiveness of solicited and unsolicited social support. *Personality and Social Psychology Bulletin* 39 (1): 88–99. https://doi.org/10.1177/0146167212465319.

Molm, L.D. (2010). The structure of reciprocity. *Social Psychology Quarterly* 73 (2): 119–131.

Molm, L.D., Whitham, M.M., and Melamed, D. (2012). Forms of exchange and integrative bonds: effects of history and embeddedness. *American Sociological Review* 77 (1): 141–165. https://doi.org/10.1177/0003122411434610.

Montoya, R.M. and Pinter, B. (2016). A model for understanding positive intergroup relations using the in-group-favoring norm: in-group-favoring norm and positive relations. *Journal of Social Issues* 72 (3): 584–600. https://doi.org/10.1111/josi.12183.

Montoya, R.M. and Pittinsky, T.L. (2013). Individual variability in adherence to the norm of group interest predicts outgroup bias. *Group Processes & Intergroup Relations* 16 (2): 173–191. https://doi.org/10.1177/1368430212450523.

Moos, R.H. and Moos, B.S. (2004). Long-term influence of duration and frequency of participation in Alcoholics Anonymous on individuals with alcohol use disorders. *Journal of Consulting and Clinical Psychology* 72 (1): 81.

Morris, S.C. and Rosen, S. (1973). Effects of felt adequacy and opportunity to reciprocate on help seeking. *Journal of Experimental Social Psychology* 9 (3): 265–276. https://doi.org/10.1016/0022-1031(73)90015-2.

Muir, D.E. and Weinstein, E.A. (1962). The social debt: an investigation of lower-class and middle-class norms of social obligation. *American Sociological Review* 27 (4): 532. https://doi.org/10.2307/2090036.

Myers, D.G. (2012). *Social Psychology*, 10e. Colombus, Ohio: McGraw-Hill.

Nadler, A. (1986). Help seeking as a cultural phenomenon: differences between city and kibbutz dwellers. *Journal of Personality and Social Psychology* 51 (5): 976–982. https://doi.org/10.1037/0022-3514.51.5.976.

Nadler, A. (1987). Determinants of help seeking behaviour: the effects of helper's similarity, task centrality and recipient's self esteem. *European Journal of Social Psychology* 17 (1): 57–67. https://doi.org/10.1002/ejsp.2420170106.

Nadler, A. (1997). Autonomous and dependent help seeking: personality characteristics and the seeking of help. *Handbook of Personality and Social Support*: 258–302.

Nadler, A. (1998). Esteem, relationships and achievement explanations of help seeking behavior. In: *Strategic Help Seeking: Implications for Learning and Teaching* (ed. S.A. Karabenick), 61–96. N.J.: Erlbaum.

Nadler, A. (2002). Inter-group helping relations as power relations: maintaining or challenging social dominance between groups through helping. *Journal of Social Issues* 58 (3): 487–502. https://doi.org/10.1111/1540-4560.00272.

Nadler, A. (2015). The other side of helping: seeking and receiving help. In: *The Oxford Handbook of Prosocial Behavior* (eds. D.A. Shroeder and W.G. Graziano), 307–328.

Nadler, A. (2018). From help giving to helping relations: belongingness and independence in social interactions. In: *The Oxford Handbook of Personality and Social Psychology*, 2e (eds. K. Deaux and M. Snyder), 465–489. New York: Oxford University Press.

Nadler, A., Altman, A., and Fisher, J.D. (1979a). Effects of positive and negative information about the self on recipient's reactions to aid. *Journal of Personality* 47: 616–629.

Nadler, A. and Chernyak-Hai, L. (2014). Helping them stay where they are: Status effects on dependency-autonomy oriented helping. *Journal of Personality and Social Psychology* 106: 58–72.

Nadler, A., Ellis, S., and Bar, I. (2003). To seek or not to seek: the relationship between help seeking and job performance evaluations as moderated by task-relevant expertise. *Journal of Applied Social Psychology* 33 (1): 91–109. https://doi.org/10.1111/j.1559-1816.2003.tb02075.x.

Nadler, A. and Fisher, J.D. (1986). The role of threat to self-esteem and perceived control in recipient reaction to help: theory development and empirical validation. In: *Advances in Experimental Social Psychology*, vol. 19 (ed. L. Berkowitz), 81–122. Elsevier.

Nadler, A., Fisher, J.D., and Itzhak, S.B. (1983). With a little help from my friend: effect of single or multiple act aid as a function of donor and task characteristics. *Journal of Personality and Social Psychology* 44 (2): 310–321. https://doi.org/10.1037/0022-3514.44.2.310.

Nadler, A., Fisher, J.D., and Streufert, S. (1974). The donor's dilemma: recipient's reactions to aid from friend or foe1. *Journal of Applied Social Psychology* 4 (3): 275–285. https://doi.org/10.1111/j.1559-1816.1974.tb02646.x.

Nadler, A., Fisher, J.D., and Streufert, S. (1976). When helping hurts: effects of donor-recipient similarity and recipient self-esteem on reactions to aid1. *Journal of Personality* 44 (3): 392–409. https://doi.org/10.1111/j.1467-6494.1976.tb00129.x.

Nadler, A. and Halabi, S. (2006). Intergroup helping as status relations: effects of status stability, identification, and type of help on receptivity to high-status group's help. *Journal of Personality and Social Psychology* 91 (1): 97–110. https://doi.org/10.1037/0022-3514.91.1.97.

Nadler, A. and Halabi, S. (2015). Helping relations and inequality between individuals and groups. *APA Handbook of Personality and Social Psychology* 2: 371–393.

Nadler, A., Halabi, S., and Harpaz-Gorodeisky, G. (2009). Intergroup Helping as Status Organizing Processes: Creating, Maintaining and Challenging Status Relations through Giving, Seeking and Receiving Help. In: *Intergroup misunderstandings: Impact of divergent social realities.* (eds. S. Demoulin, J.P. Leyens, and J.F. Dovidio), 311–331. Washington, D.C.: Psychology Press.

Nadler, A., Harpaz-Gorodeisky, G., and Ben-David, Y. (2009). Defensive helping: threat to group identity, ingroup identification, status stability, and common group identity as determinants of intergroup help-giving. *Journal of Personality and Social Psychology* 97 (5): 823–834. https://doi.org/10.1037/a0015968.

Nadler, A., Lewinstein, E., and Rahav, G. (1991). Acceptance of mental retardation and help-seeking by mothers and fathers of children with mental retardation. *Mental Retardation* 29 (1): 17–23.

Nadler, A. and Liviatan, I. (2006). Intergroup reconciliation: effects of adversary's expressions of empathy, responsibility, and recipients' trust. *Personality and Social Psychology Bulletin* 32 (4): 459–470. https://doi.org/10.1177/0146167205276431.

Nadler, A., Maler, S., and Friedman, A. (1984). Effects of helper's sex, subjects' androgyny, and self-evaluation on males' and females' willingness to seek and receive help. *Sex Roles* 10 (5–6): 327–339. https://doi.org/10.1007/BF00287550.

Nadler, A., Peri, N., and Chemerinski, A. (1985). Effects of opportunity to reciprocate and self-esteem on help-seeking behavior. *Journal of Personality* 53 (1): 23–35. https://doi.org/10.1111/j.1467-6494.1985.tb00886.x.

Nadler, A. and Porat, I. (1978). When names do not help: Effects of anonimity and locus of need attributions on help seeking behaviour. *Personality and Social Psychology Bulletin* 4: 624–628.

Nadler, A., Romek, E., and Shapira-Friedman, A. (1979b). Giving in the Kibbutz: pro-social behavior of city and Kibbutz children as affected by social responsibility and social pressure. *Journal of Cross-Cultural Psychology* 10 (1): 57–72. https://doi.org/10.1177/0022022179101004.

Nadler, A., Sheinberg, L., and Jaffe, Y. (1982). Coping with stress in male paraplegics through help seeking: the role of acceptance of physical disability in help-seeking and -receiving behaviors. *Series in Clinical & Community Psychology: Stress & Anxiety* 8: 375–384.

Nadler, A. and Shnabel, N. (2015). Intergroup reconciliation: Definitions, instrumental and socio-emotional processes and the needs-based model. *European Review of Social Psychology* 26: 93–125.

Nai, J., Narayanan, J., Hernandez, I., and Savani, K. (2018). People in more racially diverse neighborhoods are more prosocial. *Journal of Personality and Social Psychology* 114 (4): 497–515. https://doi.org/10.1037/pspa0000103.

Newman, F. (1991). *The Myth of Psychology*. New York: Castillo International.

Newman, R.S. and Schwager, M.T. (1992). Student perceptios and academic help seeking. In: *Student Perceptions in the Classroom* (eds. D.H. Schunk and J.L. Meece), 123–146. Hillsdale, N.J: L. Erlbaum.

Nicholls, J.G. (1984). Achievement motivation: conceptions of ability, subjective experience, task choice, and performance. *Psychological Review* 91 (3): 328–346. https://doi.org/10.1037/0033-295X.91.3.328.

Nier, J.A., Gaertner, S.L., Dovidio, J.F. et al. (2001). Changing interracial evaluations and behavior: the effects of a common group identity. *Group Processes & Intergroup Relations* 4 (4): 299–316. https://doi.org/10.1177/1368430201004004001.

Nozadi, S.S., Spinrad, T.L., Eisenberg, N., and Eggum-Wilkens, N.D. (2015). Associations of anger and fear to later self-regulation and problem behavior symptoms. *Journal of Applied Developmental Psychology* 38: 60–69. https://doi.org/10.1016/j.appdev.2015.04.005.

Okun, M.A., Yeung, E.W., and Brown, S. (2013). Volunteering by older adults and the risk of mortality: A meta-analysis. *Psychology and Aging* 28: 564–577.

Oliner, S.P. and Oliner, P.M. (1988). *The Altruistic Personality: Rescuers of Jews in Nazi Germany*, vol. 20, 105. New York: *Free Press.*

Oliner, P.M. and Oliner, S.P. (1992). Promoting extensive altruistic bonds: a conceptual elaboration and some pragmatic implications. In: *Embracing the Other: Philosophical, Psychological, and Historical Perspectives on Altruism* (eds. P.M. Oliner, S.P. Oliner, L. Baron, et al.), 369–389. New York: New York University Press.

Omoto, A.M. and Snyder, M. (2009). The role of community connections in volunteerism and social action. In: *Youth Empowerment and Volunteerism: Principles, Policies and Practices* (eds. E.S.C. Liu, M.J. Holosko, T.W. Lo and E. Au), 27–56. Hong Kong: City University of Hong Kong.

Onu, D., Smith, J.R., and Kessler, T. (2015). Intergroup emulation: an improvement strategy for lower status groups. *Group Processes & Intergroup Relations* 18 (2): 210–224. https://doi.org/10.1177/1368430214556698.

Osborne, D. and Weiner, B. (2015). A latent profile analysis of attributions for poverty: identifying response patterns underlying people's willingness to help the poor. *Personality and Individual Differences* 85: 149–154. https://doi.org/10.1016/j.paid.2015.05.007.

Otten, C.A., Penner, L.A., and Altabe, M.N. (1991). An examination of therapists' and college students' willingness to help a psychologically distressed person. *Journal of Social and Clinical Psychology* 10 (1): 102–120. https://doi.org/10.1521/jscp.1991.10.1.102.

Padesky, C.A. and Hammen, C.L. (1981). Sex differences in depressive symptom expression and help-seeking among college students. *Sex Roles* 7 (3): 309–320. https://doi.org/10.1007/BF00287545.

Parker, G.R., Cowen, E.L., Work, W.C., and Wyman, P.A. (1990). Test correlates of stress resilience among urban school children. *The Journal of Primary Prevention* 11 (1): 19–35. https://doi.org/10.1007/BF01324859.

Penner, L.A. (n.d.). Measuring the prosocial personality. *Advances in Personality Assessment* 10: 147–163.

Penner, L.A. and Finkelstein, M.A. (1998). Dispositional and structural determinants of volunteerism. *Journal of Personality and Social Psychology* 74 (2): 525–537. https://doi.org/10.1037/0022-3514.74.2.525.

Penner, L.A. and Fritzsche, B.A. (1993). Magic Johnson and reactions to people with AIDS: a natural experiment1. *Journal of Applied Social Psychology* 23 (13): 1035–1050. https://doi.org/10.1111/j.1559-1816.1993.tb01020.x.

Penner, L.A., Fritzsche, B.A., Craiger, J.P., and Freifeld, T.R. (1995). Measuring the prosocial personality. In: *Advances in personality assessment*, vol. 10 (eds. J. Butcher and C.D. Spielberger), 147–163. Hillsdale, NJ: Erlbaum.

Piff, P.K., Dietze, P., Feinberg, M. et al. (2015). Awe, the small self, and prosocial behavior. *Journal of Personality and Social Psychology* 108 (6): 883–899. https://doi.org/10.1037/pspi0000018.

Piff, P.K., Kraus, M.W., Côté, S. et al. (2010). Having less, giving more: the influence of social class on prosocial behavior. *Journal of Personality and Social Psychology* 99 (5): 771–784. https://doi.org/10.1037/a0020092.

Piliavin, J.A. (1981). *Emergency Intervention*. Academic Press.

Piliavin, J.A. (2009). Volunteering across the life span: doing well by doing good. In: *The Psychology of Prosocial Behavior: Group Processes, Intergroup Relations, and Helping* (eds. S. Stürmer and M. Snyder), 157–172. Chichester, UK: Wiley.

Piliavin, J.A., Dovidio, J.E., Gaertner, S.L., and Clark, R.D. (1981). *Emergency Intervention*. New York: Academic Press.

Piliavin, I.M., Piliavin, J.A., and Rodin, J. (1975). Costs, diffusion, and the stigmatized victim. *Journal of Personality and Social Psychology* 32 (3): 429–438. https://doi.org/10.1037/h0077092.

Piliavin, I.M., Rodin, J., and Piliavin, J.A. (1969). Good samaritanism: an underground phenomenon? *Journal of Personality and Social Psychology* 13 (4): 289–299. https://doi.org/10.1037/h0028433.

Pincus, A.L. and Gurtman, M.B. (1995). The three faces of interpersonal dependency: structural analyses of self-report dependency measures. *Journal of Personality and Social Psychology* 69 (4): 744–758. https://doi.org/10.1037/0022-3514.69.4.744.

Pincus, A.L. and Wilson, K.R. (2001). Interpersonal variability in dependent personality. *Journal of Personality* 69 (2): 223–251. https://doi.org/10.1111/1467-6494.00143.

Plomin, R. (1994). *Genetics and Experience: The Interplay Between Nature and Nurture*. Thousand Oaks: Sage Publications.

Poulin, M.J., Brown, S.L., Dillard, A.J., and Smith, D.M. (2013). Giving to others and the association between stress and mortality. *American Journal of Public Health* 103 (9): 1649–1655.

Pryor, J.B., Reeder, G.D., Yeadon, C., and Hesson-McInnis, M. (2004). A dual-process model of reactions to perceived stigma. *Journal of Personality and Social Psychology* 87 (4): 436–452. https://doi.org/10.1037/0022-3514.87.4.436.

Pursell, G.R., Laursen, B., Rubin, K. et al. (2008). Gender differences in patterns of association between prosocial behavior, personality and externalizing problem. *Journal of Research in Personality* 42: 472–481.

Rabbie, J.M. and Lodewijkx, H.F. (1994). Conflict and aggression: an individual-group continuum. *Advances in Group Processes* 11: 139–174.

Rand, D.G., Greene, J.D., and Nowak, M.A. (2012). Spontaneous giving and calculated greed. *Nature* 489 (7416): 427–430. https://doi.org/10.1038/nature11467.

Rasenberger, J. (2004, February 8). Kitty, 40 Years Later. *New York Times*, p. 14014001.

Raviv, A. (1993). Radio psychology: A comparison of listeners and non-listeners. *Journal of Community & Applied Social Psychology* 3: 197–211.

Regnerus, M.D., Smith, C., and Sikkink, D. (1998). Who gives to the poor? The influence of religious tradition and political location on the personal generosity of Americans toward the poor. *Journal for the Scientific Study of Religion* 37 (3): 481. https://doi.org/10.2307/1388055.

Reicher, S., Cassidy, C., Wolpert, I. et al. (2006). Saving Bulgaria's Jews: an analysis of social identity and the mobilisation of social solidarity. *European Journal of Social Psychology* 36 (1): 49–72. https://doi.org/10.1002/ejsp.291.

Riemer, J.W. (1998). Durkheim's "heroic suicide" in military combat. *Armed Forces & Society* 25 (1): 103–120. https://doi.org/10.1177/0095327X9802500106.

Rogers, C.R. (1961). *On Becoming a Person: A Therapist's View of Psychotherapy*. New York, NY: Houghton-Mifflin.

Rogers, C.R. (2004). *On Becoming a Person: A Therapist's view of Psychotherapy*. London: Constable.

Rogoff, B. (2003). *The Cultural Nature of Human Development*. Oxford university press.

Rosener, J. (1990). Ways women lead. *Harvard Business Review* 68 (6): 119–125.

Rosenhan, D. (1970). The natural socialization of altruistic autonomy. In: *Altruism and Helping Behavior* (eds. J. Macaulay and L. Berkowitz), 251–268. New York: Academic Press.

Ross, L. and Nisbett, R.E. (1991). *The Person and the Situation: Perspectives of Social Psychology*. New York, NY: Mcgraw-Hill.

Ross, L. and Nisbett, R.E. (2011). *The Person and the Situation: Perspectives of Social Psychology*. London: Pinter & Martin Ltd.

Ruble, D.N., Boggiano, A.K., Feldman, N.S., and Loebl, J.H. (1980). Developmental analysis of the role of social comparison in self-evaluation. *Developmental Psychology* 16 (2): 105–115. https://doi.org/10.1037/0012-1649.16.2.105.

Ruble, D.N. and Frey, K.S. (1987). Social comparison and self-evaluation in the classroom: developmental changes in knowledge and function. In: *Social Comparison, Social Justice, and Relative Deprivation: Theoretical, Empirical, and Policy Perspectives*, 81–104. Hillsdale, NJ, US: Lawrence Erlbaum Associates, Inc.

Rudolph, U., Roesch, S., Greitemeyer, T., and Weiner, B. (2004). A meta-analytic review of help giving and aggression from an attributional perspective: contributions to a general theory of motivation. *Cognition & Emotion* 18 (6): 815–848. https://doi.org/10.1080/02699930341000248.

Rushton, P., Chrisjohn, R.D., and Cynthia Fekken, G. (1981). The altruistic personality and the self-report altruism scale. *Personality and Individual Differences* 2 (4): 293–302. https://doi.org/10.1016/0191-8869(81)90084-2.

Ryan, R.M. and Deci, E.L. (2000). Self-determination theory and the facilitation of intrinsic motivation, social development, and well-being. *American Psychologist* 55 (1): 68–78. https://doi.org/10.1037/0003-066X.55.1.68.

Ryan, R.M. and Deci, E.L. (2001). On happiness and human potentials: a review of research on hedonic and eudaimonic well-being. *Annual Review of Psychology* 52 (1): 141–166. https://doi.org/10.1146/annurev.psych.52.1.141.

Ryan, A.M. and Pintrich, P.R. (1997). "Should I ask for help?" The role of motivation and attitudes in adolescents' help seeking in math class. *Journal of Educational Psychology* 89 (2): 329–341. https://doi.org/10.1037/0022-0663.89.2.329.

Ryburn, M. (1996). A study of post-adoption contact in compulsory adoptions. *British Journal of Social Work* 26 (5): 627–646. https://doi.org/10.1093/oxfordjournals.bjsw.a011138.

Salovey, P., Mayer, J.D., and Rosenhan, D.L. (1991). Mood and helping: mood as a motivator of helping and helping as a regulator of mood. In: *Prosocial Behavior*, 215–237. Thousand Oaks, CA, US: Sage Publications Inc.

Saroglou, V. (2006). Religion's role in prosocial behavior: myth or reality? *Religion* 31 (2): 1–66.

Saroglou, V. (2013). Religion, spirituality, and altruism. In: *APA Handbook of Psychology, Religion, and Spirituality (Vol 1): Context, Theory, and Research* (eds. K.I. Pargament, J.J. Exline and J.W. Jones), 439–457. Washington: American Psychological Association.

Saucier, D.A. (2015). Race and prosocial behavior. In: *The Oxford Handbook of Prosocial Behavior* (eds. D.A. Schroeder and W.G. Graziano). Oxford; New York: Oxford University Press.

Saucier, D.A., Miller, C.T., and Doucet, N. (2005). Differences in helping whites and blacks: a meta-analysis. *Personality and Social Psychology Review* 9 (1): 2–16. https://doi.org/10.1207/s15327957pspr0901_1.

Schnall, S. and Roper, J. (2012). Elevation puts moral values into action. *Social Psychological and Personality Science* 3 (3): 373–378. https://doi.org/10.1177/1948550611423595.

Schnall, S., Roper, J., and Fessler, D.M.T. (2010). Elevation leads to altruistic behavior. *Psychological Science* 21 (3): 315–320. https://doi.org/10.1177/0956797609359882.

Schneider, R.J., Ackerman, P.L., and Kanfer, R. (1996). To "act wisely in human relations:" exploring the dimensions of social competence. *Personality and Individual Differences* 21 (4): 469–481. https://doi.org/10.1016/0191-8869(96)00084-0.

Schneider, M.E., Major, B., Luhtanen, R., and Crocker, J. (1996). Social stigma and the potential costs of assunptive help. *Personality and Social Psychology Bulletin* 22 (2): 201–209. https://doi.org/10.1177/0146167296222009.

Schroeder, D.A. and Graziano, W.G. (eds.) (2015). *The Oxford Handbook of Prosocial Behavior*. Oxford; New York: Oxford University Press.

Schuster, M.A., Stein, B.D., Jaycox, L.H. et al. (2001). A national survey of stress reactions after the September 11, 2001, terrorist attacks. *New England Journal of Medicine* 345 (20): 1507–1512.

Schwartz, S.H. (1992). Universals in the Content and Structure of Values: Theoretical Advances and Empirical Tests in 20 Countries. In: *Advances in Experimental Social Psychology*, vol. 25, 1–65. Elsevier https://doi.org/10.1016/S0065-2601(08)60281-6.

Schwartz, S.H. (2012). An overview of the Schwartz theory of basic values. *Online Readings in Psychology and Culture* 2 (1) https://doi.org/10.9707/2307-0919.1116.

Schwartz, S.H. and Howard, J.A. (1982). Helping and cooperation: a self-based motivational model. In: *Cooperation and Helping Behavior* (eds. V.J. Derlega and J. Grzelak), 327–353. Elsevier.

Schwartz, S.H. and Rubel, T. (2005). Sex differences in value priorities: cross-cultural and multimethod studies. *Journal of Personality and Social Psychology* 89 (6): 1010–1028. https://doi.org/10.1037/0022-3514.89.6.1010.

Seligman, M.E.P. and Csikszentmihalyi, M. (2000). Positive psychology: an introduction. *American Psychologist* 55 (1): 5–14. https://doi.org/10.1037/0003-066X.55.1.5.

Seligman, M.E.P., Steen, T.A., Park, N., and Peterson, C. (2005). Positive psychology progress: empirical validation of interventions. *American Psychologist* 60 (5): 410–421. https://doi.org/10.1037/0003-066X.60.5.410.

Shaffer, P.A., Vogel, D.L., and Wei, M. (2006). The mediating roles of anticipated risks, anticipated benefits, and attitudes on the decision to seek professional help: an attachment perspective. *Journal of Counseling Psychology* 53 (4): 442–452. https://doi.org/10.1037/0022-0167.53.4.442.

Shariff, A.F. and Norenzayan, A. (2007). God is watching you: priming god concepts increases prosocial behavior in an anonymous economic game. *Psychological Science* 18 (9): 803–809. https://doi.org/10.1111/j.1467-9280.2007.01983.x.

Shariff, A.F., Willard, A.K., Andersen, T., and Norenzaryan, A. (2016). Religious priming: Meta-analysis with a focus on pro-sociality. *Personality and Social Psychology Review* 20: 47–48.

Shell, R.M. and Eisenberg, N. (1992). A developmental model of recipients' reactions to aid. *Psychological Bulletin* 111 (3): 413–433. https://doi.org/10.1037/0033-2909.111.3.413.

Shilkret, C.J. and Masling, J. (1981). Oral dependence and dependent behavior. *Journal of Personality Assessment* 45 (2): 125–129. https://doi.org/10.1207/s15327752jpa4502_4.

Shnabel, N., Bar-Anan, Y., Kende, A. et al. (2016). Help to perpetuate traditional gender roles: benevolent sexism increases engagement in dependency-oriented cross-gender helping. *Journal of Personality and Social Psychology* 110 (1): 55–75. https://doi.org/10.1037/pspi0000037.

Shnabel, N. and Nadler, A. (2008). A needs-based model of reconciliation: satisfying the differential emotional needs of victim and perpetrator as a key to promoting reconciliation. *Journal of Personality and Social Psychology* 94 (1): 116–132. https://doi.org/10.1037/0022-3514.94.1.116.

Shnabel, N. and Nadler, A. (2015). The role of agency and morality in reconciliation processes: the perspective of the needs-based model. *Current Directions in Psychological Science* 24 (6): 477–483. https://doi.org/10.1177/0963721415601625.

Sidanius, J. and Pratto, F. (1999). *Social Dominance: An Intergroup Theory of Social Hierarchy and Oppression*. New York, NY: Cambridge University Press.

Sidanius, J. and Pratto, F. (2001). *Social Dominance: An Intergroup Theory of Social Hierarchy and Oppression* (1. paperback ed.). Cambridge: Cambridge Universtiy Press.

Silverstein, M. and Bengtson, V.L. (1994). Does intergenerational social support influence the psychological well-being of older parents? The contingencies of declining health and widowhood. *Social Science & Medicine* 38 (7): 943–957. https://doi.org/10.1016/0277-9536(94)90427-8.

Simmel, G. (1950). The stranger. In: *The Sociology of Georg Simmel* (Trans. K.H. Wolff). Glencoe, IL: The Free Press.

Simpson, J.A. and Beckes, L. (2010). Evolutionary perspectives on prosocial behavior. In: *Prosocial Motives, Emotions, and Behavior: The Better Angels of our Nature* (eds. M. Mikulincer and P.R. Shaver), 35–53. Washington: American Psychological Association.

Simpson, J.A., Rholes, W.S., and Nelligan, J.S. (1992). Support seeking and support giving within couples in an anxiety-provoking situation: The role of attachment styles. *Journal of Personality and Social Psychology* 62 (3): 434–446.

Skinner, B. (1981). Selection by consequences. *Science* 213 (4507): 501–504. https://doi.org/10.1126/science.7244649.

Smith, E.A. and Bliege Bird, R.L.B. (2000). Turtle hunting and tombstone opening. *Evolution and Human Behavior* 21 (4): 245–261. https://doi.org/10.1016/S1090-5138(00)00031-3.

Smith, J.A., Braunack-Mayer, A., Wittert, G., and Warin, M. (2007). "I've been independent for so damn long!": independence, masculinity and aging in a help seeking context. *Journal of Aging Studies* 21 (4): 325–335. https://doi.org/10.1016/j.jaging.2007.05.004.

Smith, K.D., Keating, J.P., and Stotland, E. (1989). Altruism reconsidered: the effect of denying feedback on a victim's status to empathic witnesses. *Journal of Personality and Social Psychology* 57 (4): 641–650. https://doi.org/10.1037/0022-3514.57.4.641.

Sober, E. and Wilson, D.S. (1998). *Unto Others: The Evolution and Psychology of Unselfish Behavior* (4. print). Cambridge, Mass.: Harvard University Press.

Solomon, J. D. (2016). *The Witness.* Filmrise, Netflix. Retrieved from https://www.imdb.com/title/tt3568002/

Sorokin, P.A. (1927). *Social Mobility.* New York; London: Harper & Brothers.

Spinrad, T.L. and Stifter, C.A. (2006). Toddlers' empathy-related responding to distress: predictions from negative emotionality and maternal behavior in infancy. *Infancy* 10 (2): 97–121. https://doi.org/10.1207/s15327078in1002_1.

Sprafkin, J.N., Liebert, R.M., and Poulos, R.W. (1975). Effects of a prosocial televised example on children's helping. *Journal of Experimental Child Psychology* 20 (1): 119–126. https://doi.org/10.1016/0022-0965(75)90031-4.

Sroufe, L.A., Fox, N.E., and Pancake, V.R. (1983). Attachment and dependency in developmental perspective. *Child Development* 54 (6): 1615. https://doi.org/10.2307/1129825.

Staub, E. (1971). A child in distress: the influence of nurturance and modeling on children's attempts to help. *Developmental Psychology* 4: 124–132. http://dx.doi.org/10.1037/h0031084.

Staub, E. (1974). Helping a distressed person: Social, personality, and stimulus determinants. In: *Advances in Experimental Social Psychology*, vol. 7 (ed. L. Berkowitz), 293–341. New York: Academic Press.

Stavrova, O. and Siegers, P. (2014). Religious prosociality and morality across cultures: How social enforcement of religion shapes the effects of personal religiosity on prosocial and moral attitudes and behaviors. *Personality and Social Psychology Bulletin* 40: 315–333.

Stellar, J.E., Manzo, V.M., Kraus, M.W., and Keltner, D. (2012). Class and compassion: socioeconomic factors predict responses to suffering. *Emotion* 12 (3): 449–459. https://doi.org/10.1037/a0026508.

Steptoe, A., Hamer, M., and Chida, Y. (2007). The effects of acute psychological stress on circulating inflammatory factors in humans: a review and meta-analysis. *Brain, Behavior, and Immunity* 21 (7): 901–912. https://doi.org/10.1016/j.bbi.2007.03.011.

Stewart-Williams, S. (2007). Altruism among kin vs. nonkin: effects of cost of help and reciprocal exchange. *Evolution and Human Behavior* 28 (3): 193–198. https://doi.org/10.1016/j.evolhumbehav.2007.01.002.

Stroebe, M.S., Hansson, R.O., Schut, H., and Stroebe, W. (eds.) (2008). *Handbook of Bereavement Research and Practice: Advances in Theory and Intervention*. Washington: American Psychological Association.

Stürmer, S. and Snyder, M. (2009). Helping "us" versus "them": towards a group-level theory of helping and altruism within and across group boundaries. In: *The Psychology of Prosocial Behavior Group Processes, Intergroup Relations, and Helping* (eds. S. Stürmer and M. Snyder), 33–58. New York, NY: Wiley Retrieved from http://nbn-resolving.de/urn:nbn:de:101:1-201502047329.

Stürmer, S., Snyder, M., Kropp, A., and Siem, B. (2006). Empathy-motivated helping: the moderating role of group membership. *Personality and Social Psychology Bulletin* 32 (7): 943–956. https://doi.org/10.1177/0146167206287363.

Stürmer, S., Snyder, M., and Omoto, A.M. (2005). Prosocial emotions and helping: the moderating role of group membership. *Journal of Personality and Social Psychology* 88 (3): 532–546. https://doi.org/10.1037/0022-3514.88.3.532.

Svetlova, M., Nichols, S.R., and Brownell, C.A. (2010). Toddlers' prosocial behavior: from instrumental to empathic to altruistic helping. *Child Development* 81 (6): 1814–1827. https://doi.org/10.1111/j.1467-8624.2010.01512.x.

Tajfel, H. (1970). Experiments in intergroup discrimination. *Scientific American* 223 (5): 96–103.

Tajfel, H. and Turner, J.C. (1979). An integrative theory of intergroup conflict. In: *The social Psychology of Intergroup Relations* (eds. W.G. Austin and S. Worchel), 33–47. Monterey, CA: Brooks/Cole.

Tajfel, H. and Turner, J.C. (2004). The Social Identity Theory of Intergroup Behavior. In: *Political Psychology: Key Readings* (eds. J.T. Jost and J. Sidanius), 276–293. New York, N.Y.: Psychology Press.

Tan, J.H.W. and Vogel, C. (2008). Religion and trust: An experimental study. *Journal of Economic Psychology* 29: 832–848.

Taylor, S.E., Sherman, D.K., Kim, H.S. et al. (2004). Culture and social support: who seeks it and why? *Journal of Personality and Social Psychology* 87 (3): 354.

Taylor, S.E., Welch, W.T., Kim, H.S., and Sherman, D.K. (2007). Cultural differences in the impact of social support on psychological and biological stress responses. *Psychological Science* 18 (9): 831–837. https://doi.org/10.1111/j.1467-9280.2007.01987.x.

Tesser, A. (1988). Toward a self-evaluation maintenance model of social behavior. In: *Advances in Experimental Social Psychology*, vol. 21 (ed. L.

Berkowitz), 181–227. Elsevier https://doi.org/10.1016/S0065-2601(08)60227-0.

Tesser, A., Gatewood, R., and Driver, M. (1968). Some determinants of gratitude. *Journal of Personality and Social Psychology* 9 (3): 233–236. https://doi.org/10.1037/h0025905.

Tessler, R.C. and Schwartz, S.H. (1972). Help seeking, self-esteem, and achievement motivation: an attributional analysis. *Journal of Personality and Social Psychology* 21 (3): 318–326. https://doi.org/10.1037/h0032321.

Thoits, P.A. and Hewitt, L.N. (2001). Volunteer work and well-being. *Journal of Health and Social Behavior* 42 (2): 115. https://doi.org/10.2307/3090173.

Thomas, E.F., McGarty, C., and Mavor, K.I. (2009). Transforming "apathy into movement": the role of prosocial emotions in motivating action for social change. *Personality and Social Psychology Review* 13 (4): 310–333. https://doi.org/10.1177/1088868309343290.

Timko, C. and Rodin, J. (1985). Staff–patient relationships in nursing homes: sources of conflict and rehabilitation potential. *Rehabilitation Psychology* 30 (2): 93–108. https://doi.org/10.1037/h0091023.

Todorov, T. (1999). *La fragilité du bien*. Paris: *Albin Michel.*

Todorov, T. (2001). *The Fragility of Goodness: Why Bulgaria's Jews Survived the Holocaust.* London: Weidenfeld & Nicolson.

Triandis, H.C., Marin, G., Lisansky, J., and Betancourt, H. (1984). Simpatía as a cultural script of Hispanics. *Journal of Personality and Social Psychology* 47 (6): 1363.

Triandis, H.C. (1995). *Individualism & Collectivism*. Boulder, CO, US: Westview Press.

Trivers, R.L. (1971). The evolution of reciprocal altruism. *The Quarterly Review of Biology* 46 (1): 35–57. https://doi.org/10.1086/406755.

Tsang, J.-A. (2006a). BRIEF REPORT Gratitude and prosocial behaviour: an experimental test of gratitude. *Cognition & Emotion* 20 (1): 138–148. https://doi.org/10.1080/02699930500172341.

Tsang, J.-A. (2006b). The effects of helper intention on gratitude and indebtedness. *Motivation and Emotion* 30 (3): 198–204. https://doi.org/10.1007/s11031-006-9031-z.

Turner, J.C. and Brown, R. (1978). Social status, cognitive alternatives and intergroup relations. In: *Differentiation Between Social Groups: Studies in the Social Psychology of Intergroup Relations* (ed. H. Tajfel), 201–234. Academic Press.

Turner, J.C. and Reynolds, K.J. (2001). The social identity perspective in intergroup relations: theories, themes, and controversies. In: *Intergroup Processes* (eds. R. Brown and S.L. Gaertner). Malden, Mass.: Blackwell Publishers. Retrieved from http://site.ebrary.com/id/10233057.

Turner, J.C. and Reynolds, K.J. (2012). Self-categorization theory. In: *Handbook of Theories of Social Psychology* (eds. P.A.M.V. Lange, A.W. Kruglanski and E.T. Higgins), 399–417. Thousand Oaks, CA: SAGE.

Uchida, Y., Kitayama, S., Mesquita, B. et al. (2008). Is perceived emotional support beneficial? Well-being and health in independent and interdependent cultures. *Personality and Social Psychology Bulletin* 34 (6): 741–754. https://doi.org/10.1177/0146167208315157.

Uhl-Bien, M. (2011). Relational leadership theory: exploring the social processes of leadership and organizing. In: *Leadership, Gender, and Organization*, vol. 27 (eds. P. Werhane and M. Painter-Morland), 75–108. Dordrecht: Springer Netherlands https://doi.org/10.1007/978-90-481-9014-0_7.

Uranowitz, S.W. (1975). Helping and self-attributions: a field experiment. *Journal of Personality and Social Psychology* 31 (5): 852–854. https://doi.org/10.1037/h0076690.

Utz, S. (2004). Self construal and cooperation: Is the interdependent self more cooperative than the independent self? *Self and Identity* 3: 177–190. http://dx.doi.org/10.1080/13576500444000001.

Vaes, J., Leyens, J.-P., Paola Paladino, M., and Pires Miranda, M. (2012). We are human, they are not: driving forces behind outgroup dehumanisation and the humanisation of the ingroup. *European Review of Social Psychology* 23 (1): 64–106. https://doi.org/10.1080/10463283.2012.665250.

Vaish, A., Carpenter, M., and Tomasello, M. (2010). Young children selectively avoid helping people with harmful intentions: selectivity in helping. *Child Development* 81 (6): 1661–1669. https://doi.org/10.1111/j.1467-8624.2010.01500.x.

Van de Vyver, J. and Abrams, D. (2015). Testing the prosocial effectiveness of the prototypical moral emotions: elevation increases benevolent behaviors and outrage increases justice behaviors. *Journal of Experimental Social Psychology* 58: 23–33. https://doi.org/10.1016/j.jesp.2014.12.005.

van Kleef, G.A., Oveis, C., van der Löwe, I. et al. (2008). Power, distress, and compassion: turning a blind eye to the suffering of others. *Psychological Science* 19 (12): 1315–1322. https://doi.org/10.1111/j.1467-9280.2008.02241.x.

van Leeuwen, E. (2007). Restoring identity through outgroup helping: beliefs about international aid in response to the December 2004 tsunami: Restoring identity through outgroup helping. *European Journal of Social Psychology* 37 (4): 661–671. https://doi.org/10.1002/ejsp.389.

van Leeuwen, E. and Mashuri, A. (2013). Intergroup helping in response to separatism. *Personality and Social Psychology Bulletin* 39 (12): 1647–1655. https://doi.org/10.1177/0146167213499613.

van Leeuwen, E. and Täuber, S. (2009). The strategic side of out-group helping. In: *The Psychology of Prosocial Behavior Group Processes, Intergroup Relations, and Helping* (eds. S. Stürmer and M. Snyder). New York, NY: Wiley. Retrieved from http://nbn-resolving.de/urn:nbn:de:101:1-201502047329.

van Leeuwen, E., van Dijk, W., and Kaynak, Ü. (2013). Of saints and sinners: how appeals to collective pride and guilt affect outgroup helping. *Group Processes & Intergroup Relations* 16 (6): 781–796. https://doi.org/10.1177/1368430213485995.

Van Vugt, M. and Hardy, C.L. (2010). Cooperation for reputation: wasteful contributions as costly signals in public goods. *Group Processes & Intergroup Relations*13(1):101–111.https://doi.org/10.1177/1368430209342258.

Veblen, T. (1994). *Theory of the Leisure Class* (New ed). Dover Publications.

Veroff, J.B. (1981). The dynamics of help-seeking in men and women: a national survey study. *Psychiatry*44 (3): 189–200. https://doi.org/10.1080/00332747.1981.11024106.

Vezzali, L., Cadamuro, A., Versari, A. et al. (2015). Feeling like a group after a natural disaster: common ingroup identity and relations with outgroup victims among majority and minority young children. *British Journal of Social Psychology* 54 (3): 519–538. https://doi.org/10.1111/bjso.12091.

Vogel, D.L. and Wei, M. (2005). Adult attachment and help-seeking intent: The mediating roles of psychological distress and perceived social support. *Journal of Counseling Psychology* 52: 347–357.

Warneken, F., Hare, B., Melis, A.P. et al. (2007). Spontaneous altruism by chimpanzees and young children. *PLoS Biology* 5 (7): e184. https://doi.org/10.1371/journal.pbio.0050184.

Warneken, F. and Tomasello, M. (2008). Extrinsic rewards undermine altruistic tendencies in 20-month-olds. *Developmental Psychology* 44 (6): 1785–1788. https://doi.org/10.1037/a0013860.

Watkins, P., Scheer, J., Ovnicek, M., and Kolts, R. (2006). The debt of gratitude: dissociating gratitude and indebtedness. *Cognition & Emotion* 20 (2): 217–241. https://doi.org/10.1080/02699930500172291.

Wayment, H.A. (2006). Attachment style, empathy, and helping following a collective loss: evidence from the September 11 terrorist attacks. *Attachment & Human Development* 8 (1): 1–9. https://doi.org/10.1080/14616730600585292.

Weiner, B. (1980). A cognitive (attribution)-emotion-action model of motivated behavior: an analysis of judgments of help-giving. *Journal of Personality and Social Psychology* 39 (2): 186–200. https://doi.org/10.1037/0022-3514.39.2.186.

Weiner, B. (1993). On sin versus sickness: a theory of perceived responsibility and social motivation. *American Psychologist* 48 (9): 957–965. https://doi.org/10.1037/0003-066X.48.9.957.

Weiner, B. (2005). *Social Motivation, Justice, and the Moral Emotions An Attributional Approach.* Routledge.

Weiner, B. (2006). *Social motivation, justice, and the moral emotions: An attributional approach.* Mahwah, NJ: Erlbaum.

Weiner, B., Osborne, D., and Rudolph, U. (2011). An attributional analysis of reactions to poverty: the political ideology of the giver and the perceived morality of the receiver. *Personality and Social Psychology Review* 15 (2): 199–213. https://doi.org/10.1177/1088868310387615.

Weiner, B., Perry, R.P., and Magnusson, J. (1988). An attributional analysis of reactions to stigmas. *Journal of Personality and Social Psychology* 55 (5): 738.

Weinstein, N., DeHaan, C.R., and Ryan, R.M. (2010). Attributing autonomous versus introjected motivation to helpers and the recipient experience:

effects on gratitude, attitudes, and well-being. *Motivation and Emotion* 34 (4): 418–431. https://doi.org/10.1007/s11031-010-9183-8.

Weinstein, N. and Ryan, R.M. (2010). When helping helps: autonomous motivation for prosocial behavior and its influence on well-being for the helper and recipient. *Journal of Personality and Social Psychology* 98 (2): 222–244. https://doi.org/10.1037/a0016984.

Weiss, H.M. and Knight, P.A. (1980). The utility of humility: self-esteem, information search, and problem-solving efficiency. *Organizational Behavior and Human Performance* 25 (2): 216–223. https://doi.org/10.1016/0030-5073(80)90064-1.

White, R. (2016). Nietzsche on generosity and the gift-giving virtue. *British Journal for the History of Philosophy* 24 (2): 348–364. https://doi.org/10.1080/09608788.2015.1088820.

Whiting, B.B. and Whiting, J.W.M. (1975). *Children of Six Cultures: A Psycho-Cultural Analysis.* Cambridge, MA and London, England: Harvard University Press.

Wildschut, T., Insko, C.A., and Gaertner, L. (2002). Intragroup social influence and intergroup competition. *Journal of Personality and Social Psychology* 82 (6): 975–992. https://doi.org/10.1037/0022-3514.82.6.975.

Wills, T.A. (1983). Social comparison in coping and help-seeking. *New Directions in Helping* 2: 109–141.

Wills, T.A. and DePaulo, B.M. (1991). Interpersonal analysis of the help-seeking process. *Handbook of Social and Clinical Psychology* 162: 350–375.

Wilson, D.S., Van Vugt, M., and O'Gorman, R. (2008). Multilevel selection theory and major evolutionary transitions: implications for psychological science. *Current Directions in Psychological Science* 17 (1): 6–9. https://doi.org/10.1111/j.1467-8721.2008.00538.x.

Wong, R.Y. and Hong, Y. (2005). Dynamic influences of culture on cooperation in the prisoner's dilemma. *Psychological Science* 16 (6): 429–434.

Wood, N. (1992). Tabula rasa, social environmentalism, and the "English paradigm". *Journal of the History of Ideas* 53 (4): 647. https://doi.org/10.2307/2709942.

Wood, A.M., Froh, J.J., and Geraghty, A.W.A. (2010). Gratitude and well-being: A review and theoretical integration. *Clinical Psychology Review* 30: 890–905.

Zahavi, A. and Zahavi, A. (1999). *The Handicap Principle: a Missing Piece of Darwin's Puzzle.* New York: Oxford University Press.

Zevon, M.A., Karuza, J., and Brickman, P. (1982). Responsibility and the elderly: applications to psychotherapy. *Psychotherapy: Theory, Research & Practice* 19 (4): 405–411. https://doi.org/10.1037/h0088452.

Index

Note: page numbers in **bold** refer to diagrams, page numbers in *italics* refer to information contained in tables.

Social Psychology of Helping Relations: Solidarity and Hierarchy, First Edition. Arie Nadler.